AF411965

Geopolitical Economy

Geopolitical Economy examines free trade agreements (FTAs), the primary policy tool through which modern nations seek access to international markets. The book focuses specifically on how FTAs are used by South Korea, which is the world's leader in the number and significance of FTAs as well as the world's sixth largest export economy.

Jonathan Krieckhaus articulates a *geopolitical economy* perspective on FTAs, arguing that geopolitics—the struggle between nations over specific geographic regions around the globe—deeply shaped FTA strategy and economic policy in South Korea and beyond. This perspective illustrates a security approach to FTAs and adds that the geographic specificity of such security concerns often influences FTA policy.

Geopolitical Economy also looks at Korean FTAs through the lens of *development strategy*. South Korea is singularly successful in garnering FTAs with all three major loci of the global economy: the United States, the European Union, and China, and these FTAs are having a notable effect on the Korean economy. This successful FTA strategy was politically predicated upon a strong commitment from three consecutive Korean presidential administrations, each operating within a favorable state-society context and each enjoying the existence of a centralized and effective trade bureaucracy.

Jonathan Krieckhaus is Associate Professor of Political Science at the University of Missouri.

Geopolitical Economy

The South Korean FTA Strategy

Jonathan Krieckhaus

University of Michigan Press
Ann Arbor

Published in the United States of America by the
University of Michigan Press
Manufactured in the United States of America
♾ Printed on acid-free paper

A CIP catalog record for this book is available from the British Library.

Library of Congress Cataloging-in-Publication data has been applied for.

ISBN: 978-0-472-13083-2 (Hardcover : alk paper)
ISBN: 978-0-472-12388-9 (ebook)

Contents

Abbreviations   vii

Acknowledgments   ix

Part I. Perspectives

Chapter 1. Introduction   3

Chapter 2. Geopolitical Economy   14

Chapter 3. FTAs, Statistics, and Korea   38

Chapter 4. Containment and South Korean Development   46

Part II. The Korean FTA Strategy

Chapter 5. FTAs as Development Strategy   59

Chapter 6. FTA Consequences   83

Part III. The Geopolitics of FTAs

Chapter 7. South Korea and the United States   103

Chapter 8. China, the European Union, and Japan   119

Chapter 9. The Emerging Geopolitical Economy   128

Appendix: Documentation of Chapter 3 and Chapter 5   135

Notes   143

Bibliography   149

Index   171

Abbreviations

AFC	Asian financial crisis
ASEAN	Association of Southeast Asian Nations
BTSCS	binary time-series cross-sectional
BRIC	Brazil, Russia, India, and China
CGE	computable general equilibrium
COW	Correlates of War
EFTA	European Free Trade Association
EOI	export-orientated industrialization
EU	European Union
FDI	foreign direct investment
FTA	free trade agreement
GATT	General Agreement on Tariffs and Trade
ICT	information and communications technology
ISI	import-substituting industrialization
IPE	international political economy
IR	international relations
KORUS FTA	Korean-U.S. Free Trade Agreement
KPR	Korean People's Republic
MOFAT	Ministry of Foreign Affairs and Trade
NAFTA	North American Free Trade Agreement
OECD	Organization for Economic Cooperation and Development
OMT	Office of the Minister for Trade
PTA	preferential trade agreement
RCEP	Regional Comprehensive Economic Partnership
ROK	Republic of Korea

TPP   Trans-Pacific Partnership
TTIP   Transatlantic Trade and Investment Partnership
WTO   World Trade Organization

Acknowledgments

I am grateful to a large number of individuals and institutions for bringing this book to fruition. It exists because of Uk Heo, who kindly invited me to join a team of authors writing several books on one central theme: *The rise of Korea in the era of globalization.* The five annual conferences that he organized at the University of Wisconsin-Milwaukee, including a wide range of scholars from both the United States and South Korea, provided a delightful intellectual setting for learning the nuances of contemporary South Korea. These conferences were impeccably well run, thanks to Uk Heo, Sooho Song, and their remarkably well-organized staff.

I would especially like to thank the Academy of Korean Studies. This study was supported by the Academy of Korean Studies Grant funded by the Korean government's Ministry of Education, Science, and Technology (AKS-2012-AAZ-2101). The five-year grant funded the annual conferences, research assistance, and many other forms of support. I particularly thank AKS grant participant Terry Roehrig for his helpful comments on the full manuscript.

For material in chapter 4 I thank the Board of Regents of California for permission to draw upon Yamamoto Rosenbaum, Chika, and Jonathan Krieckhaus. 2016. "What Explains South Korean Interest in FTA Partners? An Empirical Analysis" *Asian Survey* Volume 56, Number 5. 982–1004. Also in chapter 4, I thank Lynne Rienner Publishers for permission to draw upon Jonathan Krieckhaus. 2017. "Geopolitics and South Korea's Economic Success." *Asian Perspective*, Volume 41, Number 1. Copyright © 2017 by Institute for Far Eastern Studies, Kyungnam University. Used with permission of Lynne Rienner Publishers.

At the University of Missouri I thank the Research Council for granting me research leave in the academic year 2016–17 so that I could finish this book. I also thank a series of effective department chairs, John Petrocik, Cooper Drury, and Moises Arce, for providing a supportive research environment.

I wish to thank a number of talented research assistants at the University of Missouri: Rebecca Miller, Michael Hendricks, Chika Yamamoto Rosenbaum, Dongjin Kwak, Timofey Kolenikov, Muinul Islam, Krisztina Pusok, and Tiffanesha Williams. I also thank a number of excellent research assistants at the University of Wisconsin-Milwaukee: ShinYoung Park, Jihye Park, Gayeon Ryu, and Wangduk Park.

More generally, I wish to thank Lael Keiser, Cooper Drury, and Stephen Quackenbush at the University of Missouri for their goodwill and their intellectual insights. I particularly thank Lael Keiser for reading the entire manuscript and providing a deeply insightful critique before this book went out for review. I thank my coauthors, Cooper Drury and Chika Yamamoto Rosenberg, for their insights into the international political economy and FTAs, which underlie the second half of chapter 5. I especially thank Chika Yamamoto Rosenbaum for sharing her Ph.D. dissertation data set on global FTAs, which underlies chapter 3. Finally, I thank Stephen Quackenbush for kindly teaching me the basics of Cox proportional hazards models.

Professionally, more than anybody else, I owe my deepest debt of gratitude to my editor, Melody Herr, at the University of Michigan Press. Melody encouraged me in this project from the start, arranged timely and extremely helpful reviews, and—most importantly—was deeply involved in helping me at each stage of the process and provided constant encouragement. At Michigan, I also thank Danielle Coty, Meredith Norwich, and Scott Ham for their kind efficiency.

Turning to my family, I thank my father, Edward Elles Krieckhaus, for his passion for big ideas. I thank my mother, Susan LaBelle, for nurturing me, intellectually and otherwise, for as long as I have known. I thank my other father, Joseph LaBelle, for a loving family filled with good humor and interesting banter. I also thank my brother, Alexander Krieckhaus. In the final days of the manuscript he provided a deep critique of the book and rewrote vast swathes of prose. I thank my friend Greg Miller, who seems more a second brother, for kindly editing the entire book line by line.

Finally, I thank the love of my life, Kim Krieckhaus. Mostly I thank Kim for living a life with me that contains more than academia. I am also grateful to Kim for giving so thoroughly of her own time as I faced various deadlines. Concerning the book itself, Kim has an excellent eye for unclear empirics or prose, such that the book is distinctly better from her ongoing ministrations.

PART I

Perspectives

Introduction

> A free trade agreement is not something that one has a right to. It's
> a privilege. But it is a privilege that must be earned via the support
> of U.S. policy goals. . . . [The Bush administration] . . . expects
> cooperation—or better—on foreign policy and security issues. (U.S.
> Trade Representative Robert Zoellick, quoted in *New Statesman*, June
> 23, 2003)

> The pursuit of FTAs is not a matter of choice for Korea, but rather, a
> necessity. Indeed, as the world's 12th largest trading nation, relying on
> international trade for more than 70 percent of its economy, Korea
> should sense the impending crisis. (Chung 2003, 73)

Imagine, if you will, that you are the president of South Korea, politically directing international trade policy. Your policy choices affect the sixth largest export value of any nation on the planet.[1] If you think carefully about the two opening quotations, you might feel that you are in a bind. The second quotation notes that the South Korean economy is unusually dependent on exports, such that obtaining FTAs is vital for its national interest. The first quotation, however, notes that the United States is demanding foreign policy convergence in exchange for such FTAs. So how do you reconcile South Korea's trading interests with its international security interests?

This book builds upon a literature demonstrating that these questions are not idiosyncratic to South Korea but rather represent a ubiquitous global policy challenge. A number of studies show that alliances and military disputes significantly influence patterns of global FTA formation, suggesting that the relationship between trade policy and international security is a general one (e.g., Mansfield and Milner 2015). Security and FTAs are clearly connected. To be effective, policymakers must work within these (often competing) constraints.

I. Why FTAs and Why Korea

A core aspiration of both citizens and nations is to increase prosperity. In the modern world, international trade has become an increasingly central component of most countries' GDPs, such that the politics of international trade policy has become a central topic of study within international relations. As Mansfield and Milner (2012, 2) note:

> Gaining a fuller understanding of international trade agreements is important because trade is crucial to the global economy and contributes heavily to many national economies. For the largest 110 countries in the world, overseas trade (i.e., the sum of exports and imports) amounted to 65 percent of total income in 1975, a figure that grew to almost 90 percent in 2005 (World Bank 2011). In 2008, furthermore, world exports amounted to roughly $20 trillion, accounting for close to a third of global output. International trade has generally grown faster than world output since the 1950s as well. (World Trade Organization 2008)

For decades most writing on the politics of international trade negotiations focused on the overwhelming centrality of the General Agreement on Tariffs and Trade (GATT) and its 1994 replacement, the World Trade Organization (WTO). These institutions successfully yielded six consecutive rounds of multilateral agreements to lower tariffs, fueling the spread of post–World War II trade. Sadly, the latest round of negotiations, the Doha Round begun in 2001, is now seen as "dead and buried" (Martin and Mercurio 2017, 49). The Doha Round faltered not on industrial tariffs, which are now relatively low, but rather on attempts to liberalize in two other sectors: agriculture and services. In lieu of a WTO multilateral solution, countries have massively turned to FTAs and other non-WTO trade agreements to meet their desire for trade liberalization.[2]

Explaining these FTAs is primarily the providence of the economist. The standard explanation relies on what is called the gravity model. The impetus for trade, as well as the impetus for FTAs, is conceived of as Newton conceived of gravity, in which large masses (read GDPs) attract one another. More specifically, the higher the product of any two potential partners' GDPs, the higher the probability that they will adopt an FTA. Just as Newton noted that this gravitational pull would fall off with distance, so too do economists view distance as weakening the pull for FTAs (distance being a proxy for transportation costs).

Political scientists demonstrate that political factors also influence FTA formation. Domestically, two political variables stand out and are detailed in chapter 2. First, democracy facilitates majority preferences and strengthens property rights and rule of law, which make FTAs more likely to be signed by democracies than by authoritarian regimes. Second, mitigating the attraction for more FTAs, a larger number of veto players in a political system (e.g., constitutional division of powers) makes FTAs *less* likely (Mansfield and Milner 2002).

Internationally, the international political economy (IPE) approach in modern international relations accommodates many viewpoints, but all give some credence to the realistic proposition that states compete for power within a global system of international "anarchy." Rational states thus prefer to form FTAs with alliance partners so that they can reap the gains from trade while excluding non-alliance countries.

My *geopolitical economy* approach is theoretically rooted in this IPE tradition. My novelty is to claim that the geographic specificity of security threats sheds light on why and where FTAs occur. For example, it is one thing to note that U.S. alliance partners *have* FTAs, but it is another thing to note *why* these FTAs exist, which is as much about the war on terror and the rise of China as it is about military alliances per se.

Korean FTAs

Why focus on South Korea? The answer, in part, is that South Korea's FTA network is the world's most elaborate. South Korea has signed FTAs with forty-nine different nations and has the vast majority of its trade under FTA provisions.[3] Moreover, South Korea has the singular honor of signing FTAs with all *three* loci of the world economy: China, the European Union (EU), and the United States.[4] This feat is stunning when one realizes that only three other countries, Malaysia, Mexico, and Singapore, have achieved FTAs with more than *one* FTA from the rich trifecta of China, the EU, and the United States.

In addition, Korea is the most important new arrival to the global trading arena. For decades, Korea had already been a development legend, sharing with Taiwan the honor of being one of the only two countries to rise from African-level poverty to Organization for Economic Cooperation and Development (OECD)–level prosperity in a mere half century. Moreover, I emphasize in this book that *Korea now operates as an equal alongside the world's largest exporting nations in global trade.* To illustrate this key point,

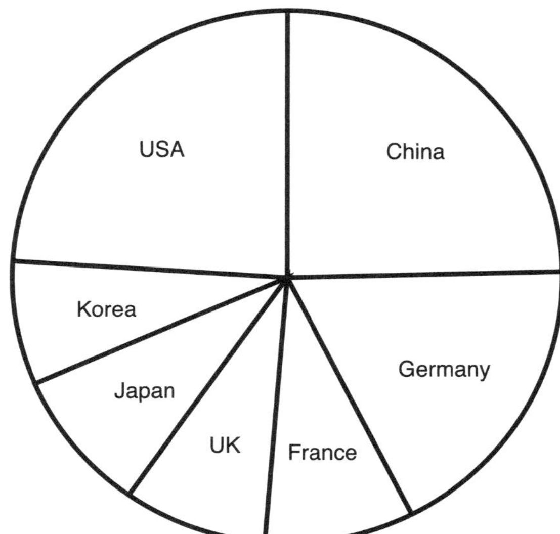

Figure 1.1. Relative Market Shares among the Seven Largest Exporters in 2013. (World Bank, World Development Indicators.)

consider figure 1.1, which depicts the relative export shares of the world's seven largest exporters. South Korea, a mere one-half of a small peninsula in the vastness of Asia, somehow shows up in figure 1.1, shoulder to shoulder with the world's Great Powers.

Think about this for a moment. South Korea is producing exports about equal to those of the United Kingdom, a former global empire upon which "the sun never set." Korea is producing exports about equal to those of Japan, its former colonial ruler and the original archetype of Asian exports as popularized by Chalmers Johnson's *MITI and the Japanese Miracle* (1982). Another way to think about the sheer magnitude of South Korea's exports is to note that when journalists speak of major emerging economies they often invoke the BRIC nations (Brazil, Russia, India, and China). The BRIC are *emerging* economies while South Korea is one of the few nations in the world to have *emerged* in the last century. Keeping in mind that all five were former developing countries, note that the *only* BRIC nation to show up in figure 1.1 is China. South Korea is more important in global trading markets than any BRIC nation other than China.

II. Geopolitical Economy

This book develops the international political economy perspective, explaining FTAs as arising, in part, from military alliances and major powers seeking security advantages. The book also extends the reach of an international political economy approach with the development of a *geopolitical economy* approach, viewing FTAs as the product of international power struggles over specific points of *geography*.

So why bring geography into the mix? Why focus on geopolitics and not merely alliances? A geopolitical economy approach posits that geography permeates most major global political and economic processes. To be more specific, but still staying at a high level of abstraction, geopolitical economy notes that the long decades of Cold War containment policy placed *certain geographic regions*, notably Western Europe, the Middle East, and East Asia, in a "privileged" global position on matters economic and political.[5]

Geopolitics brings to IPE the concept of **geography**. Indeed, "Geopolitics can be described as both the policy and the study of using geography and any factors attendant upon it, to understand, or influence, or, outright govern interstate relations, and international relations more generally" (Black 2016, 18).

A well-known illustration is Gowa's (1995) important point that the U.S.-led liberal multilateral trading order post–World War II was to a large extent a geopolitical reaction to the latest threat in Eurasia, namely, the USSR. What we call modern free trade might be better seen as the twentieth century playing out of a geopolitical battle between a maritime power, the United States, and a Eurasian land power, the USSR.

Black (2016) provides a comprehensive contemporary account of geopolitical history, and I identify in his account three modern geopolitical phenomena: (1) Cold War containment, (2) the war on terror, and (3) the rise of China. All three, I argue, have deeply shaped South Korean contemporary FTA policy as well as influenced global FTA negotiations more generally.

First, Cold War containment policy, including the U.S.-Korean military alliance and associated economic cooperation, was a necessary condition for long-run Korean economic development and export success. The U.S. occupation (1945–49) was a period when South Korean conservatives and U.S. policymakers worked together to crush the power of the political left, creating a conservative pro-capitalist political system. Then, as part of its strategy of containing Russian and Chinese communism in Asia, the United States also nurtured South Korea, offering massive foreign aid and easy access to the lucrative U.S. market.

Second, the war on terror has dramatically "securitized" U.S. international economic policy since 2001 (Higgott 2004). The world's strongest economic and military power, the United States, has ever since favored the geopolitical over the economic when initiating FTA policy. Whereas the

North American Free Trade Agreement (NAFTA) discourse of comparative advantage and regionalism would not have been inviting for South Korea, the new post-9/11 security discourse opened the window for U.S. policymakers to see the Korea-U.S. Free Trade Agreement (KORUS FTA) as a U.S. security asset in Asia.

Third, the rise of China, economically and militarily, is the overwhelming geopolitical reality of our times. It was this Chinese growth that largely led the Bush administration to deploy its "securitized" FTA policy to Asia. Naturally, South Korea felt the rise of Chinese power even more than the United States did, and this plus the threat from North Korea constituted the security backdrop that made the KORUS FTA irresistible for policymakers in both nations.

III. Method and Evidence

At heart, this book is a case study. There is an enormous body of literature on case studies, but for my purposes Gerring's (2004) piece "What Is a Case Study and What Is It Good For?" captures the essential elements. I entirely adopt Gerring's precise definition:

> A "case study," I argue, is best defined as an intensive study of a single unit with an aim to generalize across a larger set of units. Case studies rely on the same sort of covariational evidence utilized in no-case study research. (2004, 341)

In this book I provide an "intensive study" of South Korea. Consistent with the definition of case study, moreover, my goal is to "generalize across a larger set of units" by using this South Korean study to shed light on the broader phenomenon of geopolitically driven FTAs.

Gerring's definition notes the need for "covariational evidence," and later he claims more pointedly that "all empirical evidence of causal relations is *covariational* in nature" (2004, 342). This book focuses heavily on variation and covariation to uncover the causal mechanisms at work in South Korean FTA policy. By looking at variation within Korea across time and across trade partners and by looking at variation in how Korea differs from other countries, the case study approach allows us to generate knowledge about how the traditional alliance variable causes FTA agreements:

> X must be connected with Y in a plausible fashion; otherwise, it is unclear whether a pattern of covariation is truly causal in nature. The

identification of causal mechanisms happens when one puts together general knowledge of the world with empirical knowledge of how X and Y interrelate. It is in the latter task that case studies enjoy a comparative advantage. (Gerring 2004, 348)

Within the Korean case I use many forms of covariation evidence. First, I use temporal comparisons, such as showing that the Cold War containment was a necessary condition for subsequent Korean FTA policy and, on a smaller scale, that the institutional centralization of the trade bureaucracy in 1997 strongly facilitated later FTA policy. Second, I use cross-national variation in South Korean FTA agreements to assess *why* South Korea chooses some FTA partners over other potential partners. Third, I employ a "nested-inference" research design (Lieberman 2005), assessing what a global statistical model has to say about Korean FTA choices and how these either reinforce or conflict with the other findings.

In addition to providing a case study, this book also provides a number of informal small-n comparisons, that is to say, informal comparisons between a handful of similar cases. I write "informal" because I do not address the extent of inter-case comparability but simply utilize a broad range of seemingly plausible country comparisons to advance generalizations about the geopolitics of FTA formation. I conceive of these cases as the "adjacent units" to Korea, in Gerring's (2004) sense, and as such, much of this book operates at "the blurry line between a unit that is intensively studied—the case study—and other adjacent units that may be brought into the analysis in a less structured manner" (344).

Given the scope of this book there is more than the usual need for parsimony, so above and beyond all the methods mentioned above, my primary approach is that of the **analytic narrative**. This term was introduced by such "soft" rational choice scholars as Robert Bates et al. (1998, 2000) and Margaret Levi (2002, 2004) and refers to the construction of a simple model of human behavior and the application of this model to some social phenomenon, for example, agriculture policy (Bates et al.) or taxation policy (Levi).

My use of analytic narrative is driven by a desire to retain parsimony in explanation (i.e., geopolitics largely explains FTA policy) while at the same time delving deeply into the *hows* and *whys* of the causal processes by examining the case in detail. As Bates et al. (2000) argue, this is precisely the most useful function of the analytic narrative.

[An] analytic narrative is most attractive to scholars who seek to evaluate the strength of parsimonious causal mechanisms. The requirement of explicit theorizing compels scholars to make causal statements and,

> if the model is to be fully explicated, to identify a small number of
> variables. . . . The advantages of this approach are twofold. First, it pro-
> vides the researcher with some discipline. If the model is important,
> the narrative should not rely overmuch on factors outside the model.
> Hence, an explicit theory allows the scholar to distill the narrative.
> Second, research of this kind can proceed by iteration. (687)

As for the first advantage, I intentionally "distill" my analytic narrative
down to the effects of geopolitics on trade policy, so as to focus intently on
assessing the causal mechanisms. By using a case study, moreover, I am able
to conduct this distillation with attention to a broad range of alternative
explanations, statistical and comparative-historical. Given this substantial
range in coverage, I distill my analytic narrative to a single causal process—
the effect of geopolitics on FTA formation.

As for the second advantage, an "iterative" approach, what Bates et al.
(2000) have in mind specifically is an inductive approach to social science.
Bates develops this point the most, arguing that to understand well any social phenomenon we need to bring to bear a number of complementary analytic lenses, including formal theory, historical reality, statistical evidence,
comparative cases, and common sense (Bates 2009). This book embraces
this mixed-method approach.

IV. The Broader Theoretical Context

My analysis of the geopolitical economy of South Korean FTAs informs a
variety of ongoing discussions in both international political economy and
comparative political economy. Most generally, I contribute to the vast existing literature seeking to understand how and why nations engage the international economy. With international trade growing more quickly than
domestic GDP, scholars and policymakers are increasingly interested in how
nations can improve their international competitiveness. My contribution,
as per the book's title, is to demonstrate that geopolitics and geography offer
novel insights for scholars thinking about FTAs.

Geography, International Politics, and FTA Policy

A rather large literature explains FTAs with respect to international political
conditions. Some argue that declining U.S. hegemony is a cause of FTAs

(e.g., Pomfret 1988; Baldwin 1993; Krugman 1993; Gilpin 1987). Others argue that military alliances facilitate FTAs (Gowa and Mansfield 1993; Mansfield 1993; Gowa 1994). Still others argue that international conflict, by contrast, deters FTAs (Mansfield 1999).

My geopolitical approach views alliances and disputes as themselves the outgrowth of geopolitical struggles in specific geographical regions. Cold War containment policy led the United States to invest in the South Korean nation. The KORUS FTA is at least as much about the U.S. response to the rise of China as it is about an alliance per se. Moreover, such geopolitical effects are considerable. Chapter 7 shows that U.S. FTA policy is tightly tied to its projection of military power in the Middle East and Asia, while China's FTAs are part and parcel of its diplomatic and political strategy to become dominant in Asia.

Geography, Foreign Direct Investment, and Global Supply Chains

Buthe and Milner (2008) argue that FTAs facilitate foreign direct investment (FDI) by signaling stronger state commitment to free markets and a stable investment climate. This book suggests that these linkages are becoming increasingly strong due to *economic geography*. Specifically, the economic dispersion that comes with a shift from two-country trade to three-country trade helps explain why FDI increases with FTAs.

Baldwin (2013) refers to this shift from two-party trade to three-party trade as a "second unbundling," as described in chapter 2. A key point is that the production process itself is now geographically dispersed across at least two different countries, which greatly complicates production and hence requires complex information processes to coordinate sufficiently to overcome transaction costs. Modern trade, therefore, has more deeply linked trade liberalization to FDI liberalization and service sector liberalization; "to stress its interconnectedness," Baldwin "call[s] this the *trade-investment-services-IP nexus*" (2013, 24; emphasis added).

Votes and Vetoes

Mansfield and Milner (2012) note an overemphasis on the international determinants of FTA policy, and they argue that two domestic political factors are important: democracy and veto players. They argue that economic theory would suggest that the median voter benefits from free trade and that in a democratic system this voter is more likely to have his or her way than in an authoritarian regime. In addition, a larger number of veto players increases the transaction costs of FTAs, inhibiting their formation.

The Korean case sheds light on these arguments, focusing on how and why veto players matter. Examining the domestic politics of Korean FTAs, as well as selected comparisons with other countries, provides a more concrete understanding of specific veto players. I provide a detailed analysis of an important veto player that Mansfield and Milner (2012) emphasize, which is the division between the executive and legislative. My case study demonstrates, however, the extreme importance of two other veto players: the agricultural sector and veto players *within* the state apparatus. These are both highly pertinent and yet go unnoticed by existing cross-national statistical proxies of veto players.

States and Economic Development

Finally, my book speaks to the broad literature on states and economic development. Evans (1979) notes that an alliance between the domestic state and foreign capital yielded rapid industrialization in Brazil. In *Bringing the State Back In,* Evans, Rueschemeyer, and Skocpol (1985) argue more generally that efficacious states can transform societies and economies. The pinnacle of this line of reasoning is the literature on "developmental states." Specialists on East Asia, writing from a variety of disciplines, argue that rapid growth in Asia was less a free-market phenomenon and more a determined effort by states to utilize industrial policy to better take advantage of international markets (Amsden 1989; Wade 1990; World Bank 1993; Evans 1995). Even more generally, Chang (2002) argues that the developmental state played a role in almost all cases of development, including in Europe and North America.

While the central story of my book relates to the geopolitical origins of FTAs, the secondary purpose of this book is to examine how the South Korean policymaking apparatus *responded* to geopolitical and international economic constraints and opportunities. As noted in the book's abstract, the second theme of this book is to evaluate the overall coherence and efficacy of the South Korean policymaking response to global events. Chapter 5, in particular, examines "FTAs as Development Strategy" while chapter 6 examines "FTA Consequences." States manage their relationship with the global geopolitical economy, and South Korea provides lessons on how to effectively conduct such management.

Conclusions

Shortly before South Korea initiated its FTA strategy, President Jimmy Carter's Secretary of State, Zbigniew Brezezinksi, wrote a book entitled The Grand Chessboard: American Primacy and Its Geostrategic Imperatives (1997). Although America has been dominant on the "grand chessboard," all nations compete on this geopolitical economy chessboard. And all play for high national stakes: peace and prosperity. By examining South Korean FTAs through the lens of development strategy, this book assesses South Korea's play on the grand chessboard.

On the whole, South Korea has played splendidly. Under the wing of U.S. containment, South Korea has blossomed into perhaps the world's most miraculous export achievement: half of a small peninsula in Asia producing export goods in excess of such territorial behemoths as India, Brazil, and Russia.

In recent years, as explored in this book, South Korea has outstripped the rest of the world in obtaining meaningful FTAs with all three major loci of the global economy: the EU, the United States, and China. This intentional and ambitious strategy capitalized on Korea's singular geopolitical environment while drawing upon Korea's capable state and dynamic economy.

CHAPTER 2

Geopolitical Economy

This book is interdisciplinary, looking at FTAs via an intersection of political science, economics, and geography. The book also follows a mixed-method approach, utilizing both quantitative and narrative methods. I blend these disciplines and methodologies because I believe that only together, through a mixed-method geopolitical economy approach, can we arrive at a thorough understanding of the origins, purposes, and results of South Korea's FTAs. Because there are so many disciplines, I dedicate this chapter to clarifying the many important approaches that scholars take to study FTAs.

I begin with a typology, depicted in figure 2.1, which visually organizes many distinct research domains. The three circles in the figure depict three academic disciplines that trade theory draws upon: geography, economics, and politics. Geography is the broadest, given that geography is the study of the Earth's crust, its inhabitants, and the ways that these inhabitants utilize the materials and resources of the crust. The disciplines of political science and economics, under this understanding, are thoroughly informed by geography, which justifies its placement at the top of figure 2.1.

These three disciplines, each with their own literatures, also significantly overlap with one another, yielding three distinct areas of interdisciplinary academic inquiry. In figure 2.1, each of the three petals radiating from the center encompasses its own interdisciplinary literatures. Finally, the central arena in the figure, where the three disciplines overlap, pulls upon all of these literatures to provide a *geopolitical economy* theory.

This chapter examines each of the interdisciplinary petals in figure 2.1. To introduce the topics, section I provides a brief introduction to the political debate over free trade. Sections II and III examine the top-right petal in figure 2.1, discussing the "gravity model" and the "second unbundling."

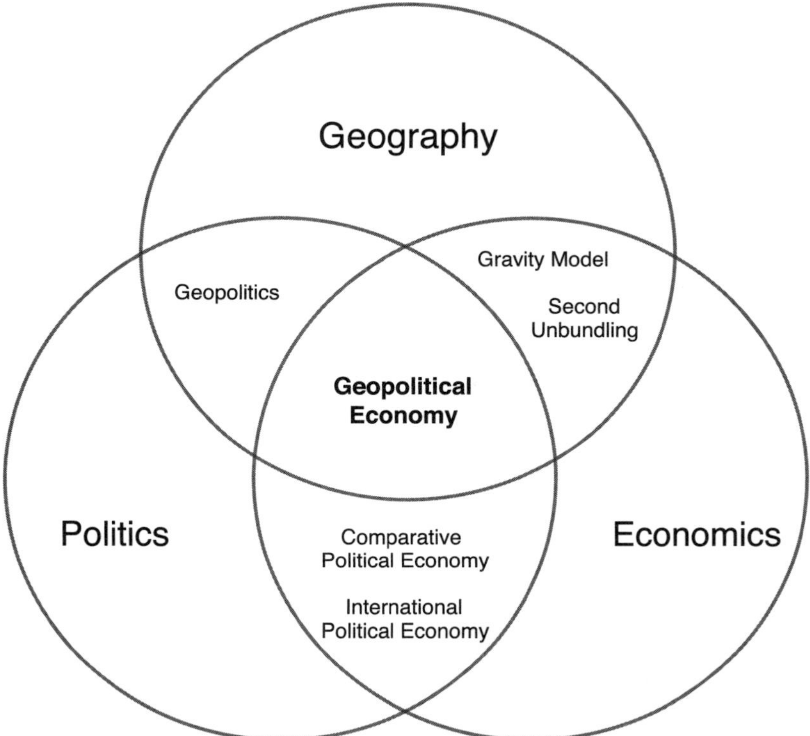

Figure 2.1. Geopolitical Economy
Geopolitical economy and its intertwining fields of inquiry: three academic disciplines, five interdisciplinary literatures, and a central geopolitical economy lens through which to study the emerging intersection of all of them.

Sections IV and V examine the bottom-most petal, focusing in turn on "comparative political economy" and "international political economy." Section VI examines the final petal, the top-left "geopolitics" petal. I argue that geopolitics—and more specifically (1) Cold War containment, (2) the war on terror in the Middle East, and (3) the rise of China—substantially influences FTA formation.

Finally, while geopolitics is the independent variable that I focus on, the broader goal of this treatise is to advance the perspective of *geopolitical economy*. This overall perspective is represented in the center of figure 2.1, a holistic approach that draws upon multiple variants of geography, economics, and political science.

I. The Politics of Trade

Trade is an inherently political topic. This was made abundantly clear to North Americans during the 2016 presidential election when much of the campaign rhetoric was heavily anti-trade. Outside of North America, Brexit demonstrates that there is a generalized controversy about, and perhaps even backlash against, globalization—by which I mean the complex processes through which people, goods, capital, and information cross international borders.

Yet international trade *has* occurred on a massive scale. Most nations *have* sought prosperity through the gains from trade. Economic growth worldwide was particularly rapid during the post–World War II liberal era, when the United States and other major powers intentionally promoted an open international trading system. The Bretton Woods agreement, the International Monetary Fund, the World Bank, and GATT generated and sustained a liberal trading system. Indeed, under GATT auspices, the world embraced seven distinct rounds of multilateral trade tariff reductions, with 123 countries agreeing to reduce barriers.

The fact that it took seven painstaking multiyear rounds of multilateral negotiations to achieve tariff liberalization also illustrates that it is politically difficult to liberalize trade. In nation after nation, both historically and in the contemporary era, every trade liberalization effort has been vigorously opposed by multiple political actors. To understand FTAs from a broad perspective, it is necessary to consider the essential elements of the historic debate over national trade policy. I begin with the classic case for free trade.

The Case for Free Trade and David Ricardo

Most economists view free trade as desirable for society as a whole. Obviously individuals vary dramatically in their politics, but professors of economics are frequently engaged in teaching free trade theory, based on Ricardo's theory of comparative advantage, which at its core concludes that free trade enhances net social welfare. As a result, millions of U.S. citizens have been educated to "appreciate" the virtues of free trade.

For those of us who study the developing world, it is easy to be sympathetic to these arguments. I, personally, am awed by the tectonically powerful force (for good or for ill) that is international trade. When one looks at major wealthy nations arising in the post–World War II era, such as South

Korea and Taiwan, one sees the incredible social power of a hypothetical idea called "free trade."

The primary argument for free trade is David Ricardo's theory of *comparative advantage* (1817). To explain this theory we start with a less sophisticated idea, the concept of *absolute advantage* (Smith 1776). A nation has an absolute advantage in a product when that country can produce it more efficiently than another country. For an example of absolute advantage, Smith (1776) gives the United Kingdom and the United States. The United Kingdom was internationally competitive in cloth exports, while the United States was competitive in wheat production, such that both countries had an absolute advantage in one of these two goods.

But what if one country is at an absolute disadvantage producing all goods? Could less efficient countries lose from trade? This question is addressed in Ricardo's famous example of Britain and Portugal. Portugal was hypothesized to have an *absolute advantage* in <u>both</u> wine and cloth, meaning that they could produce more of each at a lower cost than the British could. This might make international trade seem risky for the British. If one seems untalented *at all things*, how can one benefit from trade? Ricardo's theory of *comparative advantage* directly answers this question, demonstrating that no matter who was *absolutely* better at producing either good, both nations would benefit overall from trade. Ricardo provided a simple yet powerful arithmetical example that is well worth reading, but I will not test the reader's patience here because the intuition is simple to present verbally, with the math merely proving that the intuition holds true.

The central intuition is that even if a country is bad at making everything, it is probably *relatively* worse at producing some things (say, wine) than other things (say, cloth). Put crudely, the idea is that while Britain might be worse at making everything, it is *especially* atrocious at making wine, whereas, in comparison, Portugal produces both products more efficiently, but is *particularly* stellar at making wine. The idea, then, is that the efficient Portuguese are capable of producing so much wine that, when imported to Britain, it frees up vast sectors of (inefficient) British producers to make large quantities of cloth. The bottom line of this example, and Ricardo's mathematical example proves it, is that trade enhances material well-being even if, in a worst-case scenario, a nation is *less* skilled than *all* other countries in *all* product lines.

There are many critiques of David Ricardo's logic, and below we will discuss the most significant of the many caveats, but nobody denies the basic logic of the theory of comparative advantage. This powerful idea drives trade liberalization to this day, and it underpins South Korea's historic success.

Dynamic Trade Theory

Caveat number one to Ricardo's theory of comparative advantage is that it depends on *certain assumptions holding true,* and, as we know, assumptions are often violated in the real world. The bulk of development economics in the 1950s and 1960s, for instance, argued that a variety of different market failures in developing countries inhibited trade's full hypothetical gains. In practice, moreover, for around a half century (1930–80) the major Latin American countries experienced involuntary import-substituting industrialization (ISI) during the Great Depression and then as a matter of tariff policy after World War II. Partially as a result, Brazil and Mexico enjoyed the world's most rapid growth over the period 1930–80 (Maddison 1992).

In East Asia, in accordance with the developmental state approach, activist governments protected "infant industries" in steel, electronics, and so forth to jump-start "dynamic comparative advantage." Even in modern OECD contexts, mainstream economists such as Paul Krugman argue that dynamic trade can help create comparative advantage. These ideas even have policy influence, such as the EU's support for Airbus's challenge to Boeing's global monopoly, which itself was guided by U.S. defense spending, a kind of developmental state approach. These and many other challenges to the free trade orthodoxy have long existed, and many may continue affecting the future for a long time to come.

This huge caveat noted, most economists do, for better or worse, legitimate free trade. Economists regularly teach international trade's gains in the classroom. For instance, the gravity model, discussed further below, simply takes for granted that trade represents a "gravitational" force. Indeed, it is implicit that policymakers "understand" that trade increases net GDP, that increasing net GDP is desirable, and that trade should be pursued.

Distributional Consequences—the Stolper-Samuelson Theorem

Caveat number two to the theory of comparative advantage is that economists are keenly aware that trade policy has *distributional implications.* This conclusion, in fact, stems from the mainstream Stolper-Samuelson theorem in trade theory. The intuition, again, is reasonably simple. Going back to the British cloth versus Portuguese wine example, just consider what would happen if these two countries had no trade to begin with and then suddenly they did start trading. Cloth manufacturers in Portugal, as well as wine producers in Britain, would be seriously hurt as demand for their products fell.

Economists can reassure us that British cloth producers and Portuguese wine producers gained even *more* than the others lost, but the distributional effects still exist and, in real-world politics, are rarely fully addressed with compensatory policies, for example, retraining and relocation costs.

The core intuition is that when a nation enters into increased international trade, some factors (i.e., social groups) see significant gains from trade while some factors actually lose from trade. This imbalance explains the strong backlash against trade in nations, given that it usually entails clear losers. Nonetheless, economists continue to underscore that *total* economic production will be higher under trade, such that *with some redistribution* everyone would in theory be better off. Such redistribution, however, is a political process, not an economic one, and rarely occurs in practice.

Despite these gigantic caveats, trade theory explicitly or implicitly accepts David Ricardo's argument that nations are better off when engaged in greater international trade. With this unifying vision, economists see a powerful underlying gravitational pull between nations for FTAs. Specifically, the larger the product of the countries' GDPs, the more the countries have an incentive to negotiate and sign an FTA. As such, the metaphor of GDP as gravity is intuitive and leads us directly to the theoretical workhorse of trade theory, namely, the gravity model.

II. The Gravity Model

We now turn from the grand debate over trade in general to the much more focused question of why it is that two countries agree to sign an FTA, binding both to a more liberal set of economic transactions. Figure 2.1 provides my overall typology of theories that purport to explain FTAs.

We begin with the gravity model because it is the most common way of thinking about FTAs. The gravity model is placed in the upper-right petal of figure 2.1, between geography and economics. This is because, as we shall see, the basic intuition of the gravity model is that the economic argument favoring free trade is tempered by the geographic reality that trade is costly across distance. There is an economic pull and a geographic resistance, which in conjunction explain trade flows and FTAs.

The gravity model starts with the analogy to physical gravity, which Sir Isaac Newton noted is equal to the product of two masses divided by the square of their distance. Trade economists argue, analogously, that international trade is "attracted" by the product of the two countries' market sizes and that this effect also weakens with distance, since distance increases transport costs.[1] Only two concepts are therefore at play—size of market (proxied by overall GDP) and geographic distance (proxied by distance between capitals).

The gravity model therefore yields two hypotheses. I state both explicitly:[2]

H_{1a}: The larger the product of the **GDP** between two trading partners, the higher the likelihood that these countries will negotiate an FTA.

H_2: The further the **distance** between two trading partners, the lower the likelihood that these countries will negotiate an FTA.

Although the gravity model is a simple intuition, three subtleties deserve attention. They by no means change the logic provided so far, but they do affect statistical specifications and some parts of the analytic narrative in chapters to come. They also highlight the fact that the economic concept of "gravity" is considerably less precise than that of Newton's laws of gravity.

First, GDP captures only the most obvious sense of the gravitational pull of a "market." An alternative conception is differences in GDP per capita or, put differently, differences in prevailing levels of prosperity. GDP per capita is often used as a measure of a country's factor endowments, particularly when it is differentiated between being capital intensive (proxied as high GDP per capita) or labor intensive (proxied by low GDP per capita). This is because economic theory suggests that countries with different factor endowments are natural trading partners. Specifically, trade (and FTAs) becomes more likely "the greater the difference in capital-labor endowment ratios between two countries due to the gains from traditional comparative advantages" (Baier and Bergstrand 2004, 60). This prompts a further hypothesis, specifically a sub of H1, as follows:

H_{1b}: The larger the (absolute) difference in **GDP per capita** between two trading partners, the higher the likelihood that these countries will negotiate an FTA.

Second, Frankel, Stein and Wei (1997) propose that wealthier countries pursue trade more vigorously. They provide multiple reasons for this claim: exotic foreign goods may be a luxury good that wealthier individuals are more likely to pursue; richer countries have more advanced infrastructure, reducing the transaction costs associated with trade; and, finally, poor countries often liberalize economically as they develop, such that richer countries tend toward freer markets. These factors, in Frankel's logic, constitute multiple reasons that rich countries will be more receptive to Korean FTAs. Accordingly:

> H_{IC}: The higher the **GDP per capita** of a country, the more likely it is to engage in an FTA.

Finally, I follow Frankel (1997, 54) in distinguishing between a "basic" gravity model that considers only the variables above as opposed to "full" gravity models that also include common borders and other factors. (For a fuller set of control variables, using both basic and full sets, see the analysis in chapter 3).

To sum up, the gravity model is the primary way that economists think about FTA formation. Any narrative explanation for a particular FTA must take into account the size of each partner's GDP, as well as the distance between the two nations, as these are two strong causal effects that must be taken into account before giving credence to a geopolitical, or other, narrative explanation.

As one particularly obvious yet very important example, China's FTA with Korea is <u>much</u> less surprising than the Korea-EU FTA or the KORUS FTA, given that China is so close to South Korea. Similarly, that South Korea actively negotiated for FTAs with the United States, the EU, and China should not be at all surprising, given their enormous gravitational pull. The flip side of that question—why these behemoths would be interested in Korea—is more perplexing given that the Korean GDP, while admirable, is not truly comparable to the major loci of the world economy. All of these points, and many more developed in this book, stem from the gravity model.

III. The Second Unbundling

Paul Krugman, the *New York Times* columnist, won his Nobel prize for his work on increasing returns, trade theory, and geography. His work gave birth to what is now called the *new economic geography*. A commentary on his Nobel prize notes how important he is to modern economic theory:

> Krugman was beyond doubt the key player in "placing geographical analysis squarely in the economic mainstream" (Krugman 1998, 7) and in conferring it the central role it now assumes (Behrens and Robert-Nicoud 2009, 468).

A central contribution of Krugman's work is to show how increasing returns influence economic production throughout geographic space. The idea is that proximity encourages increasing returns, which is why production is not spread out across the globe but rather clusters in certain global regions, within certain nations, as well as within certain locales and cities within nations. Krugman explained, essentially, the clustering of production through geographic space.

This new focus on geography leads me to a second interdisciplinary literature that is relevant to South Korean FTAs, which is the literature on the "second unbundling" (Baldwin 2013). It too lays at the intersection of geography and international trade (see fig. 2.1). Baldwin notes that international trade is essentially the dispersion of economic processes across geography. The long history of trade in the nineteenth and twentieth centuries can be seen as a first great "unbundling" of production and consumption across international borders.

> In the pre-globalization world, each village made most of what it consumed. Production and consumption were forced together by poor transportation technology. The steam revolution, especially railroads and steamships, made it feasible to spatially separate production and consumption with this starting from the 1830s and accelerating in the 1870s (the Trans-America line was completed in 1869). Once feasible, scale economies and comparative advantage made separation profitable. This transformed the world. (Baldwin 2013, 14)

Baldwin points out what he calls a "second unbundling" taking place in the contemporary global political economy. Whereas the first unbundling was a geographic dispersion of *production from consumption*, the second unbundling is a geographic unbundling of *production itself* (Baldwin 2013). The *Economist* popularized Baldwin early, in 2007, providing a useful description of what happens:

> Ricardo, it seems, did only half the job. He described the first of two "great unbundlings"—as Richard Baldwin, of the Graduate Institute of International Studies in Geneva, has put it in a recent guide. Trade in wine, cloth and other goods allows production to be distanced from consumption. Countries do not need to grow grapes to enjoy the fruit of the vine; thanks to trade, they can transform cloth into wine instead.

But in Ricardo's world, a country must still take care of all of the separate tasks required to finish the goods it makes. In a country of pinmakers, to take Adam Smith's seminal example, someone must still cut, draw and straighten the wire; fashion and affix the head; then whiten and sheath the finished product, if any pins are to be made at all.

In the second great unbundling, production is spliced and diced into separate fragments that can be spread around the globe. Pin-whitening is done in one country; wire-cutting in another. Some theorists call this the "vertical disintegration of production across borders." Thankfully, Messrs Grossman and Rossi-Hansberg have a more felicitous phrase: "trade in tasks."

As globalisation has advanced, it has become easier to move some of these tasks offshore. For the workers who once carried them out, this has three possible consequences, two bad, one good. Start with the good news. Offshoring makes firms more productive. The tasks that are best kept close to home remain onshore; other tasks can be taken care of in cheaper places abroad. Everyone benefits from this gain in productivity, including the workers who have fewer tasks to perform. For example, Japanese electronics companies continue to flourish in American markets precisely because they have moved their assembly lines to China.

In essence, Baldwin's point is that international trade is increasingly geographically dispersed into three-party trade networks, as opposed to traditional two-party trade networks. Baldwin further notes that with improved technology there has been a dramatic fall in international coordination costs, making these three-country economic production networks entirely feasible. Baldwin (2013, 6) explains:

> Some of the coordination costs are related to communication, so the "coordination glue" began to melt from the mid-1980s with ICT's [information and communications technology] melding of telecommunications, computers and organizational software. In short: The ICT revolution made it possible to coordinate complexity at distance. . . . The vast wage differences between developed and developing nations made separation profitable. . . . This was globalization's second unbundling—some production stages previously performed in close proximity were dispersed geographically.

This book will discuss further the increasingly global interconnectedness of trade in the second unbundling, but for now note how complex the international *geographic* distribution of comparative advantage has become, with three-country flows and increasingly common ties with FDI and professional services.

IV. Comparative Political Economy

We must also consider the broader political and social world to understand trade policy. Thinking back to figure 2.1, we now shift attention from the top-right petal to the bottom-most petal. We are therefore leaving behind for now the realm of geography and focusing instead on the interaction between politics and economics.

This section begins with an emphasis on the domestic politics of economic policy, known more generally as "comparative political economy." Comparative political economists, at least in political science, lay claim to a different empirical domain than economists. Whereas most economists study the societal institution called "the economy," political scientists study other elements of a nation, most notably, societal interest groups, state and societal institutions, and individual behavior.

A simple state-society conceptual vocabulary is useful to cope with these topics. This vocabulary, as per the state-society tradition described in Bringing the State Back In (Evans, Rueschemeyer, and Skocpol 1985), distinguishes between *states* and *societies*. *Societies* are groups of human individuals, and these groups exhibit the great and extraordinary variation of human life, such as family, food gathering, social events, poetry, paintings, and the economy. *States* are conceived of as a narrower entity, populated by a few individuals in structured organizations, and yet having a monopoly on the legitimate use of coercion and therefore, in effect, having power to control the direction of societies.

Societies are complex, multifaceted, and ultimately composed of myriad individuals with their own interests, hopes, and fears. Reducing this complex whole into any simple typology is a gross oversimplification, and yet that is precisely the task of social science. One prominent approach is that of Marxism, which in its crudest form could be thought of as reducing society to two agents: labor and capital. Pluralist scholars, on the other hand, posit that citizens have multiple political interests (e.g., values, race, gender, and socialization) such that citizens find themselves facing each other across a variety of crosscutting cleavages rather than just a simple and divisive class system.

Economic Sectors and Political Interests

The approach of most trade theorists, as well as political scientists studying the politics of trade, is to think about society through a variety of prisms, such as pluralism and/or Marxism, but with a particular focus on the political interests of specific *economic sectors*. The Stolper-Samuelson theorem discussed above emphasized that trade has distributional consequences, and such distributional effects depend upon a country's comparative advantage, and affect each country's sectors accordingly.

In Korea it is commonly observed that the manufacturing sector is the most competitive sector and, hence, generally benefits most from increased international trade. It is not surprising, therefore, that the gargantuan Korean manufacturing firms, the *chaebol*, are generally pro-trade. The less competitive factors of production, however, are hurt by trade. Agriculture in Korea is relatively less efficient than manufacturing, and by such a large margin that it is generally agreed to be the primary loser from trade liberalization. Again, real events are more complicated, but the overall winners and losers from trade are fairly easy to see simply by examining the basic pattern of a nation's exports and imports.

More generally, it might be noted, South Korea's uncompetitive agricultural sector reflects a generally powerful economic sector. As we shall see in countries throughout Asia, and indeed the world, the agricultural sector is a particularly critical veto point in many countries, making or breaking a government's ability to enter into FTAs.

In the United States, similarly, some sectors are highly competitive internationally, such as agriculture, services, and some lines of manufacturing. Although they get less attention than job losses, the foreign demands for these sectors boost U.S. product and employment. That said, in the United States, the low-wage and low-skill manufacturing sector is less competitive internationally, such that the "returns" (econ-speak for wages) to unskilled labor have fallen. Given rising inequality in the United States for a number of decades, these distributional effects have shaped political debates over trade.

Prevailing cross-national statistical models do not, to my knowledge, provide any proxy for the differing levels of political power found between different sectors. The contentious wrangling between rival economic sectors, country by country, is largely invisible in the cross-national statistical literature, despite its well-known importance (e.g., Gourevitch 1986).

Given that this is precisely the literature to which we must look for alliance effects on FTAs, which are inherently cross-national, these two political stories often speak past each other. In the mixed-method spirit, this book takes from the qualitative and historical literature the premise that it is clear that economic sectors organize vigorously around trade polices that benefit or, especially, harm them. This assumption is utilized throughout the book, despite the lack of cross-national confirmations of the hypothesis in the statistical literature, as the premise is both intuitive and without vigorous dissent.

Democracy

A second concept that is vitally important in the comparative political economy literature is the concept of democracy. Indeed, concerning trade theory, we have rather powerful theoretical and empirical reasons to believe that *states* that are structured *democratically* with respect to societies are more likely to sign FTAs than states that are *authoritarian* in relation to societies. Given that Korea was authoritarian up until 1987, but has been democratic since, this variable needs to be taken into consideration when analyzing Korea's FTA strategy, although it only exhibits itself statistically in cross-national tests.

Democracy, in theory, facilitates FTAs because it allows citizens to express their rational (if you accept Ricardo) desire for trade. While some groups will be harmed by trade, making free trade controversial, the intuition is that if most citizens, on net, benefit from free trade, then democracy gives citizens the power to make free trade happen in public policy. In contrast, under authoritarianism, citizens' preferences for free trade can be ignored.

Contemporary readers in North America will object that presidential candidates Bernie Sanders (on the left) and Donald Trump (on the right) argued against the Trans-Pacific Partnership (TPP) and FTAs. Surely democracy can generate sentiment against free trade? Given distributional consequences and dynamic trade theories discussed earlier, reasons exist for citizens to lean in a more protectionist direction from time to time.

Although protests show visible evidence of anti-trade sentiment, however, democracies are arguably run by the *median* voter, or at least much more so than authoritarian regimes are (Downs 1957). When it comes to median voters, Mansfield and Milner (2012) present a markedly broad body of studies showing that in continent after continent, and indeed in nation after nation, majorities or *strong* majorities support free trade compared to protection. Free trade is surprisingly popular worldwide.

As an empirical matter, moreover, democracy is robustly correlated with FTAs across a variety of studies. Democracies are more likely to trade with each other and more likely to form FTAs with each other. It is these two facts—the simultaneous evidence that *most* people in *most* countries want free trade alongside the fact that democracies do in fact pursue trade and FTAs more frequently than do authoritarian regimes—that make compelling the prevailing theoretical argument that more democratic nations will be more free trade than less democratic countries. Therefore we can posit yet another hypothesis to our list:

H$_4$: The more **democratic** a country, the higher the likelihood that it will seek to negotiate an FTA with other nations.

Just as the economic gravity model had both an attractive force (GDP) and a resistance (distance), so too does political economy theory provide both an attractive force and a resistant force. Democracy pulls countries toward FTAs, but what pushes them apart? The answer lies in another prominent domestic theory of FTA formation in the cross-national literature, namely, the resistance to FTA policy caused by the number of *veto players* in a country's political institutions (Mansfield and Milner 2012).

Indeed, it is well accepted in the political science literature that any policy change (adopting an FTA is merely one example) will be less likely the greater the number of veto players in the political system (Tsebelis 2002; Henisz 2000). Empirically, the Henisz index has been extensively used in comparative political economy and international political economy given the obvious relevance of veto players to all policy topics. This index is constructed to capture veto actions, as is evident in Mansfield and Milner's succinct description of the index: the Henisz index "ranges from 0 to 1 and considers the presence of effective branches of government outside the executive's control, the extent to which these branches are controlled by the same political party as the executive and the homogeneity of preferences within these branches" (2015, 66). The idea is that the more veto points, especially when inhabited by alternative political parties and/or general policy preferences, the less likely it is that FTA negotiations will be successful. In sum, the Henisz index allows us to posit another, simple, hypothesis to our list:

H$_5$: The more **veto players** a country has, the lower the likelihood that it will seek to negotiate FTAs.

V. International Political Economy

Returning to the bottom petal of figure 2.1, we have now looked at one of the literatures in that petal, which is the comparative political economy perspective. The other literature noted in figure 2.1 is the international political economy perspective.

The first point to note is that international relations (IR) theory posits different causal mechanisms than comparative political economy, or even other parts of the field of comparative politics, the field of American politics and the discipline of economics. In economics, the unit of analysis is the individual or the firm, and in comparative politics, the unit of analysis is usually either the individual or an institution. In contrast, the unit of analysis in IR is the state. Political realism, perhaps the most long-standing theoretical tradition in IR, takes as its prime axiom that the international system is (largely) one of international anarchy. As such, realists argue states must engage in military "self-help," such as national defense spending, international alliances, and even outright war.[3]

Mansfield and Milner (2015) utilize this line of reasoning to argue that raw security-alliance politics strongly influences the likelihood of FTAs: "political relations between states may influence whether they join the same FTA. Military hostilities between states are likely to discourage economic cooperation and thus reduce states' propensity to sign FTAs, whereas political-military cooperation is likely to promote economic cooperation" (66).

This perspective is grounded in Albert Hirschman's analysis of the economic and political environment leading up to World War II. In *National Power and the Structure of Foreign Trade* (1945), he showed that geopolitics influenced trade agreements because the economic gains from trade accrued to the whole alliance, not just the individual country. Whereas supporting allies usually costs money, FTAs allow one to support allies and actually make money doing it. This makes FTAs a rather obvious and even lucrative policy tool in promoting security alliances and security interests.

Gowa (1994) stated the point perhaps most clearly, noting that trade between allies has (positive) security externalities while trade between enemies has (negative) security externalities. Given how important trade is to the economy, and how important the economy is to military capacity, the trade-alliance relationship is a major one, allowing us to add another hypothesis to our list:

H$_6$: Trading partners that share **security alliances** will have a greater probability of forming FTAs than other country dyads.

This hypothesis has been confirmed by Gowa (1995), Mansfield (1993), Mansfield and Milner (2015), and Yamamato (2016). This hypothesis obviously has significant implications for my analytic narrative, and indeed of all the hypotheses posited thus far it is the "alliance hypothesis" that most strongly informs my own theoretical perspective, which is heavily focused on security concerns.

Hegemonic Stability Theory

Most scholarly analyses of FTAs, whether using case studies, small-n comparisons, or cross-national statistical analyses, focus on the following question: *Why do some pairs* of countries sign FTAs while others do not? Chapters 3 and 5 address this same question, using novel global and Korean data sets. The rest of this book focuses on why South Korea has so many FTAs, and such quality FTAs, compared to other countries.

And yet arguably an even more fundamental question is, Why do FTAs exist at all? After all, global trade has existed for centuries, and yet the FTA phenomenon is recent, especially outside of Europe and North America. Korea's FTAs, for example, were *all* signed after 2000. The important point is that the world **did in fact** shift from the multilateral trade institutions of the GATT and WTO (circa 1950–80); most subsequent trade liberalization has occurred in a fragmented semi-multilateral and bilateral system of FTAs. Why?

This is a particularly important question because first and foremost Korea was reacting—as was much of Asia—to stagnating WTO talks and the shift from global multilateralism to regionalism that was inherent in the 1993 EU agreement and the 1994 NAFTA (Watanbe 2004, 1–3; Schott, Bradford, and Moll 2006, 1–2).

Trying to explain the world's first and only transition to an FTA environment is fraught with methodological peril so I provide no attempt myself. I do, however, briefly bring to the reader's attention a prominent theory in political science that attempts such an explanation. This is the "hegemonic stability" theory. The idea is that public goods, such as the consistent provision of open international markets even during difficult times, are most easily provided when one country reaps sufficient benefits to outweigh the costs of this systemic public goods provision (Olson 1965; Kindlberger 1973; Gilpin 1987). The basic issues at stake, and their direct relevance to the origins of the modern FTA phenomenon, are succinctly stated by Mansfield and Milner (2012, 71–73):

> Various scholars argue that international economic stability is a collective good, and that suboptimal amounts of it will be provided without a stable hegemon (Kindleberger 1973; Gilpin 1975; Lake 1988). Preferential trade arrangements, in turn, may be outgrowths of the economic instability fostered by the absence or the decline of such a country (Kindleberger 1973; Gilpin 1975 and 1987; Krasner 1976). In this vein, many observers maintain that the current wave of PTAs [preferential trade agreements] was triggered by the U.S. decision to pursue such arrangements in the early 1980s, once its economic power waned and the Uruguay Round of GATT stalled (e.g., Pomfret 1988; Baldwin 1993; Bhagwati 1993; Krugman 1993; Bhagwati and Panagariya 1996b). Other leading economic powers responded in kind to ensure that they would not be placed at a competitive disadvantage, giving rise to a set of loose economic blocs in North America, Western Europe, and East Asia (e.g., Gilpin 1987, 88–90 and ch. 10). . . . In Baldwin's (1995; see also Gilpin 1987) opinion, this development combined with the completion of the Single Market in Western Europe to set off a "domino effect" that produced the latest wave of regionalism.

In short, if one wants to understand why FTAs exist, one might turn to hegemonic stability theory. But this is a Korean case study, not a theory of hegemonic stability, so this book focuses on the first dimension of IPE, which is how security concerns and alliances influence FTAs. States seek FTAs with allies for security purposes. I bring a specific focus to the geographic nature of these security issues, in which geopolitics strongly influences the formation and effects of modern FTAs.

VI. Geopolitical Economy

This brings me to geopolitics, which is the final piece of my overall geopolitical economy perspective. Looking again at figure 2.1, we now turn to the third and last petal, in the top left. As we shall see, geopolitics was originally the field of political geography, and as Agnew and Muscarà note in a classic overview:

As a modern academic field of study, political geography came into being across Europe in the 1890s as an "aid to statecraft" on the part of the Great Powers of the day. Contemporary national political identities and reasons-of-state were taken as givens. The "needs" of territorial states and their relative locations on the earth's surface and the resources available in driving and determining the outcome of competition between them were the main concerns of the field. (2012, viii)

Many IR scholar will immediately see the clear realist tone in the above quotation. Political geography not only brings in geography, but does so from the same theoretical lens as international political economy, which is to say, a realist vision of states competing in anarchy. Indeed, as Gökmen (2010) argues at length, the theory of political realism upon which the IPE tradition relies is to a large degree an exercise in intellectual recycling. Geopolitics was the original field of study.

Geopolitics was born in the late nineteenth century and disappeared from universities with the end of the Second World War. IR as a separate academic discipline was born during the interwar period. Despite the fact that both IR and geopolitics deal with common issues and share many common assumptions, IR theory never directly mentions geopolitics or its prominent figures. This was due, at first, to the idealist character of American IR when it emerged during the interwar period. After the Second World War realists came to the fore. In place of the idealist worldview realists viewed IR as power politics and competition between self-interested states in an anarchical international system. It is ironic that the Second World War marked the victory of realism and at the same time loss of geopolitics. Just like the term race, geopolitics was erased from academic literature in accordance with its close association with Nazism.

I believe that mainstream IR theories cannot be properly understood or analyzed without addressing the theories of geopolitics that abounded and informed them during the period of their genesis. The fields of geopolitics and political geography were central to political thought long before IR grew into its own as a separate academic discipline in the aftermath of the First World War. Classical geopolitical theories, linking history and geography, were part of the wellspring out of which realist approaches to IR arose. Any history of IR that fails to address the links between classical geopolitics and realist theories of IR thus remains fundamentally flawed, historically speaking. (Gökmen 2010, 3)

This book is entitled *Geopolitical Economy* for many reasons. Following Gökmen, there is a sense in which the field of IPE, particularly those with realist underpinnings, are an offshoot of the discipline of geography. Intellectual genealogy aside, however, the more fundamental reason for this book's title is that I believe that geopolitics matters, and, more specifically, that the specificities of geography are major factors shaping both conflict and trade policy.

Geopolitics

Geopolitics has come to mean many things to many people, and its plasticity as a concept is perhaps one of its most useful rhetorical advantages. But for my purposes I intend no complexity nor any duplicity. All that I mean by "geopolitics" is the addition of geography as a pertinent variable in the study of international politics. I therefore embrace Black's precise definition of geopolitics, which defines the term in such a way as to bring no intellectual baggage and focuses instead on the single claim that geography matters for international politics: "Geopolitics can be described as both the policy and the study of using geography and any factors attendant upon it, to understand, or influence, or, outright govern interstate relations, and international relations more generally" (2016, 18).

To explain this geopolitical perspective, let me begin by introducing the primary intellectual figure in geopolitics, Harold Mackinder, also the most prominent British scholar in the discipline of geography. Mackinder is best known for promulgating the idea that eastern Europe is "The Geographic Pivot of History."

Who rules East Europe commands the Heartland:
Who rules the Heartland commands the World-Island:
Who rules the World-Island commands the World .(Mackinder 1904)

I invoke Mackinder's notion of the pivot of history for two reasons. First, it is probably the root metaphor of all geopolitical imaginings, such that throughout the twentieth century it guided U.S. containment policy specifically and global struggle for power more generally. Second, the pivot of history strongly illustrates my geopolitical point more generally, which is that policymakers' understanding of military geography heavily structures foreign policy, and this in turn shapes FTA policy.

Mackinder's dictum rests upon plausible assumptions, especially given the Eurocentric and military realities of 1904, when he presented his theory to the Royal Geographic Society. First, Europe, Asia, the Middle East, and Africa are together larger and therefore more important than the Americas, and he calls the larger land mass the World Island. Second (in the words of Agnew and Muscarà), "sea-power was declining in relation to land-power, as a result of the coming of the railroad, and there was now a pivotal area, "in the closed heartland of Euro-Asia', that was likely to become the seat of world power" (2012, 76). Finally, within Eurasia itself, Mackinder argued that eastern Europe was the concrete pivot of history in this global geopolitical struggle.

The first point to note about the pivot of history is that although few have explicitly heard the notion, Mackinder's geopolitical imagination had a strong hold on the minds conducting German statecraft and American statecraft:

> Mackinder's ideas, particularly that of the pivot, have seemed to have a prescient quality to them that later generations have found attractive. They take world politics out of the realm of the historically contingent and into the realm of the geographically predictable. Geography trumps history. Not only was the pivot idea picked up by German writers in the 1920s, though put to very different purposes than Mackinder would license, but the US policy of "containing" the Soviet Union after World War II could be seen as finding its "scientific" basis in Mackinder's heartland thesis (as in Gray, 1989). (Agnew and Muscarà 2012, 79)

The second reason I invoke the pivot of history is that it nicely captures the role of symbolism and imagination in geopolitics. As Black (2016) notes, in addition to its many objective effects on security, "geopolitics, like other forms of geographic analysis and expression, can, in part, be seen as a belief system" (6).

Black provides a comprehensive treatment of geopolitical phenomena throughout history, as well as a thoughtful treatment of contemporary geopolitical phenomena. Although he does not set out to create a vocabulary of geopolitical typologies, it is clear from his summary (2016, 19), as well as his final chapters, that he witnesses three general geopolitical phenomena in recent decades. First, and most obviously, he devotes a chapter to Cold War communist containment. Second, he discusses Fukuyama (1989, 2012) and Huntington's *Clash of Civilizations* (1999) and weaves them together into a discussion of the war on terror. Third, throughout the final portions of the book, he addresses the rise of China. I will take each in turn.

Cold War Containment

Cold War containment was at the center of U.S. foreign policy for half a century. George Kennan single-handedly formulated the policy, and he put the point powerfully and succinctly: "it is clear that the main element of any United States policy towards the Soviet Union must be that of a long-term, patient but firm and vigilant containment of Russian expansionist tendencies" (1947, 547). Containment policy was deeply endorsed by post–World War II American presidents Truman, Eisenhower, Kennedy, Nixon, Carter, and Reagan.

The sudden adoption of containment policy shifted the United States from its historical isolationism abruptly into classic European geopolitics. Political realism dominated policy-orientated thought. Simply put, U.S. policymakers engaged in global military balancing (containment) against Soviet communism because they had no other recourse in what realists call the "anarchy" of the international system (Bull 1977).

Cold War containment also brought with it the classic European emphasis on geopolitics, that is to say, concerns about power vis-à-vis specific critical pieces of geography. Given where the USSR is physically located, for instance, containment policy involved three geographic regions. The first, consistent with Mackinder's pivot of history, was Western Europe, with U.S. troops along one side of the Iron Curtain running through the heart of Europe. The second front of containment was Asia, with South Korea being the flashpoint. The third front was the Middle East. These three regions constituted the global frontline of the fifty-year Cold War between the United States and the USSR. By contrast, events in Latin America and sub-Saharan Africa were much more distant to the United States, geopolitically speaking.

A striking illustration of this disparity between Cold War containment and the twin continents of Latin America and Africa is the fact that about half of U.S. foreign aid historically went to Israel and Egypt, the former as the closest U.S. ally in the Mideast and the latter for its willingness to make peace with Israel. This concern outweighed all other aid consideration. The rest of the world was further from U.S. geographic interests, at least in a security sense.

The profound and multifaceted manner in which the United States influenced and supported Korea is documented in the next chapter, but here the point is established that U.S. policy was driven by a geopolitical imperative to contain communism, and, as a sheer accident of geography, Western Europe, Asia, and the Middle East all garnered much more attention from U.S. foreign policy than did Africa or Latin America.[4]

The War on Terror

While this book specifically studies the Far East country of South Korea, the story leading to the KORUS FTA is staged in the Mideast and scripted by the war on terror. The idea of South Korea receiving an FTA with the United States was an unlikely one after the United States turned to the Americas with NAFTA and various Central American FTAs. The war on terror, however, securitized U.S. FTA policy. Policymakers were inclined to use FTAs to address the rise of China because geopolitical FTAs had already become the norm in Washington.

The title of this book is meant to be a general one, so I also examine the world's hegemon (that is to say, the United States). Strikingly, by far the single most important factor driving U.S. FTA policy in the twenty-first century has been the war on terror. This is the book's most striking illustration of geopolitical economy.

The Rise of China

Geographically, South Korea is about as proximate to China as a country can get. This geographic proximity has contrasting economic and military effects. Economically, having the world's largest economy next door is a huge boon. China long ago displaced the United States as South Korea's top trading partner. Militarily, however, China backed North Korea during the Korean War, and, more recently, China's territorial disputes are a source of concern.

Coping with China is, of course, a ubiquitous problem in Asia and might well be the preeminent geopolitical question of our time. Chung (2009) usefully notes a continuum in Asia itself, from countries bandwagoning *with* China (North Korea, Cambodia, Laos, and Myanmar) to countries trying to balance *against* China (Taiwan, Japan, Australia, and Mongolia). South Korea attempts to avoid both extremes and falls into Chung's interesting category of hedging, in which countries seek to engage both China and the United States, enjoying benefits from both. Chung places Korea in an even smaller category of four countries engaged in "active hedging," in which the countries *aggressively* seek benefits from China and from the United States. The KORUS FTA pushes active hedging to new heights, providing strong political and economic ties with the United States and thereby allowing South Korea to pursue China economically with less fear of being subsumed by it. As Sohn and Koo (2011) argue at length, the KORUS FTA was therefore as much a geopolitical project vis-à-vis the United States and China as it was an economic project:

> For president Roh and his political cohorts, an FTA with the US meant a double-edged sword. Despite perceived economic risks, the ROK [Republic of Korea] not only wanted to hedge against US abandonment by courting economic binding, but it simultaneously wanted to hedge against Chinese predation or the possibility of Chinese economic domination by courting US entrapment. An FTA will help balance the security areas of difference between Seoul and Washington and help provide a new ground for the alliance. . . . [A]n FTA will help boost ROK's status as a middle power balancer by ensuring the US to remain a strategic and economic counterbalance to China and Japan. (447)

Having successfully concluded the KORUS FTA, and strengthened ties with the United States, South Korea felt safer pursuing a deeper economic relationship with China. Indeed, in late 2014 South Korea signed an FTA with China, facilitating yet deeper ties with its largest trading partner.

Conclusions

This chapter notes that FTA policy has many determinants: the allure of large and/or rich foreign markets, the deterrence by distance, the domestic politics of winners and losers by economic sector, the institutional effects of democracy and/or the number of veto players in national politics, the effects of alliances, and, more generally, the ubiquitous presence of geopolitics.

For the purposes of the rest of this book, three points from this theory chapter are worth underlining. First, as illustrated in Figure 2.1, there is a considerably broad range of theories in both economics and political science as to why FTAs form. Although this book focuses squarely on the geopolitics of FTAs, clearly FTA policy remains highly over-determined. As such, all of the processes in Figure 2.1 play some explanatory role in various chapters to come, even if only in passing.

Second, this book is deeply embedded in a particular theoretical tradition in FTA policy, which is the IPE approach, and more specifically, the security approach to FTAs. Inspired by Hirschman (1945), Gowa (1995), and econometric studies on alliances and FTAs (e.g., Mansfield and Milner, 2015), the security dimension of FTA policy is scrutinized in depth in the chapters to come.

Third, and what makes this book distinct even within the security tradition, is my resolute focus on the political geography of international politics. Specifically, I explore how Cold War containment, the war on terror, and the rise of China all shaped FTA policy, within South Korea specifically, and around the globe more generally.

CHAPTER 3

FTAs, Statistics, and Korea

Given that a primary purpose of this book is to examine how geopolitics shaped long-run Korean development strategy, much of this book is qualitative in nature. To balance this qualitative approach with quantitative data, this chapter provides a statistical confirmation of the theoretical claims made in chapter 2. Using a global data set of 160 countries over the period 1992–2013, I examine how geographic distance, average citizen wealth, size of GDP, political democracy, and military alliances each influence FTA formation.

I additionally apply the model to South Korea, asking the following questions: (1) How well does a global econometric model explain South Korean FTA policy? (2) To the extent that such a model <u>does</u> explain South Korea FTAs, which variables drive South Korea's predicted FTAs? (3) To the extent that such a model does <u>not</u> explain FTA policy, which specific FTAs are left unexplained and hence deserve attention?

I. Method

My unit of analysis is the dyad-year. An example of a single data point is United States–Korea in 2007, in which the United States and Korea are the dyad and 2007 is the year. The data is dyadic because FTAs are by their nature a *relationship* between two different countries. If the outcome is dyadic, then the unit of analysis must be dyadic. The data set contains 160 nations, yielding over 25,000 possible dyads each year.

The analysis starts in 1992, which marks the geopolitical genesis of FTAs, namely, the creation of the EU and NAFTA. The analysis ends in 2013 as determined by data availability. The data set is unbalanced, with some missing observations, such that the total sample size is limited to 303,540 observations.

The dependent variable is whether or not a particular dyad (in a particular year) has signed an FTA. This is a dichotomous variable (FTA = 1 or 0). Given that this is also a pooled data set—with multiple years per dyad—we must address possible distortions to the z-statistics induced by temporal dependence and/or heteroskedasticity.

The two most common techniques for analyzing such data structures (dichotomous dependent variables with temporal dependence) are Cox proportional hazards models and binary time-series cross-sectional (BTSCS) models (Beck, Katz, and Tucker 1998). BTSCS is conceptually the same as duration (event) data, and as such, a Cox proportional hazards model can be replaced with logistic regression, with splines to account for temporal dependence. This BTSCS technique seems dominant in political science, including for much of the work on FTAs (e.g., Mansfield and Milner 2015). One important nuance is that Carter and Signorio (2010) refined this BTSCS technique by suggesting a cubic polynomial in place of splines.[1] Table 3.1 provides these logistic regression results.

Concerning model specification, I utilize five theoretically inspired models. First, in the interest of theoretical parsimony, model 1 includes only the basic gravity model, with GDP and distance. Model 2 includes other definitions of "gravity" such as GDP per capita and differences between countries' factor endowments. Model 3 includes the political variables, therefore representing a test of the conventional wisdom developed in chapter 2. While theoretical parsimony is a virtue, there is an ongoing debate about the extent to which one should vigorously attempt to control for alternative explanations. Within the political science community the prevailing tendency seems to be toward lengthy specifications, so model 4 includes a number of additional controls. Finally, model 5 includes exports as yet an additional control variable. This could be considered the best model, but unfortunately the Correlates of War (COW) data set provides trade data only through 2009, so any trade analysis loses about a quarter of available observations. A case can be made for retaining full temporal data, and another case can be made for controlling for trade. I therefore report on all five analyses for the reader's discernment.

II. Results

Table 3.1 provides the results of the BTSCS model. Looking first at the parsimonious model in column 1, note that economic theory is confirmed in that the product of two countries' GDPs positively predicts FTAs, while distance between countries negatively influences FTAs.

Column 2 adds other measures of gravity that we discussed, such as a country's overall level of wealth and the difference between two countries' per capita income. Two of these forms of economic gravity are significant with the correct sign: the product of GDPs and the wealth of a country.

TABLE 3.1. Explaining FTA Formation (BTSCS estimation)

Variables	Model 1	Model 2	Model 3	Model 4	Model 5
Difference (per capita incomes)		−0.0000	0.0000	0.0000	0.0000
		(0.0000)	(0.0000)	(0.0000)	(0.0000)
GDP * GDP	0.0000***	0.0000***	−0.0000	−0.0000	−0.0000***
	(0.0000)	(0.0000)	(0.0000)	(0.0000)	(0.0000)
Distance	−0.0006***	−0.0007***	−0.0006***	−0.0006***	−0.0006***
	(0.0000)	(0.0000)	(0.0000)	(0.0000)	(0.0000)
Democracy			0.0542***	0.0283***	0.0214***
			(0.0049)	(0.0057)	(0.0061)
Alliance			0.7579***	0.6798***	0.7780***
			(0.0935)	(0.1100)	(0.1197)
GDP per capita		0.0000***	0.0000***	0.0000***	0.0000***
		(0.0000)	(0.0000)	(0.0000)	(0.0000)
Veto players			0.7131***	0.4620***	0.2304*
			(0.1143)	(0.1233)	(0.1338)
Common border				0.9059***	0.6534***
				(0.1608)	(0.1716)
WTO				0.7283***	0.7260***
				(0.0614)	(0.0634)
Shared association				0.0777***	0.0509***
				(0.0118)	(0.0140)
EU				0.4372***	0.3573***
				(0.0773)	(0.0889)
Exports (% GDP)					0.0001***
					(0.0000)
t1	−0.0450***	−0.0421***	−0.0328***	−0.0302***	−0.0286***
	(0.0032)	(0.0032)	(0.0030)	(0.0029)	(0.0030)
t2	0.0000***	0.0000***	0.0000***	0.0000***	0.0000***
	(0.0000)	(0.0000)	(0.0000)	(0.0000)	(0.0000)
t3	−0.0000***	−0.0000***	−0.0000***	−0.0000***	−0.0000***
	(0.0000)	(0.0000)	(0.0000)	(0.0000)	(0.0000)
Constant	0.5105***	0.2686***	−0.6832***	−1.2719***	−1.0598***
	(0.0570)	(0.0597)	(0.1116)	(0.1225)	(0.1317)
Observations	356,899	356,392	261,604	261,604	213,562

Robust standard errors in parentheses.
$*p < 0.1$, $**p < 0.05$, $***p < 0.01$

Column 3 is arguably the most theoretically derived model, in that it tests exactly the hypotheses in chapter 2, including the three political variables. Most importantly, alliances, as predicted by the IPE perspective, significantly correlates with FTAs. Democracy is also a significant facilitator of FTAs.

Veto players are also a significant FTA correlate, but oddly the coefficient is the opposite of what is predicted by theory. I cannot explain this finding. The dataset used here starts later than that used by Mansfield and Milner (2012) and runs somewhat later, so potentially the different sample yields differ findings. Further testing seems warranted.[2]

Model 4 provides a fully saturated model with a wealth of potential explanations for FTA formation, while model 5 adds in the potentially endogenous trade measure. The main point to pull from both models 4 and 5 is that distance, alliances, and democracy remain robust determinants of FTA formation. The economic variables, somewhat ironically, perform less well, with GDP product actually changing signs in a fully saturated specification (model 5).

Finally, a few other comments about model 5. First, the exports variable is highly significant and, as shown in the predictions section, is powerful enough that it arguably should be in the models. On the other hand, we lose much temporal variation when we include trade. Moreover, on strictly theoretically grounds, it is not clear that trade should be a control variable given that the forces leading to an FTA are also the forces leading to trade, and controlling for trade might therefore incorrectly "control" away actual causal effects.[3] Again, a case can be made either way, so I report robustness across all models.[4]

One advantage of the logit model is that it provides a few useful substantive intuitions. First, because we are making predictions for a dichotomous result, we can count the percent of correct dichotomous predictions (Count R2) and compare this with our default prediction. FTAs exist in about 7 percent of all dyad-years, so our default prediction is to assume that no FTA exists in any given dyad-year. Indeed, if we made no-FTA our formal prediction for all cases, we in effect would be "correct" 93 percent of the time (and, equally, incorrect in the 7 percent of the dyad-years where FTAs do in fact exist). Although it might seem odd, it is useful to remember that this 93 percent figure is the Count R2 of the model. More specifically, even without explanatory variables we can "explain" 93 percent of the outcomes, so any further "predictions" will be compared with that default outcome.

The question for all models of this nature, with noticeably more 0s than 1s, is whether we can increase predictive accuracy over 93 percent by shifting some predictions from no-FTA to yes-FTA. On the positive side, we might thereby increase the number of accurate predictions (we get some of the 1s correct now), while on the negative side we might also increase the number of inaccurate predictions (we can now additionally mis-predict a 0 by falsely predicting it to be a 1).

The Count R3 in column 3 is 94.5 percent, which factually tells us that we raised our predictions from a base 93 percent accuracy to 94.5 percent accuracy, or differently put, an increase of 1.5 percent from the baseline. While this may not sound like much, it is nonetheless a 21 percent reduction in the remaining 7 percent of unexplained variation (i.e., and to a great degree of decimal accuracy (1.43) / 6.93) = 20.6 percent). Comparing with column 5, finally, would be difficult since the samples are substantially different once exports are controlled for, given missing export data).

NAFTA and the EU

Given that the gravity model explains a substantial portion of the variation in FTAs across time and countries, it should also provide insight into some of the better-known FTAs. Table 3.2, happily, demonstrates that the model does predict major FTAs of the world.

Table 3.2 shows the model's predictions for a number of interesting dyads. To illustrate, consider the first row, the U.S.-Canada dyad. Under model 3, the first column provides the minimum predicted probability over the twenty-one years and the second column provides the maximum predicted probability over the same period. For model 3, then, the lowest annual prediction was .64 for a U.S.-Canada FTA, and other annual predictions rose as high as .93. Given that any prediction over .5 is a prediction of 1, the U.S.-Canada FTA was correctly predicted for all years.

Recall that model 3 had six independent variables, while model 5 added a variety of control variables albeit at the cost of a reduced sample size. In table 3.2 I report the predicted values for the model for chapter 2 (model 3), as well as the fully specified model (model 5).

In fact, these variations in specification do seem to matter. Model 3, for instance, only weakly predicts the U.S.-Canada FTA during a few years, at $p = .64$. Moreover, we see that trade matters greatly in the U.S.-Canada case, in that once we account for the large trade flows, that dyad's FTA is at least 99 percent probable in all years, because existing trade further increases the desirability of an FTA. Putting this altogether, the models seems to address the U.S.-Canada FTA satisfactorily.

The model also predicts the U.S.-Mexico FTA, but only in the fully specified model that includes trade. Those models predict the FTA at 99 percent, but the trade variable has a large role, because in model 3 the Mexico case is only slightly predicted for an FTA. The Canada-Mexico dyad, finally, seems a low probability event, suggesting the partners might owe their FTA primarily to their shared interests with the United States.

Turning to Europe, note first that the three core countries of the EU are Germany, France, and Italy. Table 3.2 shows that the models overwhelmingly predict these FTAs and that often the predictions are very high. Indeed, with just a few annual exceptions in model 3, all models predict FTAs for each dyad across all twenty-one years.

Korean FTAs

Having established that the model is statistically satisfactory and explains major highlights of the international trading order, it is time to examine how well the model explains the South Korean case specifically. The answer is—not particularly well. In fact, model 3 does not predict even a single FTA for the nation of South Korea! The first and foremost mystery about Korea,

TABLE 3.2. Predicted Probability of an FTA

		Model 3		Model 5	
		Min.	Max.	Min.	Max.
NAFTA					
US	Canada	.64	.93	.99	.99
US	Mexico	.08	.48	.99	.99
Canada	Mexico	.01	.09	.01	.19
EU					
Germany	France	.61	.93	.99	.99
Germany	Italy	.83	.90	.99	.99
France	Italy	.56	.91	.99	.99
Korea					
Korea	US	.01	.06	.03	.22
Korea	China	.00	.01	.01	.99
Korea	Japan	.00	.00	.00	.06
Korea	Germany	.00	.06	.03	.89

Note: Each entry provides minimum and maximum predicted values of an FTA between each dyad over the twenty-one-year period.

then, is why did it enter into so many FTAs? The GDP was not sufficiently large, nor distance sufficiently close, to predict Korean FTA partners. We must thus turn to a distinctively political history of Korea to understand its FTA pattern. Returning to the book's narrative, I argue that geopolitics placed Korea on a very unusual trajectory, both historically and in the contemporary era.

While the models do not generally predict Korean FTAs, model 5 is an exception in that it predicts FTAs with China, and actually predicted a Korea-China FTA at 99 percent by the last years, based overwhelmingly on the huge trade volume between these two countries. This raises a bit of a mystery. Why was this most likely FTA signed so near the end of the lineup? Why the long delay? Chapter 8 addresses this mystery, noting that Korea wanted an FTA with China but that geopolitics held it back, illustrating how geopolitics can resist even intense economic gravity.

The model also provides some noticeably high probabilities between the United States and Korea—not reaching p > .50, but still quite high given that 93 percent of dyads have no FTA and the two countries are very far part. Indeed, in some years the probability of a KORUS FTA rises as high as .22.

Finally, and particularly interesting given the security emphasis of this book, the reason that the KORUS FTA is plausible has much to do with the alliance variable. If that variable is excluded from the model, the KORUS FTA probability falls in half. To the extent that the model is capturing statistical regularities, then, it is the security effect attracting the United States and the trade effect attracting China.

Conclusions

The short discussion in this chapter cannot definitively resolve debates about Korean FTAs, but it does provide some important clues. The finding that alliances have a statistically significant and substantively large effect on FTA formation is notable and obviously consistent with the overall vision of this book.

Of more relevance to Korea specifically, the following conclusions seem warranted:

1. The variables discussed in chapter 2 are usually statistically significant determinants of FTA formation patterns in a global data set
   of all countries from 1992 to 2013. This provides additional confi-

dence in my use of these specific variables in my analytic narrative explaining Korean FTAs.

2. These variables also correctly predict some major facets of the modern trading system, such as the existence of NAFTA and the existence of FTAs between Germany, France, and Italy (i.e., the basic actors in the EU).

3. Global models generally predict South Korea poorly, usually predicting no FTAs at all. I caution about reading too much into this, given that it is possible this model failed to control for some pertinent variable, which might have thrown off all of the Korean predictions. It is nonetheless notable that the entire Korean FTA project does not arise obviously from a standard statistical model, suggesting the need for alternative explanations for South Korea's numerous FTAs.

4. While FTA predictions are generally low for Korean FTAs, the models do sometimes predict a China FTA with a high degree of probability, correctly pointing out that the raw "gravitational" attraction of these two is immense, especially divided by distance.

5. Finally, a few models come close to predicting a Korea-U.S. FTA even though the *p*-value never rose above .22. Further exploration indicates it is the alliance variable that explains much of this (almost significant) *p*-value. This provides additional legitimacy to my narrative in chapter 7, which places security concerns at the heart of the KORUS FTA.

CHAPTER 4

Containment and South Korean Development

Geography dealt Korea a particularly difficult role. Located in a strategic but dangerous neighborhood between the greater powers of China, Japan, and Russia, Korea has suffered nine hundred invasions, great and small, in its two thousand years of recorded history. It has experienced five major periods of foreign occupation—by China, the Mongols, Japan, and, after World War II, the United States and the Soviet Union. (Oberdorfer and Carlin 2014, loc. 487–90, Kindle)

South Korea is in an awkward geopolitical position. The above quotation attests to the consequences of being a peninsula among the major powers (China, Japan, and Russia). The United States last occupied South Korea, liberating the nation from Japan. Due to that occupation, and subsequent Cold War containment policy, South Korea and the United States have become inextricably linked.

This chapter explores how South Korea's stark geopolitical location encouraged rapid economic development. Section I describes in detail how the United States' postwar policy objective (containing communism) shaped South Korea's development. Section II recaps the "Korean miracle." Section III provides a brief history of the Korean developmental state (1961–87), while section IV examines economic policy during South Korea's early period of democracy (1987–97).

I. Cold War Containment

Without the U.S. Cold War containment policy, there would not be an impressive South Korean FTA strategy. Indeed, if one had applied a gravity model in 1945, the start of the current liberal international order, it would have predicted an extremely low probability of an FTA between South Korea and the United States. South Korea had a per capita income as low as impoverished Africa, yielding little economic gravitational pull, and the significant distance between the two nations made an FTA even less likely.

Although South Korea was distant from a gravity model perspective, from a geopolitical perspective South Korea is at the heart of U.S. foreign policy doctrine. Indeed, it was because of the Korean War that Cold War containment became a cornerstone of U.S. foreign policy.

Containment as a concept is often associated with George Kennan. He was the deputy chief of staff of the U.S. embassy in Moscow and had long been skeptical of future USSR policy. His "long telegraph" of February 22, 1946, "became the conceptual foundation for the strategy the United States—and Great Britain—would follow for over four decades" (Gaddis 2011, 227). Cold War containment policy, in essence, follows Kennan's idea that the USSR was inherently anti-West but not quickly expansionist, such that it could effectively be contained.

But in a war-weary population there was naturally reluctance among U.S. citizens and U.S. politicians to commit to such containment. Containment went from intention to the bedrock of U.S. foreign policy only after North Korea's invasion of South Korea and the ensuing three-year war that deeply embroiled both the United States and China. The outbreak of the Korean War demonstrated that communism was a potential border changer and that U.S. policy should contain that threat.

After the United States liberated South Korea from Japan, it occupied South Korea for three years (1945–48) and then fought alongside South Korea for three years fending off North Korea and its powerful allies (1950-53). This intense influence placed American officials close to the heart of South Korean policymaking following decades of Japanese rule. As Cole and Lyman (1971, 59) argue:

From 1945 on—through the American military government of 1945–1948, the leading role in the Korean War, and the massive aid programs thereafter—American influence extended directly into nearly every aspect of Korean political and economic development. Thus in the first few years after World War II the United States largely shaped the structure of the independent government, the postwar educational system, the country's internal and external relationships; and increasingly thereafter, through its training and education programs, it shaped the attitudes and abilities of key groups, especially in the education sector, bureaucracy, military, and business community.

Believing that a strong economy supports a strong military, the United States wanted South Korea to succeed on both dimensions. Finally, politics is also symbolic, especially in the increasingly globalized media-centric world of the twentieth century, such that U.S. policy officials wanted South Korea to succeed as part of the broader optics war against communism:

> Korea is the only area in the world in which democratic and communist principles are being put to the test side by side and in which the U.S. and the U.S.S.R. have been, and no doubt in the estimation of the world, will continue to be, the sole contenders for the way of life of 30,000,000 people. The entire world and especially Asia is watching. (American official quoted in Brazinsky 2009, 2)

Given its motivation in strengthening a bastion of Cold War containment policy, the United States, to no surprise, shaped the very nature of the Korean political economy. Most profoundly, the United States intentionally and forcefully set South Korea on a course of capitalist development.

Prior to U.S. occupation, various left-wing forces had united to proclaim a Korean People's Republic (KPR). This communist movement had gained considerable legitimacy not only for its advocacy of social justice but equally for its steadfast opposition to Japanese colonial occupation. As occupier of South Korea, however, the United States marginalized leftist forces and "consciously and systematically root[ed] out" the committees of the KPR, thereby destroying the communist movement (Cumings 1981, 350). Overall, in Moon and Rhyu's (2010, 445) words, U.S. occupation led to an "American implantation of the capitalist system" in South Korea.

Because it is not enough to just remove the communist influences, the United States provided South Korea with preferential access to the huge U.S. trade market. "The alliance with the United States has not only provided South Korea with a credible military deterrence against North Korea, but also helped normalize its economy through extensive military and economic assistance and assertive policy intervention for macroeconomic stabilization and export drive. South Korea was also one of major beneficiaries of the American-built liberal international economic order" (Moon and Rhyu 2010, 441).

Economic growth is difficult without access to capital, so the United States aggressively provided it: South Korea received the third-highest level of U.S. foreign aid in the early post–World War II period, surpassed only by two equally critical geopolitical allies, Vietnam and Israel (Kang 2002, 43). Obviously, this aid was an enormous boon to South Korean development.

Indeed, according to Haggard (1990, 55), "the significance of U.S. support for the regime can hardly be overstated. Aid financed nearly 70 percent of total imports between 1953 and 1962 and equaled 75 percent of total fixed capital formation" (1990, 55). While it is impossible to know what would have happened without U.S. foreign aid, the sheer magnitude of this aid in the economic processes suggests economic growth would have been substantially lower in its absence.

In all, the South Korean economic miracle, while built by the ingenuity and sacrifices of the Korean people, must also be understood in a geopolitical context. The Korean economic miracle would not have occurred if not for the United States' Cold War containment policy.

II. The Economic Miracle

The American geopolitical bid to support South Korea's economy succeeded, quite possibly beyond anyone's expectations. As recently as 1960, per capita incomes were as low as those prevailing in Africa, whereas today South Korea is not only a member of the OECD but, strikingly, the world's eleventh largest economy.[1] Economic success of this magnitude requires extremely rapid economic growth rates over a period of many decades. Williamson and Haggard (1994, 544) note that Korea is "perhaps the most dramatic case of an underdeveloped country turning itself into an industrial powerhouse in a mere third of a century."

Figure 4.1 starkly illustrates South Korea's remarkable economic success over a five-decade period from 1960 to 2014. The figure compares nominal per capita GDP in South Korea against three baselines. First, relative to sub-Saharan Africa, we can see the minimal GDP from which South Koreans have come and where they would be today if they had followed Africa's trajectory. Figure 4.1 also compares Korea's income with the global average. South Korean incomes were substantially below world averages in 1960, making the country a relatively "poor" nation, and yet Korea went on to surpass world income averages as early as 1982. As figure 4.1 illustrates, current incomes are now *three times* higher than world averages. This represents a dramatic surge through the world's economic hierarchy.

The most challenging comparison one could make is with the OECD, the organization containing the world's most wealthy countries. Figure 4.1 demonstrates that South Korea, although not yet quite at the level of the overall OECD average, is nonetheless well over 75 percent and continues to catch up. Moreover, I only used GDP statistics in figure 4.1 to capture the

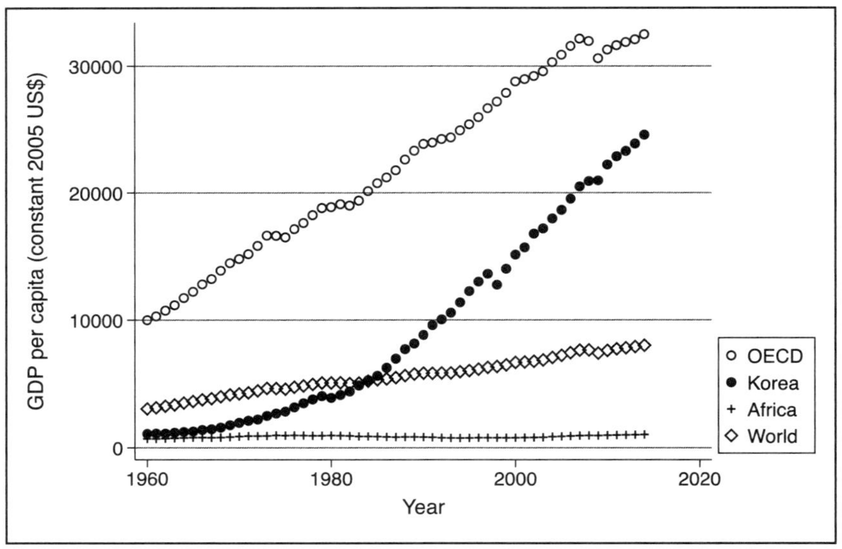

Figure 4.1. Korean GDP Per Capita in Global Perspective
Korean GDP per capita grew at a remarkable rate compared to OECD and
African nations from 1960 to 2014. In just a few decades Korea levered its
near bottom poverty to near OECD GDP per capita. (World Bank, World
Development Indicators.)

long run. Purchasing power parity is arguably better data and shows even
less discrepancy between South Korea and OECD countries. South Korea is
now a robustly *developed* country.

While it is widely understood that South Korea has done well for itself,
it is less commonly appreciated that this success has propelled South Korea
into its role as a major global economic actor. Kalinowski and Cho (2012,
43), for instance, recently observed that South Korea's "global political role is
still under-appreciated and understudied as most attention was captured by
the BRIC countries, that is, Brazil, Russia, India and China."

Table 4.1 shows the top ten exporting countries, ranked by exports, but
with additional data on land mass, population, and income per capita. Note
first that two of the BRIC countries, India and Brazil, are entirely missing
from the top-exporting list.

Russia, China, and the United States are in a category of their own in
table 4.1. They have vast geographic scope being 3 of the top four countries
in land mass size. They also have the largest populations among top exporters, with 1.35 billion in China, 316 million in the United States, and 144
million in Russia.

There are some underlying similarities across the remaining seven top exporters. We suddenly drop from the four biggest countries to much smaller countries, with land mass size ranging in rank from 41 (France) to 131 (the Netherlands). Population fluctuation is also much more homogenous, and with the exception of the Netherlands (17 million), the other six countries have strikingly little variation in total populations, with 50 million in South Korea on the low side to 127 million in Japan on the high side, and Germany, France, Italy, and the United Kingdom all in between.

South Korea, in just a few decades, not only emerged from poverty but also economically outstripped geographically larger countries. To whatever extent GDP is power, geographically small South Korea is the eleventh most powerful nation in the world.

I conclude this geopolitically grounded success story with an empirical point. We already know that South Korea has always been extraordinarily dependent on exports for its economic growth. Figure 4.2 graphs these Korean exports as a percentage of Korean GDP. A flat line would indicate that the proportion of exports has remained constant, rising equally rapidly as Korea's overall phenomenal economic growth. Instead, it is clearly evident that exports have become an increasingly large portion of the Korean economy, rising as a share of GDP from under 5 percent in 1960 to over 50 percent by 2012.

South Korea entered the new millennium, in short, with a highly suc-

TABLE 4.1. Geography and Demography of Top Ten Global Exporters

Country	Land mass (rank)	Land mass (km²)	GDP per capita	Population (millions)	Exports (% GDP)	FTA coverage
China	3	9,596,961	5652	1,357	24.8061	0.17
United States	4	9,629,091	49849	316	13.5824	0.45
Germany	62	357,137	43433	82	45.4882	0.72
France	41	551,500	41268	66	28.6081	0.72
Japan	61	377,930	44327	127	16.1877	0.15
United Kingdom	78	242,495	39504	64	30.0319	0.59
South Korea	107	100,148	23784	50	53.8751	0.68
Netherlands	131	37,354	49820	17	82.6266	0.85
Italy	71	301,339	33882	60	28.8512	0.68
Russia	1	17,075,400	11616	144	26.6265	0.13

Source: World Development Indicators. FTA coverage is calculated as per footnote 4 of chapter 5.

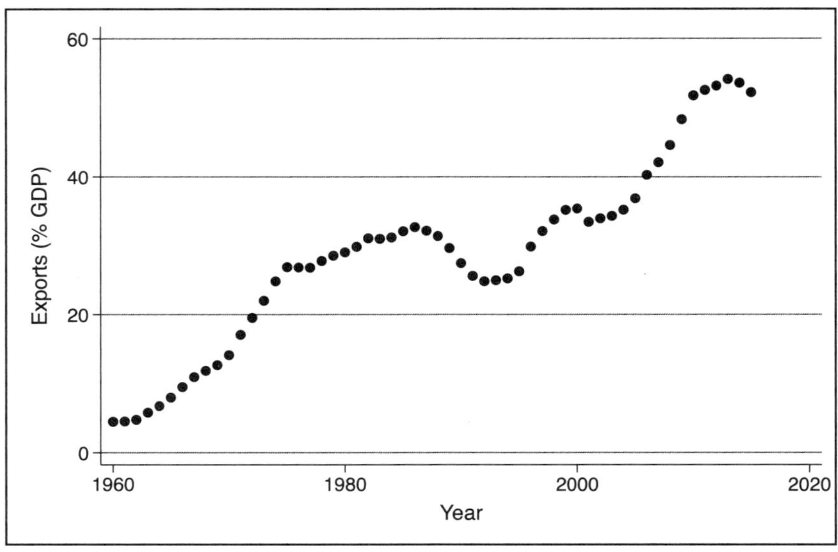

Figure 4.2. Korean Exports as a Percentage of GDP
Accompanying Korea's meteoric rise in GDP, even faster export growth resulted
in an increase in exports from 5 percent of Korea's GDP to 50 percent.

cessful export machine. Whatever the specifics, figure 4.2 makes clear that exports were going to be absolutely central to any national strategy.

III. The Developmental State (1961–87)

Cold War containment policy was a *necessary* condition for the South Korean export miracle, and therefore a necessary condition for the successful Korean FTA strategy. To be a necessary condition is far from being a sufficient condition, however, and, as noted earlier, it was the Korean people, with their education, ingenuity, sacrifice, and hard work, who embodied the efficient Korean economy and the growth-promoting state.

This was the period in which a developmental state pushed Korea into its well-known export-oriented industrialization (EOI) developmental strategy. The domestic policies driving the Korean economic success are complex and debatable.

During the 1960s and 1970s South Korea enjoyed extraordinarily rapid economic growth, and by the early 1980s the economic literature on this nation was primarily pro-market in perspective. A wide range of studies emerged indicating that Korea grew rapidly because of liberal virtues such as free international trade, market exchange rates, and low government consumption (e.g., Balassa 1978; Krueger 1979).

During the late 1980s scholars from a diverse set of fields challenged this neoliberal interpretation and argued that state-led industrial policy drove Korean success. Amsden (1989) argued provocatively that Korea intentionally got "prices wrong" by subsidizing key industrial sectors. Woo-Cumings (1991) argued analogously that the Korean state possessed extensive control over industrial finance and used these resources to promote industrialization. More generally, a wide range of scholars, including but certainly not limited to Deyo (1987), Evans (1994), Jones and Sakong (1985), Wade (1993), and Kohli (2004), have argued that a Korean developmental state drove its economic success.

Due to the ideological nature of the state versus market debate, the neoliberal and developmental state perspectives are usually seen as antagonistic. Given that the two approaches emphasize somewhat different aspects of economic policy, however, they can also be seen as complementary explanations (Krieckhaus 2006, 136–42). Neoliberals are largely correct that Korean government spending was lower than in most developing nations, and tariffs were reduced much earlier than in Latin America (e.g., Haggard 1990). At the same time, however, it is also the case that trade protection was used at an early stage of Korean development, and a vast array of loans and tax breaks were utilized to advance economic growth (e.g., Amsden 1989; Kohli 2004). These explanations are not mutually inconsistent, but rather complementary.

Moreover, at a deeper level of analysis, neoliberals and statists provide remarkably similar political explanations of Korean development, focusing especially on the state's autonomy from societal interest groups. Neoliberals note that this allowed for tough free-market policies, given that policymakers faced a "virtual lack of constraints on the ability to make decisions and carry them out" (Kwang Suk Kim, quoted in Krueger 1979, 85). Statists also emphasize the state's autonomy from societal actors. Amsden (1989), for instance, emphasizes that "where Korea differs from most other late developing countries is in the discipline its state exercises over private firms," such as the ability to cut off support to major firms if they were unable to achieve export success. Labor was similarly unable to control policy in Korea (Haggard 1990, 63–64).

Another characteristic of the South Korean model, going back to the consensus among neoliberals and developmental statists that the state maintained considerable autonomy, is that the South Korean state was authoritarian from 1960 until 1987, and it was not until 1997 that an opposition figure won the presidency. For many decades, in short, South Korean economic policy was conducted by a centralized bureaucracy that itself was embedded in an authoritarian state (Haggard, 1990).

IV. Early Democracy (1987–97)

I end this chapter by describing how the economy and political institutions fared under democratization in 1987 and the Asian financial crisis (AFC) in 1997. The short story is that in the closing days of the twentieth century South Korea was economically and politically stable and hence ready to pursue a robust FTA strategy.

Democratization nonetheless posed new challenges to the Korean developmental state. As indicated in the last section, scholars, whether neoliberal or statist, frequently view an autonomous state as an important political foundation for South Korea's effective policymaking. Although autonomy and authoritarianism are different concepts, there is little doubt that authoritarianism facilitated the Korean state's autonomy, and for this reason we could expect democratization to reduce autonomy and lead to a diversion from economic growth as the central political goal of the nation.

Indeed, a variety of scholars suggest that democratization reduced Korean state autonomy, policy effectiveness, and economic growth. First, in contrast to the authoritarian period, when the state could "discipline" business (Amsden 1989), "Democratization led to increased demands for political payoffs, as politicians began to genuinely compete for electoral support, and to a decrease in the state's ability to resist or constrain the demands of the business sector" (Kang 2002, 193).

Furthermore, democracy reduced the state's autonomy not only from business but from the electorate. While normatively this is desirable, the structural adjustment literature notes that elections often lead governments to postpone painful and yet necessary economic adjustments (e.g., Haggard and Kaufman 1992). This phenomenon beset Korea after democratization. Haggard and Mo (2000), for instance, note that democratic elections contributed to delaying necessary financial reforms and hence exacerbated Korea's financial crisis in 1997.

In the end, however, the democratization challenge was met successfully. Despite fears of weak economic policy, when Korea faced its first severe test, namely, the AFC of 1997, Korea recovered very rapidly, and "this swift recovery can be attributed to decisive reform efforts by the Kim Dae Jung Government" (Haggard, Pinkston, and Seo 1999). So how did a state with weakened autonomy implement such good policies?

Haggard, Pinkston, and Seo (1999) provide a compelling explanation that notes the important intersection of two events. The first is the election of President Kim Dae-Jung in December 1997, the first opposition figure to win the presidency in democratic Korea. Kim represented the popular sector as opposed to the military-business alliance, making him in many ways a figure of the left, but his policy preferences were liberal. At root Kim viewed the state-capital alliance that had propelled Korea's growth as an exclusionary system, leaving out the people. This version of left politics led him to *reduce* subsidies to the *chaebol* and *weaken* in other ways the long historical alliance between the state and capital. Surprising many Western observers and media, President Kim vigorously pursued economic liberalism starting from the very first days of his administration (Haggard, Pinkston, and Seo 1999).

Haggard, Pinkston, and Seo (1999), however, go on to note that while Kim's liberal preferences were a necessary condition for reforms, they were far from a sufficient condition. Indeed, the prospects of Kim achieving reform looked highly improbable, given that he did not have a majority in the legislature, and, furthermore, many of his reforms had been earlier rejected by his own party.

Haggard, Pinkston, and Seo's (1999) second explanation of the successful Korean policy response is that Kim's election coincided with the AFC of 1997. When Kim was elected on December 8, stocks had fallen by 50 percent in value and the value of the won had fallen by an equal amount. Indeed, there was a general sense that the Korean economy was simply falling apart on election eve. Just two days after the election, therefore, outgoing president Kim Young-Sam met with incoming president Kim Dae-Jung, and they agreed to jointly oversee a twelve-member economic guidance council. This council was composed of both presidents, along with six members from each administration, but de facto left President Kim Dae-Jung making the major decisions. In effect, the AFC provided President Kim Dae-Jung with sufficient autonomy from veto players to pursue liberal reforms.

This, of course, is consistent with a broad literature in comparative political economy that notes how external economic crises frequently provide domestic politicians with the autonomy to promote radical policy change (e.g., Waterbury 1992; Gourevitch 1986). Ironically, then, the AFC, despite its severe damage to the Korean economy, was critical in allowing the Korean state to regain some of the policy autonomy it had lost during democratization. In short, "the crisis . . . had the effect of weakening the political clout of vested interests, which otherwise might have blocked reform. A newly elected reformist president took advantage of the crisis atmosphere to push major bills through the National Assembly, even though his coalition did not have a majority" (Lim and Hahm 2006, 111).

Finally, and importantly, note that the crisis not only allowed Kim Dae-Jung to move forward his liberal policy preferences but also gave him the wherewithal to create and empower the state economic bureaucracy (Haggard, Pinkston, and Seo 1999; Lim and Jang 2006; Koo 2010; Solís 2013b). As discussed in subsequent chapters, this somewhat *statist* shift toward bureaucratic empowerment and centralization was just as important for South Korea's trade strategy as was the *liberal* shift toward freer markets.

Conclusions

What have we learned from this chapter? First, that geopolitics, and specifically Cold War containment, was a necessary condition for South Korean economic success. Second, that there was in fact an economic miracle, launching Korea to the eleventh largest economy today. Third, that a developmental state utilized liberal markets and (arguably) industrial policy to create growth. Fourth, that democratization provided new challenges, but on the whole Korea responded well, ironically because the AFC coincided with Kim Dae-Jung's arrival as the first opposition politician in power in democratic Korea. Korea entered its recent FTA strategy with a strong prior history of economic success as well as a successful economic transition to democracy.

PART II

The Korean FTA Strategy

CHAPTER 5

FTAs as Development Strategy

Chapter 4 examined South Korea both as an agent—a developmental state successfully pursuing rapid industrialization—and as a subject, under pressure from its geopolitical location and yet incentivized by an economically rewarding trading system. The present chapter overwhelmingly looks at South Korea as an agent, free to choose among policy options. This chapter, in short, looks at FTAs as an intentional development strategy.

To begin, it is important to note that the FTA strategy is a variant of the long-standing EOI strategy and, moreover, that the FTA strategy represents another shift toward economic *liberalism*, most notably liberalization of banking, insurance, and professional services. The goal, inherently, is liberal international economics.

Despite the FTA strategy's liberal goals, its origins, execution, and political basis were highly statist. As will become clear in this chapter, FTA policy rested upon an executive commitment across three consecutive presidential administrations, utilizing an active state bureaucracy that operated with autonomy from the agriculture sector, the national legislature, and even other important state bureaucratic actors.

Organizationally, section I explains what I mean by a "development strategy," while Section II then examines the politics of the South Korean FTA strategy. Section III describes the vast scope of the South Korean FTA strategy, and section IV examines the politics of South Korean partner choice. Finally, section V provides an overall summary of the South Korean FTA strategy.

I. Development Strategy

This book takes a very different approach to FTAs than the vast majority of the existent literature, which routinely examines FTAs through the lens of an "economic policy" variable. Most of the economic literature, for instance, is focused on looking at FTA policy as an independent variable, calculating the policy effects of any given FTA on economic output, trade flows, FDI flows, and other purely economic outcomes. Meanwhile, political scientists tend to look at FTAs as a policy outcome to explain. Much of the political science literature focuses on specific FTAs, describing the political calculus that went into their emergence. Cross-national statistical literatures are more inclined to look at a variety of economic and political determinants of FTA adoption, but the conceptualization is the same, namely, that FTAs are *economic policies*, worthy of explanation just like other economic policies. In this sense the study of FTAs gets buried among the immense body of literature on economic policy more generally. Most nations adopt thousands of different economic policies, including tax policy, expenditure policy, monetary policy, trade policy, investment policy, labor policy, and environmental policy.

In this book, I look at FTAs as something distinctly larger than economic policy. But what then is the appropriate frame of reference? Economic policies may be more or less important, but what is the broader conceptual category we should use rather than economic policy? The prevailing term for a larger category of economic planning is the concept of development strategy. This phrase is widely used yet remains poorly defined and operationalized. Perhaps the best-known statement is from Hirschman's (1958) *The Strategy of Economic Development*, which describes poor nations' struggle to utilize public policy to catch up with wealthier regions of the world.

The classic development strategy is the ISI strategy that many developing countries adopted for decades. Although this strategy was made up of hundreds of component policies, the overarching vision was that a nation might industrialize rapidly if it cut industrial imports by imposing tariffs, thereby "substituting" from imports of industrial goods to the domestic production of said industrial goods. In practice, a vast array of tariffs were buttressed by large development loans, tax breaks, and other state subsidies further promoting domestic industrial projects. Moreover, many governments placed ISI at the core of their political coalitions, thus elevating the policies into a national strategy for development with major economic goals and a supporting political base.

The alternative development strategy, again at a high level of abstraction, is the EOI strategy that East Asia pursued in contrast to the ISI strategy pursued in Latin America and Africa.[1] South Korea exemplified this EOI model, privileging exports as the cornerstone of economic growth and demonstrating how EOI countries aggressively utilized the liberal trading system. By aggressively, I mean state policy conformed to and catered to international market forces <u>and</u> states extensively used industrial policy to promote the export sectors with cheap credit, tax breaks, subsidized inputs, and so forth. It was a highly efficacious state-market synergy, often referred to as a *developmental state*.

Although ISI and EOI are different development strategies, they are nonetheless *both* development strategies. Central planning, as in the communist countries, as well as an attempt at liberalism, as in the Latin American Southern Cone countries in the 1970s, also count as development strategies. So what is the broader commonality that constitutes a development strategy? Three characteristics seem to hold true for both ISI and EOI.

First, both are designed to have major long-run economic effects. ISI provided decades of rapid economic growth while EOI is said to have launched East Asia to unprecedented growth rates. To rise from an "economic policy" to a "development strategy," in short, requires that the country's long-run GDP growth rate potentially be at stake.

The second attribute that ISI and EOI hold in common is an activist state. For ISI, this activist role is incontrovertible, given that the state's tariffs, state-owned enterprises, investment banks, and taxation policies constitute active government on a massive scale. Concerning EOI, there is more debate (as we saw in the last chapter). Developmental state scholars, for the most part, view activist states as an essential requisite for rapid growth. Neoliberal scholars, on the other hand, place primary causal emphasis on liberal markets and, while noting that states did act extensively, call into question how much this mattered. Given that the South Korean government did utilize extensive promotional policies, I tend to view EOI strategies as having an activist state just as do ISI strategies. Overall, it seems fair to say that development strategies are associated with more activist states.

Third, and finally, both ISI and EOI have in common the presence of broad national political coalitions. To some extent this third characteristic follows from the first two. That is, insofar as a nation-state intends the prolonged use of public policy (and on a large scale) to boost long-run economic activity, such a project requires some social and political consensus. This consensus, moreover, must continue through more than one administration. When we speak of a development strategy, therefore, we usually speak of an underlying coalition of the state and/or business and/or labor and/or other actors that provides substantial support for the state's promotional activities.

Development strategy, to sum up, includes (1) an attempt to influence long-run economic growth, using (2) an activist state that is, itself, (3) embedded in a prolonged political coalition. Not all countries engage in development strategies. "Failed states" are one such category, as are countries in constant political turmoil. These states either have no state bureaucracy or are unable to focus on a coherent economic growth strategy.

Among the countries that do manage to have a development strategy, whether central planning, EOI, ISI, or even overt liberalism, some subset of these states is referred to as *developmental states*. By *developmental state*, I mean a state that is not only pursuing a *development strategy* but, additionally, doing so with a state that can be said to possess both state *autonomy* and state *capacity*. The developmental state not only is active but also has high state capacity (ability to get things done) and high autonomy (ability to implement a policy without being stymied by veto players). An activist state with such characteristics, such as South Korea and Taiwan most notably, is often labeled the *developmental state.*

Johnson's classic, *MITI and the Japanese Miracle* (1982), interpreted Japan as a different kind of economic model than the Western variant, in which a developmental state of meritocratic state technocrats is able and willing to promote industrial exports and industrialization more generally. Amsden's (1989) work on South Korea and Wade's (1990) work on Taiwan, both of which explore the state's nuanced and pervasive promotional policies, are the canonical developmental state citations, along with a general treatment of state types by Evans (1994).

II. The Politics of FTA Strategy

The post-1997 South Korean trade bureaucracy possessed high state autonomy and high state capacity and even utilized aspects of industrial policy. These three political attributes help explain the unusual extent to which South Korea has been able to pursue FTAs. Given that these three traits are also intrinsic to the concept of a "developmental state," this chapter exposes the statist side of a seemingly liberal policy, one that required an activist state pursuing a coherent long-term strategy.

The first point to make is that the Korean FTA strategy was definitely a state-led project. As Koo (2010, 101) concludes, Korea's FTA policy "has been driven by a top-down political initiative rather than a bottom-up demand from business groups and the general public." Indeed, the primary explanation for Korea's ambitious FTA pursuit is the strong commitment by three consecutive presidents to the FTA strategy (Yoshimatsu 2012). I first document each president's commitment and then describe how this policy commitment was largely autonomous from societal actors.

Kim Dae-Jung's (1997–2003) contribution to the Korean pursuit of FTAs was threefold. First, he initiated liberal policy momentum through broad re-forms, including liberalizing FDI and labor markets. Second, and important for subsequent events, he created an autonomous and empowered Ministry of Foreign Affairs and Trade (MOFAT) with far-reaching powers (Haggard, Pinkston, and Seo 1999). MOFAT was to become the "pilot agency" for the ambitious FTA policy. Third, it was under Kim that MOFAT first began pursuing FTAs, beginning with Chile.

The Roh Moo-Hyun administration (2003–8) accelerated this initial FTA strategy. In August 2004 MOFAT released an *FTA Promotion Road-map*, noting the importance of FTAs for the Korean economy and laying out a three-stage plan to pursue FTAs. The plan began with learning FTA negotiation with practiced FTA leaders (e.g., Chile and Singapore), then shifting to a second stage of FTAs with larger economies (e.g., Mexico and Canada), and, third, concluding FTAs with the global loci of the United States and EU. While parts of the roadmap were eventually changed (e.g., the proposed FTA with Japan stalled), much of the roadmap was accomplished under President Roh.

Under the Lee Myung-bak administration (2008–13), the political coalition drew upon different groups compared with Presidents Kim and Roh. Lee Mung-bak's supporting bases were more from the business sector than the popular sector. Lee, nonetheless, continued and further accelerated South Korea's FTA strategy. Lee pushed for FTA negotiations with China, Korea's single largest trading partner, and, perhaps most critically, he expended a tremendous amount of political capital to get the KORUS FTA passed by the national legislature.

State Autonomy

The fact that presidents from a variety of political affiliations were able to pursue FTAs so systematically is partially rooted in the autonomy of the Korean trade policymaking process. Specifically, Korean presidents were able to pursue FTAs without facing a meaningful veto from the agriculture sector or the legislature.

The Korean state possessed considerable autonomy from these actors during the period of military dictatorship (1962–79) (Haggard,1990). Perhaps the biggest difference compared to most developing countries of the time was that the agriculture sector was particularly weak due to a combination of U.S.-imposed land reform and the defeat of communism before and during the Korean War (Haggard 1990). More generally, the ongoing external threat from North Korea facilitated society's deference to the state, and the military government had high autonomy to pursue its goals (Kang 1995).[2]

Korean democratization in 1987 was seen as eroding the state's autonomy from society, but as noted in chapter 4, the AFC gave Kim Dae-Jung transitional and temporary legislative power to build a strong economic bureaucracy with more autonomy as well as other reforms.

Perhaps the most important sector with respect to FTA policy was agriculture since it was this sector that had the most to lose from trade liberalization. The most competitive sector of the Korean economy in the international market is industry while the least competitive sector is agriculture (e.g., Cheong 2007). The potential loss to agriculture was severe, and as Choi and Oh (2011) note, the Korea agriculture sector had far more to lose from FTAs than even the Japanese agriculture sector, since most Korean farmers are full-time farmers whereas Japanese farmers tend to be involved in other economic activities as well.

Yet while the Japanese state was unable to ignore the agriculture sector, the Korean state was able to do so. This was partially rooted in the historical weakness of agriculture, as noted above. Moreover, Korea's long industrial success further weakened the relative power of agriculture, with the sector falling from 18 percent of GDP in 1990 to 8 percent of GDP in 2004. It was the 1997 crisis, however, that proved to be the turning point. "In the immediate aftermath of the Asian financial crisis, South Korea's protectionist veto players, such as labor unions and farmers' organizations, were temporarily disorganized due to President Kim Dae-jung's (1998–2003) liberal reform and the austerity program imposed by the International Monetary Fund" (Koo 2010, 110), based on the analysis of Kyun-Sup (2007).

Another possible restraint on FTA policy might have been the legislative branch, as often occurs in the U.S. case. Indeed, the U.S. Congress has overcome its tendency toward vetoing trade agreements by partially tying its own hands through "fast track" authority, which gives the president wide latitude to conduct trade negotiations. In Korea, however, the legislature does not have the formal power to influence FTA negotiations, such that the executive branch already has the constitutional equivalent of "fast track authority." Moreover, with democratization being relatively recent, the Korean legislature is still institutionally weak. Lee (2010, 292), for instance, laments that whereas the executive branch has heavily invested in bureaucratic capacity to regulate economic globalization, the legislative branch has fallen far behind, such that "the weight of foreign-policy power has moved more and more towards executive branch, thereby taking power away from the legislative branch." This is not to deny that the legislature has legal veto power over

FTAs nor to deny that there was considerable legislative controversy over the FTAs with both Chile and the United States, but the South Korean executive branch was not as constrained by the legislature as was the case in the United States and many other nations.

South Korea's FTA strategy arose from within the state and was pursued autonomously from societal actors. This is not to say that the state was completely insulated. Evans (1995) notes that autonomy should be coupled with "embeddedness," in which the state extensively consults with business and collects information before it acts autonomously in executing policy. South Korea did precisely this, in that MOFAT engaged in extensive consultation with business over FTA policy. Nonetheless, it was ultimately state actors that conceived, initiated, and implemented FTA policy and thereby elevated South Korea into the vanguard of world FTA activity.

State Capacity

In contrast with the explicit attention given to state autonomy in the literature, attention given to the concept of state capacity is limited and less explicit. A few comments are therefore warranted. First, South Korea undoubtedly inherited much of the effective bureaucracy enjoyed by so many earlier administrations. Indeed, in a recent statement, Im (2013) notes that the Korean government, unlike the U.S. government, continues to attract the highest caliber of applicant: "in the Korean context, bureaucrats play a leading role in society, solicit significant respect from it, and have high levels of esprit de corps in the bureaucracy."

Second, as already noted, the crisis conditions of 1997 allowed Korea to create a powerful bureaucratic actor in MOFAT. The spearhead was a newly established Office of the Minister for Trade (OMT). The OMT was in charge of trade negotiations, and the head of the OMT held a minister-level position, putting trade policy at the highest level of executive governance (Choi and Oh 2011, 515).

Third, to facilitate rapid and effective policy, the executive mandated a regularly occurring ministerial Meeting on External Economic Affairs in 2001. Indeed, this new ministerial meeting process was a fascinating instance of the power of groupthink. As Choi and Oh (2011, 517) argue,

> The ministerial meetings critically alter the negotiation leverage of individual ministries. Since ministries engaged in repeated discussions during the monthly ministerial meetings, it became difficult for one

ministry to consistently oppose and thus stall negotiation efforts. . . . For example, MOA [Ministry of Agriculture] would risk bearing the blame for sabotaging FTA negotiations if they continued to oppose agricultural liberalization.

Fourth, descriptions of how FTA policy unfolded in South Korea attest to the *capacity* of MOFAT bureaucrats. MOFAT recognized the importance of bureaucratic learning and intentionally targeted FTA learning experiences (e.g., Chile and Singapore) before strategically following up with more ambitious FTAs. Various scholars have confirmed that these early FTAs were useful for preparing Korean policymakers for the later FTAs (e.g., Park and Koo, 2007).

Fifth, MOFAT was extremely proactive about pursuing the critical KORUS FTA. This included convincing the president to make concessions to the United States even prior to FTA negotiations (Choi and Oh 2011).

More generally, MOFAT was highly proactive throughout the process, resembling Johnson's notion of a "pilot agency" in the state bureaucracy, which like the Ministry of International Trade and Industry, could get things done. As Solís (2013b, 8) puts it:

MOFAT's power of initiative reached new heights when it advocated for leapfrogging its own roadmap and negotiating sooner than originally planned with a major economy like the United States. The trade minister Kim Hyun-chong made a strong argument for using a trade agreement with the United States to enhance domestic structural reforms and shift the developmental model further towards a liberal market economy. Despite the fact that incoming President Roh Moohyun's base of support was largely on the anti-FTA camp, he was swayed by these arguments.

In sum, it is clear that Korean FTA policy formulation and implementation was characterized by high levels of state autonomy and state capacity. In these respects, Korea exhibits two key characteristics of a developmental state.

Industrial Policy

So far Korean FTA policy looks analogous to the developmental state model, in that an autonomous and high-capacity state was at the heart of the FTA strategy. But can FTAs be considered industrial policy?

It is easy to make the case that FTAs are neoliberal policies. FTAs are essentially legally binding agreements between nations to reduce government restrictions on international trade. In this sense, FTA policies increase the power of the market and reduce the power of the government. Indeed, as Wade (1991) notes, free trade is considered the crown jewel of neoliberal ideology.

A first caveat to thinking about FTAs as liberal, however, is the reality that FTAs are inherently bilateral rather than multilateral. This means that states selectively seek out some partners with whom to sign an FTA while leaving other candidates out. Many economists, therefore argue, that FTAs discriminate against third parties. Moreover, since FTAs are often driven more by political factors than by economic factors (e.g., Sohn and Koo 2011), FTAs should perhaps be considered just as much a political effort to drive trade flows as they are a form of economic liberalism. Indeed, Mansfield and Milner's (2014, 178) very last footnote addresses the commonly noted truth that FTAs are associated with free-market ideology: "This is somewhat ironic since PTAs themselves . . . imply government intervention in the trading system."

Koo (2010) views FTAs as being closely associated with industrial policy, noting a resurgence of industrial policy in major industrial countries alongside active pursuit of FTAs. If we accept the World Bank's definition of industrial policy as "government efforts to alter industrial structure to promote productivity-based growth" (World Bank 1993, 304), then the Korean case looks even more like industrial policy. The traditional justification for free trade is Ricardo's theory of comparative advantage, suggesting static benefits from free trade as each country specializes in its comparative advantage. Korean officials, however, had a very different vision in mind. They focused on the dynamic benefits of free trade, believing that competition with major industrial countries such as the United States and the EU would increase economic efficiency in South Korea and hence propel the nation further up the ladder of productivity. Choi (2009), for instance, notes this productivity motivation with respect to the KORUS FTA.

> Korea has embarked on aggressive regionalism because it wants to upgrade its internal economic environment. If Korea simply wanted to reduce the cost of trade with a big economy, it would have been better off negotiating a FTA with China rather than with the US. . . . Korea understood that its economic problems were internal, and it decided to eliminate domestic inefficiencies by forcing its system to compete with the U.S. economy, the most efficient economy in the world. (694)

In this conception the state is strategically and actively guiding the Korean economy and seems to fit the above World Bank definition of industrial policy. Whether or not we view Korea as a developmental state, then, depends largely on how one wants to define industrial policy. The broader picture, however, is clear. Although FTAs are a liberal policy, obtaining this liberal goal is a thoroughly statist project, in which such attributes as planning, bureaucratic capacity, and state autonomy are helpful in obtaining FTAs.

III. The Scope of Korean FTAs

South Korea's FTA strategy has vast scope compared to other countries. To validate this point, I examine the role of international trade and FTAs more generally around the world. The data shows that South Korea is substantially *more influenced by trade* than most countries and that their *proportion of total trade subject to FTAs is higher* than in most countries. Few countries achieve this status, and I compare South Korea with that select sample to see how unusual South Korea appears.

A nation's exposure to trade is often measured by its exports as a percentage of GDP. Indeed, if one views Asian development as an overall EOI development strategy, then this simple export variable becomes a crude proxy for EOI. The significance of exports for South Korea is demonstrated in figure 5.1, which provides 2013 export data for the world's seventy-seven most populous countries.[3] The y axis provides the conventional measure, exports as a percentage of GDP. This variable reveals that exports play a huge role in South Korean GDP. Only eight out of the seventy-seven countries shown have a higher trade share on the y axis. Indeed, more than half of what the South Korean economy produces is meant for foreign markets.

FTA Coverage

Turning now to FTAs explicitly, the x axis in figure 5.1 is an innovation that I introduce for this book, namely, to measure the proportion of each country's trade that is regulated by FTAs.[4] The x axis therefore ranges from 0 to 1, with the latter signifying that 100 percent of a nation's trade is regulated by FTAs. The country that most approximates this extreme is Mexico, on the far right of which figure 5.1, with over 95 percent of its trade regulated by FTAs—

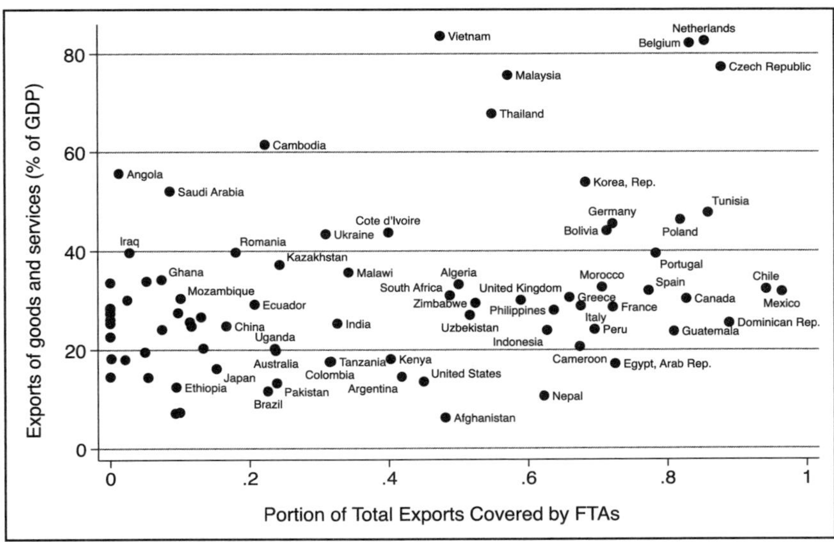

Figure 5.1. Exports and FTA Coverage
Exports as a percentage of GDP and the percentage of their exports covered by FTAs for the seventy-seven most populous countries. Those measuring more than 40 percent of GDP in exports *and simultaneously* more than 40 percent of exports covered under FTAs are considered FTA intensive. (Source: footnote 4.)

mostly a powerful testament to the scope of NAFTA but also an indication of Mexico's active FTA network.[5]

In figure 5.1 the further up the country is on the y axis, the larger its exposure to international markets. The further right on the x axis the country is, the greater the percentage of its trade regulated by FTAs. Those countries in the top-right corner of figure 5.1, therefore, are most FTA-intensive, loosely defined as simultaneously at least 40 percent of their GDP in trade and 40 percent of their trade under FTAs.

Korea appears in the top-right quadrant and is hence correctly considered an FTA-intensive country. Six other countries, however, have an even higher percentage of GDP from exports with similar levels of FTA to Korea. These are conveniently clustered in two groups, one in the extreme top-right corner of figure 5.1 and the second in the approximate middle of the x axis. These six countries, as well as the four additional countries just below Korea in figure 5.1, raise important social science questions when thinking about Korean FTAs. How analogous is Korea to these countries? Do they demonstrate similar patterns, idiosyncratic causal processes, or some composite between the two? Put more pointedly, is Korea unique or just one more FTA-intensive country?

FTAs as Development Strategy

It is here that the concept of a "development strategy" again becomes useful. One way of assessing Korea's distinctiveness is to answer the following question for each of the ten countries in the top-right quadrant of figure 5.1: Is their placement there due to an intentional economic development strategy or due to happenstance?

On the one hand, Belgium, the Netherlands, and the Czech Republic all have their position in figure 5.1 through happenstance. These nations' societies voted to join the EU, as did all of their neighbors. They all have high export ratios (y axis) due to their small size and are highly FTA-intensive countries because almost all of their trade occurs with the EU.[6] This was no state-led FTA strategy but rather the consequence of being a very small economy in a very large FTA.

Given this clear "EU effect," it is important to assess more generally how many of the countries in figure 5.1 are driven solely by European integration. By filtering out countries in the EU as shown in figure 5.2, the answer is evident: a disproportionate number of the FTA-intensive countries in figure 5.1 are EU countries. Indeed, while only eleven of the seventy-seven most populous countries are in the EU, the FTA-intensive category falls by nearly half, leaving only seven nations.

What about the other FTA-intensive (non-EU) countries in figure 5.1? Mexico's export economy is dominated by NAFTA but also has an economically significant FTA with the EU. Chile is legitimately on the far right given its strong commitment to a broad FTA strategy. Chile, however, is only half as dependent on trade as Korea, making Chile's FTA strategy only half as relevant to its economy. Finally, note that Tunisia and Bolivia, which appear close to Korea in figure 5.2, are both heavily dependent on a single FTA. Tunisian exports are overwhelmingly dominated by EU partners while Bolivian trade is dominated by Mercosur partners.[7]

On the whole, once one removes the EU cases (again, figure 5.2), Korea is rather unusual. Among countries with substantial FTA coverage, it is at the highest point on the y axis, meaning that trade is noticeably more important for Korean economic growth than for the remaining countries. Korea is also relatively far to the right in figure 5.2, suggesting it has extensive FTA

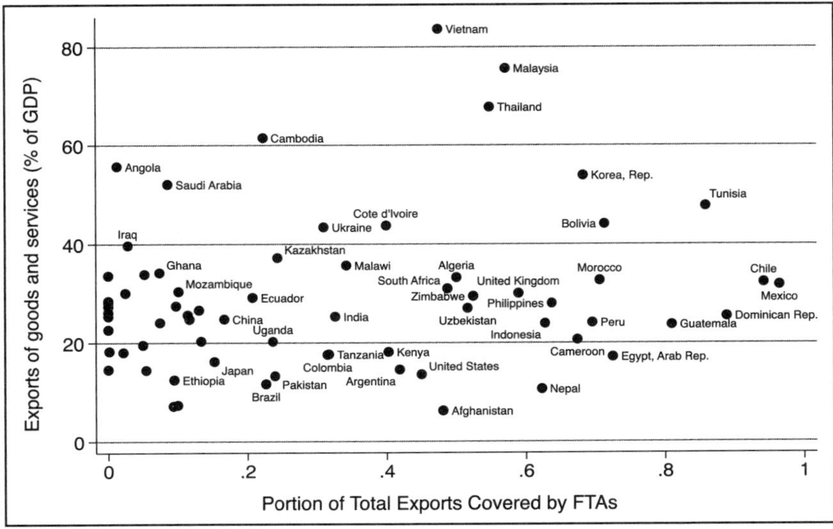

Figure 5.2. Exports and FTA Coverage (without EU)

coverage. Although some countries do have higher FTA exposure, this rarely stems from a development strategy but instead stems from being dependent primarily on a single multilateral regional trade zone (e.g., Mexico, Tunisia, and Bolivia). Figures 5.1 and 5.2, in short, reinforce the fact that Korea is unusual—with the important exception of the one cluster we have not yet discussed, the three outliers (Thailand, Malaysia, and Vietnam) at the top of both figures.

Korea as Subset of Export Orientated-Industrialization

Whether examined through figure 5.1 or figure 5.2, the countries of Thailand, Malaysia, and Vietnam clearly are in a league of their own. Again, these three outliers are evident as a small cluster at the top of figure 5.2, in the middle of the x axis. Exports constitute over two-thirds of GDP in these countries, and they are the extremes in the sample.[8] Along with Korea, these Asian exporters constitute a theoretically comparable group, with unusually high trade dependence and reasonably high FTA coverage.

When comparing Korea with the other three Asian EOI countries, a few things become clear. First, the other three Asian countries are noticeably more export intensive than even Korea. A second, less obvious, but still important, distinction is that the other three countries are members of the Association of Southeast Asian Nations (ASEAN) while Korea is not. China and then Japan and Korea all jumped to sign FTAs with ASEAN after the 1997 financial crisis. It was not a strategy to pursue FTAs with China and Japan that connected Thailand, Malaysia, or Vietnam, but rather ASEAN's collective bargaining with Japan and China that led to FTAs.

Korea was the only one of the four Asian EOI countries (Thailand, Malaysia, and Vietnam) with an FTA strategy that reached either the United States or the EU. Is this a more general finding? Is Korea unique globally in its outreach to the two Westerns nodes of the world economy?

A Western Strategy

The major centers of the world economy have been rather loath to sign FTAs with other major economies around the world. Table 5.1 illustrates this, listing the top twenty trading partners of the world's three economic cores: the EU, the United States, and China. All countries with *more* than one FTA with a major economic center are in bold.

What is striking about this list is how few countries have FTAs with more than one of the major foci of the world economy. This is especially apparent for each region's top twenty list. Only four countries have managed the feat of signing more than one FTA with any of the three regional centers. Singapore, a particularly active trading state, has FTAs with both China and the United States. Korea has the unique distinction of being the only country on all three top ten lists, having signed FTAs with China, the United States, and the EU. This makes South Korea the world's FTA leader—being the only major exporter with FTAs with all three centers of the world economy, the United States, the EU, and China. This trifecta of FTAs vividly demonstrates Korean success in planning, negotiating, and ratifying major FTAs on a global scale.

Most important, the list of countries possessing FTAs with multiple economic centers remains largely unchanged. Singapore still stands out as a global player, having FTAs with two centers of the world economy, and Mexico now joins this list, at twentieth with the EU and second with the United States. Nonetheless, Korea remains singular in being the sole country with FTAs with all three centers of the world economy.

Indeed, only Mexico, Singapore, Australia, and Malaysia are even remotely comparable to Korea, with two FTAs each from the Korean trifecta of FTA partners: the United States, the EU, and China. In the case of Mexico, FTA is dominated by NAFTA, and even the EU FTA was NAFTA related, so Mexico is not a good example of a global strategy. Singapore, on the other hand, has trading relations with China and the EU. It is perhaps most comparable to Korea, although it is important to keep in mind that Singapore is a city-state, and as essentially a port city it is inherently predisposed toward trade.

To sum up, Korea is the sole winner of the FTA trifecta, and few other countries even come close in terms of having a diversified FTA strategy. Some are comparable, however, so this book makes reference to Mexico, Singapore, and Taiwan at times. Nonetheless, South Korea clearly has a unique FTA footprint.

A Map and a List

Now that we have gained a sense of how unique Korea's FTA strategy has

TABLE 5.1. Three Loci of Global Trade and Their Top Twenty Trading Partners

	(1)	(2)	(3)	(4)	(5)	(6)
	EU	%	United States	%	China	%
1	United States	13.8	Canada	20	United States	28
2	China	13.3	Mexico	13	Japan	10
3	Russia	9.5	China	7	Germany	5
4	Switzerland	6.6	Japan	6	**South Korea**	5
5	Norway	4.4	United Kingdom	5	United Kingdom	4
6	Turkey	3.7	Germany	4	Netherland	4
7	Japan	3.6	**South Korea**	3	Canada	3
8	India	2.5	Netherlands	3	**Singapore**	3
9	Brazil	2.3	**Singapore**	3	**Mexico**	2
10	**South Korea**	2.1	France	2	Taiwan	2
11	Saudi Arabia	1.7	Taiwan		Italy	2
12	Canada	1.6	Brazil		**Australia**	2
13	Singapore	1.4	**Australia**		France	2
14	Algeria	1.4	Belgium		**Malaysia**	2
15	South Africa	1.3	**Malaysia**		**India**	2
16	Australia	1.3	Switzerland		Spain	1
17	UAE	1.3	Italy		**Thailand**	1
18	Hong Kong	1.3	UAE		UAE	1
19	Taiwan	1.2	India		Belgium	1
20	**Mexico**	1.2	Venezuela		Russia	1

Source: EUGene.

Note: Percentages refer to the percent of trade that each partner captures of that locus (i.e., EU, United States, or China). For example, in the top left, the United States accounts for 13.8 percent of EU trade. Countries are in **bold** if they have signed an FTA with that world center (EU, U.S., and China) and at least one other center.

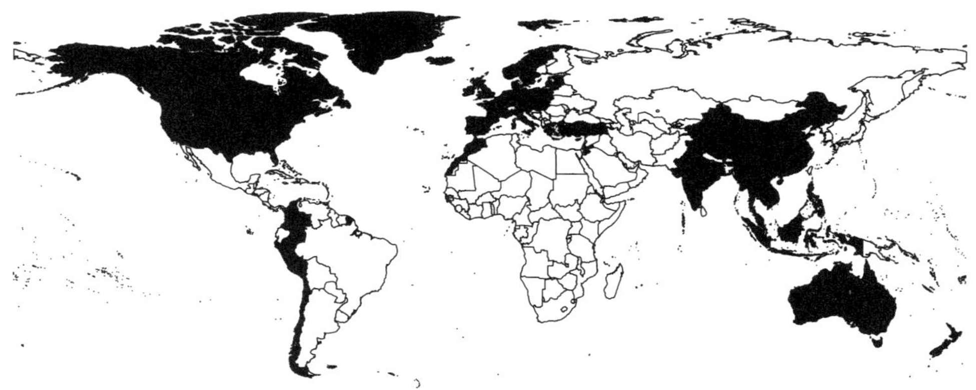

Figure 5.3. Korean FTAs
Shaded areas indicate the global scope and diverse range of nations with which
Korea has successfully negotiated and signed FTAs.

been, we can turn to the actual data set of South Korea's FTA partners. I
present the data first as a map and then as a list, noting that both formats
contain useful information.

Figure 5.3 portrays Korea's remarkable FTA activity on a global map, illustrating all signed FTAs. Clearly Korea has a global FTA vision. Indeed,
the sheer geographic extent of South Korean FTAs is striking. Korea has
FTAs in six continents, covering most of Europe as well as the vast territories
of India, the United States, and China.

Table 5.2 portrays Korea's FTA strategy in list form. The first point to
note about table 5.2 is that it contains three semi-multilateral FTAs and a
dozen bilateral FTAs. This illustrates the point that many of South Korea's
important FTAs are semi-multilateral. The ASEAN FTA included ten country commitments, the EU FTA included numerous commitments, and the
European Free Trade Association (EFTA) included four country commitments. This multitude of partners through only three agreements provides
much of the visual power of figure 5.3.

When it comes to bilateral FTAs, Korea has signed twelve such agreements. Korea first sought out two well-known FTA leaders—Chile (2003)
and Singapore (2005). Of the remaining bilateral agreements, three are easily
understood. The United States, China, and India are three massive economies. A bilateral FTA with each seems imperative for a successful FTA strategy.

So in the end what is to be concluded about the extent of Korea's FTA strategy? The scale of this strategy is amazing, and Korea is the only country to rival the world's Great Powers for market share of global trade. Korean FTA policy, moreover, is substantial and unique in that exports constitute the majority of Korea's economy, which places trade policy at the core of Korea's economic strategy. In this context, it is important to remember that Korea has an unusually high share of its trade under FTA, particularly for a country outside of the EU. Finally, Korea's FTA policy is comprehensive in that Korea forged FTAs with all three centers of the world economy, constituting a truly diverse FTA network.

IV. Explaining Partner Choice

The prior section detailed Korea's FTA profile by identifying the country's FTA partners, noting the nation's extensive reliance on trade, and emphasizing the breadth of the nation's FTA network. In what follows I focus on a *specific* choice involved in FTA strategy, namely, with which countries to sign. Why did South Korea enter into FTAs with some countries but not with others?

TABLE 5.2. South Korea's Signed FTAs (year/month/day)

Partners	Proposed date	Signed date	Ratified date	Effective date
ASEAN	2004	2006	2007–04–02	2007–06–01
EFTA	2004	2005	2006–06–30	2006–09–01
EU	2006	2010–10–06	2011–05–04	2011–07–01
				2015–12–13
India	2005	2009–08	2009–11–06	2010–01–01
Singapore	2003	2005–08	2005–12–01	2006–03–02
Chile	1999	2003–02	2004–02–16	2004–04–01
Peru	2007	2011–03–21	2011–06–30	2011–08–01
USA	2005	2007–06	2011–11–22	2012–03–15
Turkey	2008	2012–08–01	2012–11–22	2013–05–01
Colombia	2009	2013–02–21	2014–04–29	2016–07–15
Canada	2004	2014–09–23	2014–12–02	2015–01–01
New Zealand	2006	2015–03–23	2015–11–30	2015–12–20
Australia	2009	2014–04–08	2014–12–02	2014–12–12
Vietnam	2010	2015–05–05	2015–11–30	2015–12–20
China	2012	2015–06–01	2015–11–30	2015–12–20

Source: http://www.fta.go.kr/main/situation/kfta/ov/ ; http://www.archives.go.kr/next/search/list-SubjectDescription.do?id=003500&pageFlag

Note: all FTAs are bilateral with the exception of the first three: ASEAN, EU and EFTA

A simple cross-sectional logistic analysis captures the central question of interest, namely, why it is that South Korea chose some countries as FTA partners but did not choose other countries. Drawing upon the hypotheses developed in Chapter 2, I conducted a cross-sectional logistic analysis of signed South Korean FTAs in a sample of 139 trading partners. To address the lack of independence of observations in multilateral FTAs, such as the ASEAN FTA, all standard errors were calculated by clustering on the multilateral FTA groupings.

Based upon chapter 2, I pose five hypotheses that can be operationalized with the following five explanatory variables: **(1)** the logged total GDP of South Korea's 139 trading partners in U.S. millions of dollars (from the 2015 World Bank *World Development Indicators*); **(2)** the distance variable as logged distance between Seoul and the capital city of a trading partner, where distance is being conceived of as a proxy for transportation costs (from EUGene, as described in Bennett and Stam 2000); **(3)** the income per capita of Korea's trading partners (from the 2015 World Bank *World Development Indicators*); **(4)** the total number of FTAs each nation has signed, to proxy trade diversion effects (calculated from Mölders 2012); **(5)** the levels of democracy among the South Korean trading partners (from the *Polity IV* score, developed by Marshall et al. 2013).[9]

Table 5.3 applies these five variables to the Korean data set. The model performs satisfactorily. Four of the five variables are statistically significant and

TABLE 5.3. Logit Analysis of Korean FTA Partner Choice

Variables	(1)
Distance	−3.0337*
	(1.5574)
GDP	0.4501***
	(0.0441)
GDP per capita	0.2033
	(0.1251)
Democracy	0.1869***
	(0.0721)
Prior FTAs (#)	0.2123***
	(0.0194)
Constant	10.0072
	(14.6436)
Observations	139

Robust standard errors in parentheses.
$*p < 0.1$, $**p < 0.05$, $***p < 0.01$

have the correct signs, which is a nice confirmation of theory. The model confirms our prior sense that Korea pursues large GDPs as well as closer countries. The model also picked up on significant effects from two subtle causal mechanisms, namely, the positive incentives stemming from democracy as well as strategic effects stemming from third-party FTAs. The only mechanism not to receive support is the idea of comparative advantage, given that differences between Korean incomes and other incomes have no effect on FTAs, although the sign of the coefficient is at least consistent with theory.[10]

Pseudo R2 is .64, which suggests that the model captures close to two-thirds of the variation. The other common measure-of-fit, namely, the percentage correctly predicted, is 94 percent of the outcomes. Given that there are 139 countries in the sample, this means that merely eight countries are incorrectly predicted.

Residual Analysis and the Chilean Case

It is generally good practice to examine mis-predictions to see if they contain counterintuitive findings or otherwise shed light on model specification. Table 5.4 lists the eight mis-predicted countries, along with their predicted

TABLE 5.4. Comparing Actual Korean FTA Partner Choice with Predictions

Panel A—Categorization

	Actual FTAs	Actual ~FTAs	Total
Predicted FTAs	38	3	41
Predicted ~FTAs	5	93	98
Total	43	96	139

Panel B—Five False Negatives

Peru	.1112815
Chile	.0530011
Sri Lanka	.3729411
Cambodia	.2914436
Laos	.1043053

Panel C—Three False Positives

Dominican Republic	.7849071
Mongolia	.5807697
Japan	.9984704

values of having an FTA with Korea. Panel B lists the five false negatives, where the model predicted no FTA and yet an FTA was in fact signed. Panel C lists the three false positives, where the model predicted an FTA and yet none in fact was signed.

Looking first at the five false negatives, Laos and Cambodia do not have sufficiently large economies to be attractive FTA partners, but the findings remind us that the ASEAN FTA was an all-or-nothing affair, and hence the two countries became Korea's FTA partners due to the simple "collective bargaining" element inherent in ASEAN.

There are two major intrigues in table 5.4. Chile, despite only having a 5 percent predicted probability, does in fact have an FTA with South Korea. Japan, which does not have an FTA with Korea, was predicted to have a 99.8 percent chance of having an FTA with Korea.

The Chilean FTA is an absolutely counterintuitive and fascinating mis-prediction. Chile was the very first FTA that Korea pursued, and a number of studies that I discuss below explain why it was a wise choice. The fact that the model mis-predicts Chile therefore demands explanation. Serendipitously, a closer look at the Chilean case also sheds considerable light on the South Korean FTA strategy more generally.

The literature provides a persuasive, interesting, and methodologically satisfying explanation for the Chilean choice (e.g., Solís and Katata 2007; Park and Koo 2007; Park 2008). Park and Koo (2007) provide the most thorough discussion: a plausible threefold explanation for why Chile does in fact exist as an FTA instance in table 5.2. First, much was due to Chile's own pro-FTA orientation: Chile was one of only six nations with any interest in discussing FTAs with South Korea in the immediate aftermath of the AFC.[11] Second, this FTA was justified by neoclassical trade theory since Korea is capital rich while Chile is resource rich and land rich, such that the two countries should profit from complementary comparative advantages. Third, politically, agriculture is Korea's uncompetitive sector, such that a gentle treatment of that sector would be welcome. Putting these three considerations together, Park and Koo (2007, 267) note that "in an inter-ministerial meeting held in November 1998, an FTA with Chile was given top priority, mainly because of the country's complementary industrial structure and the potentially low level of threat to South Korea's agriculture due to the seasonal differences."

Park and Koo (2007) not only provide a compelling explanation for why Chile was in fact Korea's first FTA partner but also note the important role of the Korea-Chile FTA in the politics of Korean FTAs more generally. As Korea's first FTA, the Chilean case would obviously set a precedent. Oversimplifying greatly, Korea is a developed country and hence has internationally competitive industry but internationally *uncompetitive* agriculture. The natural and most politicized opposition was going to come from agriculture. All actors knew this. For the government to advance the cause of future FTAs, therefore, it had to pull off a delicate balancing act. Korea had to liberalize agriculture by a sufficiently *substantial amount* to be seen as a credible signal, and yet at the same time it had to successfully sign this FTA, which meant that it could not generate *too much* domestic opposition from agriculture and/or other actors. In short, "South Korea's choice of Chile as its first FTA partner had a lot to do with the potentially minimal costs for South Korea's uncompetitive sectors such as agriculture" (Park and Koo 2007, 270).

In articulating their political explanation, Park and Koo are aware that they are providing an alternative to the standard economic explanation, and they do so intentionally. Concerning gravity models they note: "From this perspective, the South Korea-Chile FTA is a typical example of an unnatural trading bloc, not only because an ocean separates the two countries, but also due to the fact that Chile's economy is relatively small" (Park and Koo 2007, 265). What is economically a disadvantage, as Park and Koo argue, is politically an advantage, meaning that Chile was too small and too far away to generate enough opposition to derail Korea's first FTA. From a development strategy perspective, this was shrewd political logic, given the ferocious opposition to the subsequent U.S. FTA.

The other surprising mis-prediction is Japan. Korea has no FTA with Japan despite a prediction of over 99 percent for a Korea-Japan FTA. This high prediction is obviously due to Japan's large GDP, which is a major determinant of Korean FTAs. Moreover, distance further suggests that Japan would be a natural FTA partner. I explore this nonevent in detail in chapter 8.

To sum up, common sense, statistics, and anecdotal evidence yield complementary confirmations. All point to the idea that Korea pursues FTAs with countries with large GDPs, once again suggesting that the single most distinctive feature about the Korean strategy is the diversity of major economic hubs with which it has FTAs. These various methods also give us complementary insights. The qualitative literature emphasizes the tremendous importance of the Chilean case and explains why it is an outlier in the statistical model. The quantitative findings reinforce our sense that a large GDP motivated Korea but also pick up on subtleties such as the role of geographic distance as well as the positive incentive effects stemming from democratic partners and partners with many existing FTAs. Residual analysis gives additional confidence that there are no serious mis-predictions to cast doubt on the conclusions just listed. In all, Korean FTA strategy seems intelligible, conforming with both economic theory and common sense.

FTA Proposals

So far I have discussed Korean signed FTAs, because they are the outcome with real direct effect on the Korean development strategy. I turn now to see what can be learned from Korean FTA *proposals*. The first point to note is that the data set is richer in two different ways. First, there were more FTA proposals to countries (seventy-five) than there were signed FTAs (forty-four), giving us more variation. Second, most of the proposals were bilateral and hence provide more independence in the observations than does the signed FTA data. Given the greater richness of this "proposed" FTA data set, I investigate whether the parsimonious model developed for FTA signatures provides insight into the timing of Korea's FTA proposals.

Table 5.5 presents the results from Cox proportional hazards models for proposals, again clustering on multilateral FTA groupings to address the potential lack of independence between observations in each FTA grouping.[12] The main point to note is that theory again is vindicated, with variables other than physical distance being statistically significant determinants of South Korean FTA policy, in this case referring to all countries with which South Korea negotiated rather than signed.

TABLE 5.5. Cox Proportional Hazards Models

Variables	(1) FTA proposal
Distance	−0.1585
	(0.4326)
GDP per capita	−2.3575***
	(0.8726)
Logged GDP (US$ million)	0.2282*
	(0.1378)
Democracy	0.0862***
	(0.0194)
Japan	0.8241*
	(0.4451)
China	0.9305***
	(0.2733)
GDP per capita * t	1.5261***
	(0.4936)
Observations	1,179

Robust standard errors in parentheses.
*$p < 0.1$, **$p < 0.05$, ***$p < 0.01$

Conclusions

Examining the broad scope of South Korean FTA policy, it seems fair to say that it resembles in many ways a full-fledged development strategy. The economic goals were major, addressing the major portion of the Korean GDP (exports) and bringing it almost entirely under FTAs.

The state was extremely active, not only in the sense that it possessed autonomy from the legislature and from agriculture, as well as other actors. The FTA strategy was also carried out by extensive presidential commitment, a strong trade bureaucracy, and even bureaucratic initiative. It took state activity on a complex scale to achieve what South Korea accomplished.

I close this chapter on the Korean FTA strategy by noting two further characteristics. First, taken as a whole, the strategy seems fairly rational. Second, South Korea was unusually effective in obtaining FTAs with the trifecta of the United States, the EU, and China, and this is perhaps the most distinctive aspect of the nation's FTA strategy.

Economically Rational

Concerning development strategy, Korea's choice in FTA partners appears to be economically rational. I do not mean anything technical by the word *rational* and hence hope to sidestep the deep debates in political science over both the meaning and the utility of that word. I have in mind instead two other senses of the phrase *economically rational*. First, does it meet our everyday sense of the word? Specifically, was Korean FTA policy conducted in a way that corresponds with common sense, basic theory, and simple facts? Second, does Korean FTA policy correspond with economic theories of FTA policy and, in particular, with econometric models proxying these theories?

Thinking first in terms of common sense, I submit that when one looks over the list in table 5.2, it is a sensible list. ASEAN was chosen to keep up with China and Japan, as well as for its geographic proximity. Chile and Singapore were both chosen as test cases to improve negotiation skills and to set domestic political precedents. Finally, because Korea is a global and competitive trading power, it signed FTAs with all major centers of the world economy, namely, the EU, the United States, China, and India. This is effectively the story of Korea's FTA strategy, other than the nuances of its various other bilateral FTAs. Korea joined in the ASEAN rush, gained more FTA negotiation experience with Chile and Singapore, and then followed through with the large GDP trifecta of the EU, the United States, and China.

This FTA strategy corresponds closely to economic theories of rationality. Using common econometric models to proxy these theories, we find that fully four of five are significant correlates of signed Korean FTAs in tables 5.3 and 5.4. Then examining the *temporal* patterns of FTA *proposals*, I again find results consistent with a parsimonious political economy explanation.

Not only do both common sense and statistical modeling suggest the Korean strategy was rational and effective, but looking at the model's mispredictions actually improves our confidence in the model rather than reducing it. Laos and Cambodia, for instance, can be explained by the all-or-nothing nature of the ASEAN agreement. The Japanese case is a huge exception and will be discussed in chapter 8. The other major exception is Chile, which upon close examination was intentionally *chosen to be contrary* to the gravity model so as to minimize the actual economic impact and hence to limit the political fallout. In all, Korea not only adopted an intentional strategy to seek out major FTAs but executed this strategy rather effectively and sensibly, regardless of whether one evaluates the strategy qualitatively or statistically.

FTA Trifecta

Finally, the most distinctive aspect of Korea's FTA policy is the country's precious ability to sign FTAs with all three major centers of the world economy. No other country has achieved this, and only a few other countries have even managed to sign with two centers. Other than these four countries, all other countries are relegated to, at most, one FTA with a regional economic center.

Although neither section II nor section III above was making strong causal claims, it is interesting to note that the theoretical setup of these sections provided somewhat different visions of how these major FTAs came about. The political narrative in section II suggests that South Korea, Singapore, Mexico, and Malaysia are unusual as countries able to *entice* more than one core region of the world economy into an FTA. In this view, Korea is exceptional. Section III, by contrast, notes that gravity models predict that all countries seek out larger GDPs, and in those models the theoretical conception is that Korea is *drawn* toward larger GDP. So, was Korea simply lured into a common pattern, or did Korea ambitiously create this FTA trifecta through unusually effective state action? Chapters 7 and 8 address these central questions through an in-depth analysis and comparison of these important FTAs with China, the EU, and the United States.

CHAPTER 6

FTA Consequences

Did South Korea's FTA development strategy work? If so, in what ways? This chapter attempts to answer these questions by analyzing the specific content of each FTA, while organizing the conclusions topically: Sections I through III examine three different mechanisms through which FTAs influenced the South Korean macroeconomy. Section I examines FTA effects on economic growth, section II examines FTA effects on exports and imports, and section III examines FTA effects on inward FDI to South Korea and outward FDI, especially to China and Vietnam. Section IV examines how FTAs have enhanced the efficiency of the Korean service sector while section V examines strategic first-mover advantages from being an FTA hub.

Before turning to the detailed effects of Korea's FTAs, recall from chapter 4, section II, that Korea's rate of economic growth since World War II has been, in a word, outstanding. I now address twenty-first century growth to provide a contemporary economic context for thinking about the consequences of South Korea's FTA strategy.

While South Korean economic growth is not nearly what it once was, it is critical to note that its recent economic growth performance is very respectable. Consider, for instance, the first decade of the twenty-first century, when South Korea experienced 3.9 percent annual growth, which outperformed the world average of 2.5 percent.[1] But South Korea is now a developed economy, and hence it is more appropriate to compare Korea's growth rates with those of the rest of the OECD countries. It is well known in economic growth theory that richer countries, all else being equal, have a more difficult time maintaining rapid growth than poorer countries.[2] To wit, OECD growth rates have been historically low at 1.1 percent annually in the twenty-first century, and thus Korea's 3.9 percent annual growth rate remains extremely successful compared to its OECD peers.

I. FTA Effects on Economic Growth

Disaggregating the Korean FTA strategy is necessary given the heterogeneity of its FTA partners, in terms of both quantity and quality. A high-quantity FTA with the EU, the United States, or China, for instance, dwarfs the Chilean FTA in trade value. A high-quality FTA with authority to enforce substantial economic liberalization will be more meaningful than a partial or symbolic FTA. The rest of this chapter assesses the nuances of these FTAs, including their authority, but let us start by reviewing South Korea's major trading partners and how much of this trade is covered by FTAs. Table 6.1 lists Korea's trading partners in order of export importance and divides the list into two categories: those that trade with Korea under FTAs and those that do not. Table 6.1 is revealing in a number of ways.

TABLE 6.1. Korean Exports by Country (by percentage)

Partners	2012	2013	2014	2015	2016	Average (2012–16)
Under FTA						
China	24.5	26	25.4	26	25.1	25.4
ASEAN	14.4	14.7	14.8	14.2	15	14.6
US	10.7	11	12.3	13.2	13.4	12.1
EU	9	8.8	9	9.1	9.3	9
Singapore	4.2	4	4.1	2.8	2.5	3.5
Vietnam	3	3.8	3.9	5.3	6.6	4.5
India	2.2	2	2.2	2.3	2.3	2.2
Australia	1.7	1.7	1.8	2.1	1.5	1.8
Turkey	0.8	1	1.2	1.2	1.1	1.1
Canada	0.9	0.9	0.9	0.9	1	0.9
Chile	0.5	0.4	0.4	0.3	0.3	0.4
EFTA	0.3	0.4	0.4	1.2	0.8	0.6
Peru	0.3	0.3	0.2	0.2	0.2	0.2
Columbia	0.3	0.2	0.3	0.2	0.2	0.2
New Zealand	0.3	0.3	0.3	0.2	0.3	0.3
Subtotal	73.1	75.5	77.2	79.2	79.6	76.9
Not under FTA						
Japan	7.1	6.2	5.6	4.9	4.9	5.7
Hong Kong	5.9	4.9	4.8	5.8	6.6	5.6
Taiwan	2.7	2.8	2.6	2.3	2.5	2.6
Mexico	1.7	1.7	1.9	2	2	1.9
Rest of World	9.5	8.9	7.9	5.8	4.9	7.4
Subtotal	26.9	24.5	22.8	20.8	20.4	23.1

Source: Korea Customs Service (https://unipass.customs.go.kr:38030/ets/)

First, the sheer extent to which Korean FTAs dominate the Korean trading system is striking. By 2016, almost 80 percent of all Korean trade is covered by FTAs, leaving just over 20 percent for the rest of the world, including Japan.

Second, no FTA partner in particular dominates South Korean exports. Whereas the vast majority of Mexico's exports go to the United States, only 25 percent of South Korean exports go to its primary trading partner, China. Moreover, ASEAN, the United States, and the EU are all major—and strikingly equal—export markets (15 percent, 13.4 percent, and 9.3 percent, respectively) for Korea. Although China (at just over 25 percent) is the greatest in this quadrangle of markets, Korea's trade portfolio is remarkably diversified.

Third, and finally, Korea has an FTA with all its major trading partners, except Hong Kong and Japan. Hong Kong is no surprise, as it maintains free trade with all nations and therefore has little need to engage in FTAs. Japan is more of a puzzle and is addressed in more detail in chapter 8.

Computable General Equilibrium Models

Most of the important South Korean FTAs are just now getting under way, such that we will not know the true long-run effects of Korean FTAs on economic growth for some time. We can make some inferences, however, based on economic theory as expressed in existing computable general equilibrium (CGE) studies.[3] These models calculate how much GDP should rise in a country once an FTA becomes implemented.

The static benefits are calculated from a model with comparative statics, using what is known about the size of, productivity of, and inputs to all economic sectors in two countries to calculate the total gain in productivity once both economies are fully in conformity with Ricardo's principles. In this process we are essentially comparing a "static snapshot" of production and other economic qualities, and then once all of the factors of production have been moved to reflect comparative advantage we calculate a second static snapshot (hence, the phrase "comparative statics").

Dynamic models include in addition any costs or benefits from the transitions between pre-trade versus with-trade periods. For instance, the loss of jobs, whether transitional or permanent, would be a negative dynamic effect. When focusing on economic growth outcomes, economists tend to focus on investment and technological change as major dynamic positive effects. Theoretically the dynamic model is preferable, taking into account the fuller set of costs and benefits, but computationally it requires an *a priori* selection of dynamic change, for instance, assuming *a priori* a 10 percent increase in FDI from a South Korean FTA and then calculating the complicated growth interactions with the existing static model.

When thinking about these models, my personal takeaway is that the comparative statics models are more objective, and therefore it is our single best calculation of a change in production. And yet, the *full* effects of trade gains do require dynamic models. This makes sense so long as we avoid overly optimistic assumptions that artificially inflate trade effects. Rather than make a case for either type of method, I report all results and reflect upon important differences between the two.

Tables 6.2 and 6.3 summarize the results of the literature's CGE analysis. To simplify what is admittedly a lot of information, table 6.2 reports just the mean estimates for each country, while table 6.3 provides the full set of studies on each country to help resolve discrepancies. The third column shows static benefits, while the fourth column shows dynamic effects.[4]

Static Effects

Column 3 of table 6.2 suggests that China's FTA has a large static effect on Korean GDP, increasing it by 2.68 percent. ASEAN, Japan, the EU, and United States are all expected to have positive effects but the Chinese FTA is in a league of its own, due largely to South Korea's extremely highly interdependence with the Chinese economy.

However, if we dig through the disaggregated set of studies in table 6.3, we find considerable variation across studies within each country. Excepting the U.S. and Chinese cases, all the other three major economies have been found by at least one study to have a negative effect on GDP, even though most of studies found substantial positive effects as is expressed in Table 6.2

TABLE 6.2. CGE Estimates (mean)

Country		Static effects (% GDP)	Dynamic effects (% GDP)
US	Mean	0.78	2.92
Japan	Mean	0.77	0.37
China	Mean	2.68	3.75
EU	Mean	0.97	−0.27
ASEAN	Mean	1.53	1.86

Dynamic Effects

If we turn to dynamic effects, the results again suggest that China has a major influence, although this time the United States effect (2.92 percent) is close to the size of the China effect (3.75 percent).[5] Obviously, all of these models come with considerable uncertainty, but the U.S. finding is consistent with the narrative about the KORUS FTA later in this chapter, specifically, that it was designed to increase economic efficiency as much as trade volume.[6]

Japan

The first CGE study of Korea was done by Cheong and Wang (1999). They examined the effect of an FTA with the United States, NAFTA, and Japan and found substantial effects from the former two, at over 1 percent of GDP. What is more interesting about this early study is that its prediction for a Japanese FTA was actually negative in terms of welfare implications and only slightly positive in terms of GDP implications. This first Korean study, then, already casts doubt on a Japanese FTA.

TABLE 6.3. CGE Estimates (individual studies)

Country	Authors	Static effects (% GDP)	Dynamic effects (% GDP)
US	Yaylaci and Shiker (2013)	0.27	NA
	Li (2012)	0.74	0.82
	Song and Lee(2008)	0.32	5.97
	Kiyota and Stern (2007)	1.26	2.62
	Lee and Lee (2005)	0.59	2.27
	Cheong and Wang (1999)	1.47	NA
Japan	Li (2012)	−0.17	−0.36
	Nakajima (2002)	0.29	1.09
	Cheong and Wang (1999)	0.15	NA
	Sohn (2001)	2.81	NA
China	Li (2012)	2.65	3.75
	Asian Development Bank	2.70	NA
EU	Li (2012)	−0.24	−0.27
	Deceux, Milner, and Perídy (2010)	0.84	NA
	Francois, Norberg, and Thelle (2007)	2.32	NA
ASEAN	Li (2012)	−0.24	−0.36
	Ando and Urata (2007)	0.00	−0.03
	Choi et al. (2003)	4.83	5.96

These findings provide one plausible explanation for Japan's anomalous status (not under FTA) in table 6.1. Table 6.3 shows that one estimate (Sohn 2001) has a positive impact of 2.81 percent of GDP, which is large and consistent with Japan's size, but all the other estimates show near zero or even negative effects. Why bother pursuing an FTA when studies show it will not overly benefit the nation? Though this is not necessarily the best explanation for why Korea did not pursue an FTA with Japan, it must go into the basket of plausible explanations to be examined in more detail in chapter 8, where I discuss large FTAs.

How Big Is the FTA Effect?

The estimates in table 6.3, admittedly, vary greatly, but if we accept the mean figure in column 3 of table 6.2, and then sum estimates across all countries and regions, it comes to a 8.9 percent larger GDP for Korea as a result of its FTAs. Taken over a ten-year period, this would be 0.89 percent higher economic growth per year. While not an economic miracle or a panacea for other economic problems, this is nonetheless a significant boost to annual economic growth, especially considering that overall OECD average growth rate in the last decade was only slightly higher at 1.1 percent.

A recent analysis by Kim (2015) graphically presents these CGE predictions annually and utilizes a complete model of FTAs in a dynamic CGE setting to estimate the effect on economic growth. Two points are notable, both of which are consistent with common sense.

First, FTAs are predicted to constitute a noticeable and growing share of contemporary Korean economic growth. Kim (2015) disaggregates the various FTAs by how much each one is predicted to influence overall Korean GDP growth. Table 6.4 reproduces the results.

The difference in the GDP growth rate calculated with and without the FTAs is shown in figure 6.1. Again, every model is subject to many limitations, so I do not wish to make too much of table 6.4 and figure 6.1, but taken at face value the recent FTA effect is striking. As Kim (2015) notes with respect to the figure: "by comparing the overall growth effect of FTA on total economic growth in 2013, the growth impact of FTAs accounts for 1.19% among 3% of total economic growth in Korea" (3). The subsequent year shows an even larger effect.[7]

This CGE study, taken at face value, estimate that FTAs are currently single-handedly responsible for one-third of South Korean economic growth. This is one reason I compare FTAs to a development strategy. FTAs arguably are having a notable effect on South Korea's economic growth.

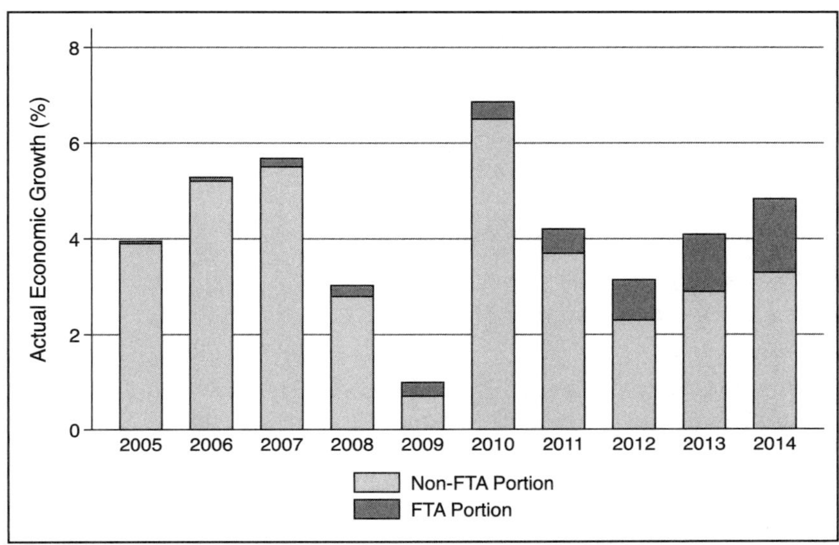

Figure 6.1. Comparing Korea's GDP Growth Rate with FTA versus without FTA
Disaggregating growth attributable to FTAs from total GDP growth shows the
increasing proportion of growth derived from Korea's FTA strategy.

TABLE 6.4. Estimated Effect of FTAs on Annual Economic Growth

Year	Chile	EFTA	ASEAN	India	EU	Peru	US	Total	Growth rate %
2005	0.048							0.048	3.9
2006	0.054	0.026						0.080	5.2
2007	0.061	0.029	0.086					0.176	5.5
2008	0.068	0.033	0.129					0.231	2.8
2009	0.075	0.037	0.176					0.288	0.7
2010	0.082	0.040	0.225	0.010				0.358	6.5
2011	0.088	0.044	0.276	0.011	0.079	0.003		0.502	3.7
2012	0.095	0.047	0.326	0.013	0.358	0.004	0.003	0.847	2.3
2013	0.101	0.050	0.376	0.015	0.630	0.004	0.012	1.190	3.0
2014	0.107	0.053	0.426	0.017	0.897	0.005	0.021	1.526	NA

Source: KIEP 2014, 284, appendix 7.

Note: All data is estimated growth effects using a global CGE model that simultaneously takes into account all of Korea's FTAs. The last column is the actual economic growth rate, to provide some comparison.

Note, lastly, that the ASEAN has had the strongest effect so far, being one of the largest FTAs and also having been signed over a decade ago. Indeed, exports from Korea to ASEAN more than doubled between 2006 and 2016 (*Korea Herald,* May 31). Moreover, as the full effects of the South Korean FTA strategy continue to unfold, the latest and largest FTAs, with China, the EU, and the United States will increasingly influence overall South Korean economic performance in years to come.

II. FTA Effects on International Trade

Some of the earlier FTAs were less important to the economy but have been around long enough to have demonstrable trade effects. Other FTAs—and here I have in mind those with the EU, China, and the United States—are only recently coming into full effect, making it impossible to conduct full-scale statistical tests, but nevertheless a simple before-and-after comparison suggests positive effects on trade.

The most comprehensive empirical study of exports shows some rather extensive FTA effects. Specifically, Kim (2015) utilizes a fully specified gravity model to explain imports as well as exports. After taking into account fixed effects, instrumental variable regression, and other nuances, he finds that FTAs had statistically significant effects on trade in five separate FTAs, namely, Chile, Singapore, EFTA, ASEAN, and the EU.

This same study finds statistically significant effects from each of the individual FTAs on trade with Korea: Chile, ASEAN, India, and Peru. Given that each of these FTAs had demonstrable effects, in the aggregate, it appears clear that FTAs had export effects across a range of countries. While the recent FTAs with the EU, the United States, and China do not show significant effects on trade, this is not surprising given that we they are relatively recent FTAs.

The Chilean example is often mentioned because it was Korea's first FTA and the effect on trade in the long run is so notable. Yoon (2015, 1–2), for instance, notes that after the FTA "Korea's exports to Chile reached US$2.5 billion in 2012, up from US$0.5 billion in 2003, with an average annual growth of 19%. Korea's imports from Chile increased to US$4.7 billion in 2013, up from US$1 billion in 2003, with an annual average growth of 18%."

Concerning the United States, most evaluations show strong trade effects, with Korean exports to the United States up about 50 percent and U.S. exports to Korea up about 10 percent. Clearly the FTA led to a dramatic surge in Korean exports, and given that CGE models assume no trade deficit, this imbalance has particularly benefited Korean GDP. This point is also made in the U.S. evaluation of the KORUS FTA (Williams 2014), as well as by economists (e.g., Polo and Viejo 2016) and media outlets *(Korea Herald,* October 29, 2015).

Concerning the EU, predicted growth effects are positive, but following the FTA Korea faced mounting trade deficits with the EU, reminding us that CGE models assume balanced trade deficits whereas in fact Korean demand for EU goods rose much faster than EU demand for Korean goods. "In 2010, a year before the implementation of the FTA, bilateral trade amounted to $92.23 billion, with Korea having a trade surplus—exports stood at $53.51 billion and imports from EU at $38.72 billion. By 2014, bilateral trade showed a growth of 23.65 percent to reach 114.05 billion. However, everything is not so rosy. Korea now has a trade deficit—exports of 51.66 billion and imports of 62.39 billion" (*Korea Herald,* July 27, 2015).

On the whole, Korean FTAs clearly have had major effects on trade flows, and the evidence is equally clear that early partners had a statistically significant positive effect on exports. The large increase in trade volume after the U.S. and EU FTAs similarly suggests positive trade effects.

III. FTA Effects on Foreign Direct Investment

Although one might think that the point of an FTA is to obtain more trade, the modern global system is complex, such that FTAs are perhaps just as much about encouraging FDI flows as they are about encouraging trade flows per se. One reason for the close connection between trade and FDI is the growth of international production networks. As discussed in chapter 2, these consist of what Baldwin calls "globalization's second unbundling— some production stages previously performed in close proximity were dispersed geographically" (2013, 17). An excellent example, discussed below, is Samsung's investments in Vietnam to serve U.S. markets.

First, it is worth noting how deeply South Korea is involved in these global supply chains. A Standard Chartered Report (2005) concluded that South Korea was one of four countries with the highest percentage of their gross exports going towards global chains (15), attesting to the depth to which the Korean engaged in this new production process. The same report also measures the presence of global chains in terms of global market trade in these chains, in which South Korea is again on the list, this time behind only such economic behemoths as China, Germany, and the United States (16). This combination of South Korea's sheer volume in global supply chains, as well as its high degree of specialization in these chains, makes Korea unusual in world trade.

Concerning the role of FTA in driving the investments to further these global supply chains, clearly much of South Korea's integration preceded the FTA boom. That said, the South Korean FTA strategy has had notable additional positive effects on FDI. Bae and Jang (2013), for instance, show a systematic correlation between the two variables in a global data set from 2000 to 2010. Specifically, they correlate Korean FTAs with increases in both outward FDI and inward FDI and that these effects were also statistically significant compared to countries without FTAs. Kim et al. (2014) use a more fine-grained measure, creating a zero-to-one index in which they code five criteria related to investment provisions to determine which Korean FTAs were "most FDI-friendly" and which were less friendly. They again find significant effects from Korean FTAs on inward FDI as well as outward FDI.

Disaggregated by country, table 6.5 shows the top sources of inward FDI for Korea in seven years. The United States has been the largest investor, but many other countries also invest heavily in Korea, most notably Japan.

When it comes to FDI outflows, we again find the United States is the first on the list. The next two largest destinations of Korean FDI are China and Vietnam.

To get a better sense of the dynamics of FDI flows, the following sections examine three particularly important Korean investment partners (China,

TABLE 6.5. FDI Flows to Korea by Country (in US$1,000)

Country	2010	2011	2012	2013	2014	2015	2016
Total	13,073,054	13,673,089	16,285,905	14,548,344	19,000,084	20,910,280	21,298,790
US	1,974,549	2,371,796	3,674,116	3,525,455	3,606,131	5,478,886	3,875,956
Singapore	772,977	611,306	1,405,407	431,044	1,672,654	2,521,026	2,347,378
Hong Kong	92,527	572,405	1,669,800	976,484	1,061,042	1,514,920	2,118,098
China	414,125	650,853	726,952	481,186	1,189,362	1,978,346	2,049,170
Netherlands	1,184,839	1,011,004	634,621	618,008	2,380,448	475,663	1,546,983
Japan	2,084,335	2,289,134	4,541,610	2,689,660	2,487,648	1,665,074	1,245,867
United Kingdom	648,956	918,614	360,811	115,876	432,424	258,813	359,933
Canada	480,345	739,268	393,769	387,599	572,071	1,268,362	326,230
Ireland	325,884	70,625	267,801	78,405	447,680	18,910	297,349
Taiwan	208,476	10,908	21,617	54,954	103,003	204,216	125,398
Indonesia	752,097	6,240	68,270	9,155	55,634	882	3,702
India	371,436	4,255	10,945	98,719	1,558	2,537	1,411

Source: Korean Ministry of Trade, Industry, and Energy (http://www.motie.go.kr/motie/py/sa/investstatse/investstats.jsp)

Vietnam, and the United States) to see Korea's international production networks in action.

China

China is by far South Korea's most important trading partner. China is also by far the world largest player in global supply chain services (OECD 2013). These two facts are not coincidental. China and South Korea have long been interconnected in global supply chains:

> Historically, Korea has primarily exported intermediate goods such as electronics to China for final assembly, and China has exported finished goods to third markets. More than three quarters of Korea's exports to China are in electrical machinery; optical, measuring, and medical instruments; chemicals; nuclear reactors and parts; and plastics. (Schott, Jung, and Cimino-Isaacs 2015, 4)

South Korean FDI has long been aimed at taking advantage of low Chinese wages to sell to final markets, especially in automobiles. Not surprisingly, South Korean FDI in China has also been unusually high. "Korean FDI abroad rose 349 percent in the past decade, and Korean investment in China increased almost seven-fold" (Schott, Jung, and Cimino-Isaacs 2015,

TABLE 6.6. FDI Flows from Korea to Partner Country (in US$1,000)

Country	2010	2011	2012	2013	2014	2015	2016
Total	34,442,348	45,737,888	39,652,738	35,634,888	35,000,297	40,232,511	30,353,139
US	5,101,058	16,582,192	6,919,679	5,861,137	9,221,681	10,421,650	8,720,752
China	4,401,050	4,797,135	6,650,973	4,700,611	3,757,828	4,299,824	2,703,334
Vietnam	2,158,201	1,510,933	943,968	1,460,560	2,106,206	2,875,011	2,242,281
United Kingdom	3,667,841	1,183,914	464,360	556,027	1,019,802	892,271	1,500,753
Hong Kong	1,516,450	1,710,688	2,067,708	1,033,748	1,083,112	3,491,251	1,267,761
Singapore	515,229	1,049,954	538,698	814,579	874,237	2,035,101	1,108,179
Japan	344,528	268,223	660,573	855,848	486,207	1,810,068	525,682
Canada	953,524	1,887,055	878,314	882,061	1,518,674	660,300	511,372
Indonesia	1,817,549	1,415,343	1,004,848	606,807	809,663	840,726	335,401
India	199,815	649,671	443,212	384,159	341,007	270,554	283,399
Netherlands	2,095,948	311,472	2,921,223	2,874,366	454,868	84,529	83,361
Taiwan	13,915	47,355	9,548	68,102	42,140	43,958	37,547

Source: Export-Import Bank of Korea (http://211.171.208.92/odisas.html)

4). During the period up until 2005 especially, both Chinese and Korean firms were utilizing their relationship to sell to third markets, particularly the U.S.

Things changed around 2005. Schott, Jung, and Cimino-Isaacs (2015) note that "demographic shifts and a growing middle class, however, have transformed China into the largest global market, creating increased opportunities for exports of Korean finished goods in which Korea has a competitive advantage, such as televisions and automobiles." Kotbee and Choi (2016) similarly argue that China is reducing its reliance on imported intermediate products and turning to domestic sourcing.

The authors provide econometric evidence consistent with this set of conclusions: prior to the financial crisis of 2008, changes in Chinese exports to advanced economies had a statistically significant effect on Korea's exports to China, consistent with the idea that South Korea was being carried along by China's export machine. After the 2008 crisis, however, Chinese exports to third parties no longer had this effect, whereas Chinese *domestic* fluctuations in demand did have an influence on Korean exports. In short, South Korea is increasingly looking at China as a growing domestic market rather than as part of an export-oriented production network.

Concerning Chinese FDI, South Korea was never a major player, despite geographic proximity. In 2010 China ranked eighth as a source of South Korean FDI, albeit at a not trivial $414 million. Just five years later, however, in 2015 FDI had rocketed to $2 billion and "the authorities credited the Korea-China free trade agreement as the largest contributor" (*Korea Herald*, December 23, 2015).

Interestingly, China is investing in sectors where South Korea wishes to build comparative advantage. "China's investments in Korea are mostly concentrated in service industries. . . . After the Korea-China FTA went into effect, China's investment professionals and sciences accounted for the largest share, at 40.5%, followed by real estate at 17.6%, and print, broadcasting, and telecommunications at 17.3%" (Yub, Won, and Min-Chirl 2017, 4).

Vietnam

Another major Korean trading partner is Vietnam, and here the story is a more traditional one of Korea outsourcing capital to obtain cheaper labor. As shown in table 6.6, Vietnam, with which Korea signed an FTA in 2015, has recently had a sharp rise in Korean FDI. Indeed, as of 2016 Vietnam is the third largest destination for Korean FDI.

This FDI is part of an international production network involving Korean capital, Vietnamese labor, and global export markets. Much of this is from Samsung, leading to some rather stunning statistics. Samsung alone is responsible for 14 percent of the entire Vietnamese GDP and 16 percent of all total Vietnamese exports (Lee 2016). This boom in FDI began around 2006 and centered on international production networks, namely, Korean capital using Vietnamese labor to produce cell phones for sale globally. Given the long-standing nature of this relationship, it is probably better to view the FTA with Vietnam as a confirmation of FDI flows rather than as the major cause, but certainly it made this ongoing FDI all the more attractive.

United States

Another major Korean trading partner is the United States, and, again, an FTA had a major effect on FDI. Kim, Eom, Lee, and Kim (2015, 4) in a third-year assessment of the KORUS FTA note that "FDI from the U.S. stabilized after a sharp increase following FTA effectuation." Table 6.5 confirms this point. FDI in 2010 was about $2 billion and then showed a sharp increase to over $3.5 billion in 2013, just after the 2012 KORUS FTA effectuation.

The United States was not investing in South Korea as an export platform, so where was this FDI aimed? Much was aimed at transport vehicles with the idea of producing them for the Korean market, but the sector with the largest increase was the service sector.

> FDI from the U.S. in services jumped to 6.51 billion dollars (an increase of 79.1% compared to the period of the previous year) since the FTA entered into force. In the case of business services, investment from the U.S. was 340 million dollars before the FTA but has risen 455% after its effectuation, specifically to 1.88 billion dollars. (Kim, Eom, Lee, and Kim 2015, 5)

This strong U.S.-investor interest in business services indicates an important reform in the Korean business sector, a theme discussed further in the next section.

In sum, Korean FTAs led to FDI flows, both outward and inward. This is true whether we focus on anecdotal evidence or aggregate statistical patterns.

IV. The Service Sector

The Korean service sector has suffered from low productivity compared to its OECD peers. The service sector refers not only to low-paying (and non-tradable) service jobs such as those in fast food or positions such as cashier and manicurist but also to high-paying (and internationally tradable) jobs in sectors such as finance, insurance, legal, and other professional services. For years the OECD has issued an annual *Going for Growth* publication, in which it provides suggestions to each member on how to accelerate GDP growth. For Korea, it consistently has suggested its top priority should be to reform the service sector, allowing competition with foreign banking, insurance, and law firms.[8]

Interestingly, while Korean FTA policy was largely initiated to retain access to markets that were retreating into regional blocs, the logic of the KORUS FTA was justified in policymaking circles less as a mechanism to maintain market share and more as a key driver of future productivity growth. As Choi (2009, 604) notes, "Korea understood that its economic problems were internal, and it decided to eliminate domestic inefficiencies by forcing its system to compete with the U.S. economy, the most efficient economy in the world." Lee and Lee's CGE (2005, 103) empirical study provides a similar conclusion:

> From our CGE analysis of the service industry, we concluded that almost all service industries will enjoy increased output and employment. In terms of output, in particular, construction, education, and the public and social sectors will see the largest increases. Those are areas of which we are now eager to increase the efficiency, which we believe is a result of higher productivity in the service sectors.

The service sector reforms inherent in the KORUS FTA are sweeping. Consider Schott's vivid description of U.S. market access; more generally, here are the core benefits of the KORUS FTA for Korea:

> For the United States, FTA provisions on trade and investment in financial services, express delivery, and professional services (such as legal and accounting services), create significant new business opportunities. Insurance companies, in particular, will benefit from broad ranging rights of establishment as well as increased cross-border trade in a wide range of insurance products. The FTA also bars customs duties on electronic commerce and lifts investment restrictions in

Korean telecommunications companies. In addition, Korea further liberalized or locked in changes in broadcasting and cable quotas undertaken just before the formal negotiations began. . . .

All these Korean "concessions" are good news for the Korean economy and for Korean companies and workers. **Indeed, the services provisions of the KORUS FTA could well be the most important aspect of the deal for Korea.** By committing to greater transparency of administrative and regulatory procedures and by removing obstacles to investment and the provision of services (where restrictions often raise production and distribution costs for producers of goods and services alike), **the Korean government will help promote a more conducive environment for investment from both domestic and foreign sources.** The ancillary benefits of the required investment and regulatory reforms, as well as **the increased productivity of service industries, should accrue across the Korean economy.** In this regard, the KORUS FTA can help **address one of the key challenges facing the Korean economy** recently highlighted by the Organization for Economic Cooperation and Development (OECD 2007): the gap between Korea and the best performing countries due to Korea's low level of productivity growth. (Schott 2007, 8–9; emphases added)

In sum, the KORUS FTA has deep economic effects on the Korean service sector. While many inefficient South Korean firms may be eliminated, in the context of dynamic trade theory, such losses could have positive (or negative) effects on long-run international economic performance, depending on many other exogenous and endogenous political, economic, and geographic causal effects. What is clear is that South Korea has committed to transforming its service sector, setting forth on a yet more liberal voyage.

V. Hub Effects

A central theme of this chapter is that South Korean FTAs are designed to reap many more advantages than merely tariff reductions. A further illustration of this point is that by signing more FTAs than other Asian nations South Korea intentionally set out to build itself as a "FTA hub" in East Asia. To the extent that all countries join a broad FTA—in which all nations have equal trade access to the other nations—then all members benefit. In contrast, to the extent that one nation acts as a "hub" country—where other nations sign FTAs with that hub nation but not other nations—then this hub country enjoys additional benefits in comparison with the "spoke" countries (Wonnacott 1996).

Wonnacott (1996) gives the example of NAFTA. The U.S.-Canada FTA provided freer trade between those two nations, and Mexico had to choose whether to pursue a bilateral FTA with the United States or a broader FTA with both Canada and the United States (NAFTA). One reason Mexico pursued the NAFTA option is that a bilateral FTA would have excluded it from benefits that only the hub country (here the United States) would have obtained. The United States would have had privileged access to both Mexican markets and Canadian markets, as well as the additional advantage of receiving intermediate inputs from both countries at lower tariff rates. This would have put Mexican and Canadian exporters at a disadvantage vis-à-vis each other, creating economic incentives for both countries to trade with the United States and thereby benefiting the United States as the hub nation. Further, these trading advantages might have lead to additional FDI in the United States to take advantage of such trade, leading to yet further economic benefits.

Deltas, Desmet, and Facchini (2006) argues that Israel instituted similar hub effects from its FTA with the EU in 1975, followed by an FTA with the United States in 1985. Alba, Hur, and Park (2010, 12) generalize the finding in a global panel data analysis, concluding not only that FTAs have positive effects on exports but also that "in addition to the direct trade-liberalizing effect of FTAs, the hub-and-spoke nature of FTAs has an additional positive effect on trade."

Park (2015) argues at length that Korea created such an FTA hub system. I have already documented that Korea obtained FTAs with a much broader set of countries than most other nations in Asia and indeed throughout the world. Park (2015, 384) invokes a speech by the Korean trade minister in 2012, noting that Korea intentionally set out to reap the benefits of being an FTA hub:

> Once Korea's global FTA hub network is completed, it will bind the three largest economies of the world into a free trade arrangement through Korea. Such an arrangement will make Korea one of the most attractive investment destinations in the world. . . . As a global FTA hub nation, Korea will emerge as the gateway for a multitude of American, European and Chinese investors seeking access to these enormous and dynamic markets.

Cheong (2014) captures these hub effects in a CGE context for the nation of South Korea specifically. Although the gains are not large, he does find some additional benefits from hub effects. Korea's unusual FTA web, in short, not only brought benefits per se but, by being an FTA hub, brought *additional benefits* to the exports and FDI effect discussed above.

Conclusions

Chapter 5 demonstrated how unusually important FTAs are to the South Korean economy, purely in terms of their magnitude, as compared with other countries. This chapter has reinforced our sense that South Korea's FTA strategy has had large economic consequences.

In short, the South Korean FTA strategy is a big deal. It has substantially altered the nature of South Korean imports, exports, FDI, services, and even economic growth for the foreseeable future. So how did this big deal come about? The last two chapters discussed South Korea's motivations, but what explains why the United States, China, and the EU were motivated to sign FTAs?

PART III

The Geopolitics of FTAs

CHAPTER 7

South Korea and the United States

The KORUS FTA clearly shows how countries can simultaneously pursue economic benefits and strategic interests in trade negotiations. In addition to the goal of maximizing the gains from trade and investment, the ROK wanted to hedge against the growing strategic uncertainties in Northeast Asia by cementing its economic ties with the United States. For its own part, the United States realized that an FTA with the ROK would give Washington a strong foothold to maintain its strategic and economic presence in the region increasingly dominated by its strategic competitor—or vital partner—China. (Sohn and Koo 2011, 435)

I. The Americas

As an undergraduate I was trained in neoclassical economics, including trade theory, and as a graduate student I watched NAFTA come into existence. My education led me to view NAFTA sympathetically, because what I saw happen with NAFTA meshed theoretically with what I had learned. Although I did not think explicitly in terms of a gravity model, it was clear that NAFTA was large-scale comparative advantage at play, with three geographically close and economically large countries. I therefore started this book project with the naive assumption that the rest of American FTA policy has been concordant with the precepts of trade theory.

As the reader will soon learn, my assumption was incorrect. This chapter argues that geopolitical security concerns have been the *primary* determinant of U.S. FTA policy. Graphically illustrating this, note that more than half (five of eight) of all U.S. FTAs on the World Island are within the lone geographic of the Middle East. This has everything to do with the war on terror and nothing to do with gravity models or other economic rationale.

Moreover, the three remaining U.S. FTAs outside the Americas are all in Asia and related closely to China's economic and political rise.

To shed some light on the vast topic of U.S. FTA policy, I use a summary table prepared by Aggarwal (2013a). He coded the fifteen U.S. FTAs across twelve different explanatory variables. His expert coding is necessarily a subjective judgment, but it constitutes a fairly comprehensive overview of the major factors at play in all of the U.S. FTAs.

Aggarwal's coding in shown in table 7.1. I do not discuss the politics of NAFTA or the politics of the four other agreements that the United States formed in the Western Hemisphere. These consist of FTAs with Peru, Panama, Colombia, and the Central America Free Trade Agreement group. Most of these had a strong regional security component, as indicated in Column 1, but had other motivations at work as well (Aggarwal 2013).

I focus here on the geopolitics of the eight FTAs pursued and signed by the United States on or near the World Island. The primary takeaway point is in column 1, which indicates that traditional security concerns, more than any other factor, have driven U.S. FTA policy on the World Island. Specifically, Table 7.1 codes all eight US FTAs outside the Western Hemisphere as being +++, the highest level, in the security column. In what follow, I provide country vignettes illustrating what these strong security motivations looked like in practice.

II. The Middle East

Figure 7.1 provides a graphical representation of these eight U.S. FTAs outside of the Americas. The first point to note is that FTAs are a *modern* policy tool. In the U.S. case, other than Israel (1985), Canada (1987), and NAFTA (1992), all other twelve FTAs signed in U.S. history were pursued by the George W. Bush administration (2000–2008) (see table 7.1). Concerning the World Island, the United States has a grand total of eight FTAs. As noted below, for each of these eight FTAs, the U.S. decision was driven more by security considerations than economic considerations.

1. Israel

The Israel FTA (1985) was the first one signed by the United States, and it is also the FTA that best foreshadowed the future. From the gravity model perspective, the FTA with Israel is an odd choice. The country is clearly a long distance from the United States, and its economy is much smaller than most other nations, making the gravitational pull relatively low. From a geopolitical perspective, on the other hand, Israel is at the center of U.S. foreign policy interests. Israel is the primary U.S. ally in the Middle East, which in turn was a vital region of U.S. containment policy.

The 1985 FTA was largely driven by the Reagan administration's close military relationship with Israel. Aggarwal (2013, 183), for instance, notes that the agreement had "significant security overtones. . . . the [Reagan] administration very much saw this agreement as a means of supplementing its military aid to Israel with an economic package. . . . As William Cooper of

TABLE 7.1. Determinants of U.S. FTA Policy

US FTA partner (year negotiations concluded)	Traditional Security			Human Security				Economic				
	Allies (reward or secure)	Bal. of Power / Regional Sec.	Support Econ. Reforms	Democracy Promotion / Rule of Law	Environment	Labor	Human Rights	Classical Trade Gains / Investment	Objections by US Domestic Producers	Widen Issue scope	Catalyze broader negot. / Template	Counter Economic Discrim.
Israel (1985)	+++	++	+++	0	0	0	0	0	-	+++	+++	+++
Canada (1987)	+	0	0	0	0	0	0	++	-	+++	+++	0
NAFTA (1992)	+	0	+++	++	---	---	-	+++	---	+++	+++	0
Jordan (2000)	+++	+++	+++	0	---	---	0	0	-	+++	0	0
Chile (2002)	+	0	+	+++	- -	- -	0	0	-	+++	+++	+
Singapore (2003)	+++	+++	0	0	-	-	0	++	-	+++	+++	0
Australia (2004)	+++	++	0	0	0	-	0	+	- -	+	++	0
Morocco (2004)	+++	+++	++	+	-	-	0	+	-	0	+++	+
DR-CAFTA (2004)	++	++	+++	++	---	---	- -	++	---	+	+++	++
Bahrain (2004)	+++	+++	+++	+++	0	-	-	0	0	+	++	0
Oman (2005)	+++	+++	++	+	0	-	0	++	-	0	++	0
Peru (2005)	++	+	++	++	---	---	-	+	-	0	++	0
Colombia (2006)	+++	+	+++	+++	---	---	---	++	- -	0	0	0
Panama (2007)	+++	++	++	+++	-	-	0	+	0	0	0	+
South Korea (2007)	+++	+++	0	0	-	-	0	+++	---	0	+++	++

Source: Aggarwal 2013a.

Note: "plus signs indicate that this factor was driver for the agreement; minus signs indicate that this factor constrained negotiations. The range is from 0 to plus 3 for both. (Aggarwal 2013, 94).

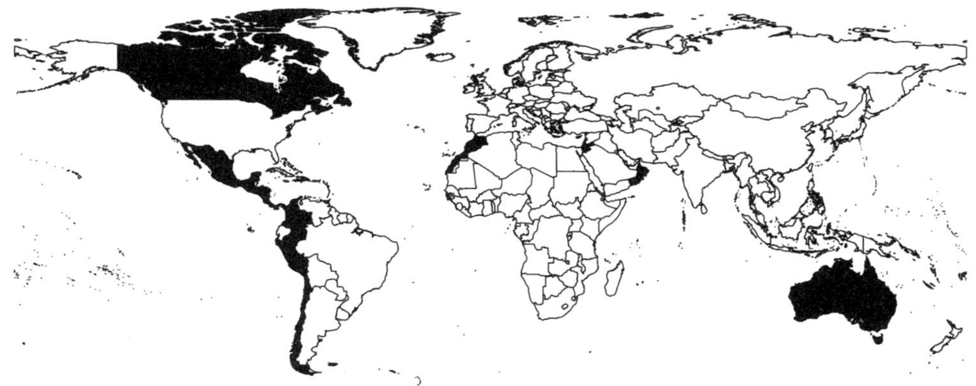

Figure 7.1. U.S. FTAs
Geopolitics influenced all eight U.S. FTAs on the World Island: five in the Middle East and North Africa (Israel, Jordan, Morocco, Bahrain, and Oman) and three in Asia (Australia, Singapore, and South Korea).

the Congressional Research Service notes, the U.S.-Israel FTA (and later, the U.S.-Jordan FTA) was undertaken due to 'political considerations' in order 'to reaffirm American support for those countries and to strengthen relations with them' (Cooper 2006, 4). Indeed, President Reagan was explicit in underscoring the security importance of the agreement for Israel" (Aggarwal 2013, 182).

Israel set the precedent. But to understand how and why U.S. FTA policy is so driven by security concerns, we must start by understanding how the war on terror led to the overt "securitization" of U.S. FTA policy (Higgott 2004).

The War on Terror

The attacks on the United States on 9/11 are said to be a defining moment in modern American history, although this may be due more to subsequent American behavior than to the event itself. One outcome was that the subsequent war on terror thoroughly securitized FTA policy. By using the term securitized I follow Higgott's point that, for the United States, "economic globalization is seen not only as an economic benefit, but also as a security 'problem'" (2004, 432).

This securitization of U.S. economic policy was no secret but rather something the Bush administration actively signaled to other governments. The following public statement, also quoted in the introduction to this book, explicitly linked U.S. FTA policy to security concerns: "A free trade agreement is not something that one has a right to. It's a privilege. But it is a privilege that must be earned via the support of U.S. policy goals. . . . [The Bush administration] . . . expects cooperation—or better—on foreign policy and security issues" (U.S. Trade Representative Robert Zoellick, quoted in *New Statesman*, June 23, 2003).

FTA policy, in short, became an active arm of foreign policy under the Bush administration, with FTAs being driven by *geopolitical* significance rather than by *economic* significance. "[The Bush] administration put into effect FTAs with Jordan, Chile, Singapore, Australia, and Morocco, and completed free trade deals with Costa Rica, the Dominican Republic, El Salvador, Guatemala, Honduras, Nicaragua, Peru, Oman, Bahrain, Panama, and Colombia. . . . **For the United States, all were of strategic significance**" (Sohn and Koo 2011, 421–22; emphasis added).

Israel is not unique in being distant both geographically and in terms of GDP gravity yet nonetheless very close geopolitically. Aggarwal points more generally to "Israel, Jordan, Morocco, Bahrain, and Oman, where security considerations were paramount. From an economic standpoint, all were relatively unimportant" (2013, 195).

2. Jordan

Jordan is a second instance where economic incentives play little role. As Aggarwal notes, "The lack of an economic rationale from the US perspective was clear: a USITC [United States International Trade Commission] study concluded that a FTA with Jordan would 'have no measurable impacts on total US exports, total US imports, US production, or US employment'" (2013, 189).

On the security dimension, however, Jordan is a close U.S. ally. Indeed, the U.S.-Jordan FTA reflected "a long-standing bipartisan security interest to reward Jordan for signing the July 1994 Washington Declaration, which normalized relations with Israel. This normalization with Israel was a major U.S. diplomatic success, and during the subsequent five years (1995–99) "the US provided Jordan with extensive military and economic aid and considerable debt forgiveness in the wake of the Washington Declaration." The year after that (2000) an FTA was signed (Aggarwal 2013, 189).

3. Morocco

Concerning Morocco, White (2005) wrote an entire article on the security aspect of the U.S.-Morocco FTA, entitled "Free Trade as a Strategic Instrument in the War on Terror? The 2004 US-Moroccan Free Trade Agreement." The abstract alone sufficiently makes the point:

> In June 2004, the United States signed a Free Trade Agreement (FTA) with Morocco. FTAs are typically thought of as economic agreements, but the agreement with Morocco has an explicit security component. Indeed, US officials have cast the agreement as an opportunity to support a close ally in the region, and its signing coincides with Morocco's denomination as a non-NATO ally of the US. (597)

4. Bahrain

Bahrain is perhaps the least discussed case but also one of the most extreme cases of security-driven FTAs. A Congressional Research Service study notes how geopolitically close Bahrain has been to the United States: "The U.S.-Bahrain security relationship dates to the end of World War II, well before Bahrain's independence, and has been central to U.S. military efforts to address regional threats" (Katzman 2016, 17).

More recently, the United States has had a major naval operation running out of Bahrain. The trade literature assumes that the U.S. FTA was driven by these security considerations (Aggarwal 2013a). A lengthy report on U.S. security ties with Bahrain pointedly concludes: "To encourage reform and signal U.S. appreciation, the United States and Bahrain signed an FTA on September 14, 2004" (Katzman 2016a, 29).

5. Oman

Katzman wrote a Congressional Research Services report on Oman, and in the opening sentences of the report he captures the powerful relationship between security concerns and FTAs:

> The Sultanate of Oman has been a strategic ally of the United States since 1980, when it became the first of the Persian Gulf monarchies to formally allow the U.S. military to uses bases there. The facilities access accord represented a long-term Omani shift

from reliance on Britain for its security, although Oman continues to maintain close military ties to Britain. Oman has hosted U.S. forces during every U.S. military operation in and around the Gulf since then, and it is a partner in U.S. efforts to counter the transit of terrorists through regional waterways. Oman has consistently supported U.S. Middle East peacemaking efforts by publicly endorsing peace agreements reached and meeting with Israeli leaders, even when doing so ran counter to the policies of Oman's Gulf state allies. It was partly in appreciation for Oman's support that the United States entered into a free trade agreement (FTA) with Oman. . . . (Katzman 2016b)

To summarize, after the events of September 11, 2001 the Bush administration overwhelmingly securitized FTA policy into a geopolitical tool in the Middle East. Following the Israeli precedent from a few decades earlier, the Bush administration signed four more FTAs in the Middle East region, including Oman. Each was designed to help facilitate the war on terror. None of these had any important motivation rooted in the economic gravity model.

III. Asia

From a geopolitical perspective the primary issue of our time is undoubtedly the rise of China. "There is likely no greater challenge for American foreign policy than finding a way to sustain a strong, robust and productive relationship with China" (Campbell and Andrews 2013, 4).

With its newly securitized foreign economic policy in the forefront, the Bush administration approached the classic question of China through the lens of geopolitical FTA policy. The United States has signed three FTAs in Asia, and all were driven heavily, albeit not exclusively, by geopolitical considerations. "Indeed, bilateral PTAs in Asia are seen in Washington foreign policy circles to reflect a desire on the part of the Bush administration to contain what it sees as the rising politico-economic influence of China in the region" (Higgott 2004, 437).

The U.S. legislature, to some extent, sympathized. One strong voice for balancing China through FTA policy came from Max Baucus, U.S. senator and chairman of the Committee on Finance. He gave a speech at the First Asian Annual Forum in 2004 critiquing the inability of the United States to rise to the Chinese challenge:

> In the absence of strong U.S. trade policy in the region, Asian countries are looking inward. Increasingly, they look toward China. And China is looking toward them. . . . No country has capitalized on this U.S. policy drift more than China. . . . Asian economic integration can help create a larger market for U.S. goods and improve U.S. competitiveness, but not if we cede that potential to others. The United States is a Pacific power, as well. And many Asian countries would like us to be more engaged in Asia, if only to *check the rising power of China*—a partner to many countries in the region, but also a major competitor. (Baucus 2004; emphasis added)

6. South Korea

For geopolitics, the logical choice of FTA partner was Japan, as the largest Asian economy outside of China and, partially as a result, the United States' most important ally in Asia. Armitage and Nye, for instance, explicitly linked the geopolitical and economic dimensions, suggesting that the United States and Japan cosign an "economic alliance agreement" (Armitage and Nye 2007, 17–18). Sohn and Koo note the broader security and trade interest in Japan. "For the US, Japan was naturally the first choice as a security-embedded FTA partner. The US urged Japan to move toward bilateral FTA negotiations for a combination of commercial and strategic reasons. A US-Japan FTA would constitute a critical part in an emerging web of FTAs that the US had worked on in the region" (Sohn and Koo 2011, 442).

But a U.S.-Japan FTA did not happen. Most observers point to the agriculture sector as the critical veto point (e.g., Sohn and Koo 2011). Yoshimatsu (2012) accepts that agriculture was a veto point but notes two other aspects of Japanese FTA policy that help explain the failure of negotiations: (1) Unlike Korea, Japan lacked a centralized economic policymaking bureaucracy geared toward FTA policy. (2) Unlike Korean President Roh, who went to extraordinary lengths to counter falling public opinion through an extended public relations campaign to promote the KORUS FTA, the Japanese prime minister made no such effort.

From a geopolitical point of view, if an FTA with Japan was not possible, then Korea became the next logical choice for an FTA with a close ally in Asia. As with most government trade reports, the US trade report on the KORUS concluded that both nations would reap more economic growth. What is more striking from the security point of view is that the trade report clearly states that "In addition to these solid economic benefits, the KORUS FTA will strengthen a strategic alliance forged in war and growing in peace.

As Korea and other Asian nations establish strong trade and investment, the KORUS FTA will serve the United States' vital interest in maintaining and expanding our partnerships in Asia" (USTR 2008, 14).

7. Singapore

Lee (2013, 143–46) argues below that linkages between security concerns and FTAs are common in Asia and that Singapore is in many ways an archetype for strictly security-driven FTAs without much economic motivation:

> Singapore is most explicit in implementing its linkage strategy. Singapore does not have great motivations for pushing for FTAs because Singapore, with near zero tariffs, expects limited economic gains from trade liberalization. Therefore, security considerations are highly incorporated into the FTA strategy of Singapore, of which survival has been the foremost preoccupation since independence and "has been its credo in its foreign policy." (Leifer 2000, 68)

All nations have their own geography, and in the case of tiny Singapore, Malaysia and Indonesia are the giants to its north and south.

> First, surrounded by big Islamic countries such as Malaysia and Indonesia that occasionally aligned to pose a security threat, Singapore tried to court regional great powers. China and Japan are natural candidates that could easily fulfill Singapore's goal of reducing security vulnerability. Singapore concluded an FTA with Japan in 2002. . . . The Singapore government thought that attracting the two regional powers was an effective means to reduce its vulnerability.

In addition, of course, there is the larger geopolitical portrait of Asia, in which China could become powerful indeed. Here, Singapore also has an FTA strategy.

> Second, Singapore has also been active in attracting great powers outside East Asia. The primary motivation for this has to do with the rise of China. Although China repeatedly made clear that its peaceful rise would not be detrimental to the core interests of Southeast Asian countries, Singapore was not certain about China's intentions in the region. Singapore chose to attract extra-regional great powers. . . . It is against this backdrop that Singapore sought a US-Singapore

FTA even if it had to make concessions in key industries such as finance. . . . (Lee 2006a, b). With the commencement of the USS-FTA [United States–Singapore Free Trade Agreement], both countries agreed to sign a strategic partnership agreement. This shows that Singapore's policy objective was to link FTAs to security.

8. Australia

The United States and Australia have always had strong relations and are close military allies. Their cultural affinity is rooted in language and shared British colonial heritage more generally. The two nations have allied frequently against mutual threats, including World War I, World War II, the Korean War, the Vietnam War, the Gulf War, and the war on terror (Vaughn 2011, 167).

The literature on U.S. FTA policy often notes that Australia was rewarded by the Bush administration for its support in the war on terror while New Zealand was punished for its lack of support and would get no FTA (e.g., Higgott 2004).

Also, and relevant from a realist perspective, after the U.S. close allies of Japan, South Korea, and Taiwan, the next plausible large economy in the Pacific Rim is Australia, making it fairly important. Indonesia is even more important economically, but it prefers a non-active form of hedging between the United States and China, forgoing any security cooperation with the United States (Chung 2009).

IV. The KORUS FTA

The KORUS FTA (first signed in 2007 and renegotiated in 2010) is South Korea's most significant FTA. For the United States, it represents the second most important FTA ever signed, following only NAFTA. Moreover, the provisions are far-reaching. For example, "Under the KORUS FTA's agricultural provisions, South Korea immediately will grant duty-free status to two-thirds of U.S. agricultural exports. Tariffs and import quotas on most other agricultural products will be phased out within 10 years" (Barnes et al. 2012, 7). Similarly, "95% of U.S.-South Korean trade in consumer and industrial products would become duty-free within five years after the agreement enters into force, and virtually all remaining tariffs will be lifted within 10 years" (10). Furthermore, a vast array of provisions address U.S. beef exports, financial services, foreign investment, automobile exports, worker rights, environmental protection, and trade enforcement mechanisms (Barnes et al. 2012).

On the U.S. side, I noted earlier in this chapter that FTA policy has been heavily driven by geopolitical concerns, especially the war on terror and the rise of China. On the South Korean side, I discussed at length in chapter 5 how South Korea wanted FTAs with all trade partners as a general rule, and in chapter 8 I will reinforce the prior economic analysis with a geopolitical explanation of South Korean motivations, specifically, an attempt to hedge in light of growing Chinese power.

Having thereby provided a multifaceted explanation for the KORUS FTA, I turn now to another important dimension of the agreement, using Putnam's (1988) two-level game as a way to think about it. The two-level game was particularly pertinent for the KORUS FTA because on both the South Korean and U.S. sides legislative passage of the KORUS FTA was precarious. Geopolitics would have been moot, as would this book, if legislatures had not passed the KORUS FTA in both nations.

Put differently, "At the pre-negotiation and negotiation stages, we highlight security and strategic calculations held by top policy-makers on both sides of the governments catalyzed the official launch of FTA negotiations" (Sohn and Koo 2011, 435; see also Schott 2007). At the confirmation stage, however, legislatures were involved, and it is to this final stage that I now turn.

The KORUS FTA: The U.S. Perspective

I provided the fundamental U.S. logic for the KORUS FTA earlier, namely, that the securitization of FTA policy after 9/11, combined with the rise of China, made an FTA with South Korea desirable. The U.S. Congress does have substantially more power than the Korean legislature, however, so while geopolitics explains why the KORUS FTA was brought to the table, we need to look at domestic U.S. politics to understand why it passed.

In bold strokes, the domestic politics of the KORUS FTA were similar to those of NAFTA. In both cases a Republican president (first George H. W. Bush and second George W. Bush) signed the FTA and was succeeded by a Democratic president who honored the agreements, relying more on the Republican votes in Congress than the Democratic votes. For the KORUS FTA vote, Seo (2015) provides a useful study of congressional voting.

Seo (2014) confirms that Republicans supported the KORUS FTA more than Democrats and that Democrats were particularly concerned about the trade imbalance in automobiles between the United States and South Korea as well as barriers to U.S. beef exports. Seo then provides a careful multivariable logit analysis of congressional votes and concludes that, while partisanship clearly mattered, legislators' political views on security also strongly influenced votes on the KORUS FTA.

> Two main findings stand out from the empirical analyses of congressional voting on the KORUS FTA. First, foreign policy conservatism as a measurement of trade–security nexus figures prominently in both chambers. Particularly, in the House side, neither overall ideological position nor party membership drowns out lawmakers' security motivations in terms of trade voting. Second, the influence of constituency signifies the House voting on the KORUS FTA. Lawmakers from the districts with a significant number of college graduates or Korean immigrants tend to be highly supportive of free trade with South Korea. (Seo 2015, 234)

Domestic and international politics always intermix, and there is no doubt that different groups viewed the KORUS FTA differently in the two countries. Opposition was also much stronger in South Korea. In the end, however, both countries' geopolitical security desires, as well as Korea's desires for economic efficiency, were sufficient to overcome domestic political resistance.

KORUS: The Korean Perspective

Chapter 5 described how the state directed South Korea's FTA strategy. This state-led strategy faced few societal or institutional checks and further benefited from strong executive preferences for FTAs as well as a coherent centralized trade bureaucracy. The state is not all-powerful, however, such that societal actors and legislative institutions also possessed power. Indeed, another reason to examine the domestic politics of the KORUS FTA is to note how close anti-trade groups came to stopping the KORUS FTA from being signed.

The most powerful domestic societal actor in South Korea has been the business sector, especially the chaebol, Korea's huge export-oriented manufacturing firms. Kim (2011) argues at length that the business sector was firmly in support of the KORUS FTA, such that state and capital were united on this matter. All the major business groups supported the U.S. alliance (and the KORUS FTA), and they engaged in considerable advocacy and education to bring it to fruition. "Korea's big business has functioned as a stronghold of support for the ROK-US alliance" (Kim 2011, 478).

MOFAT, the government trade bureaucracy, invited business into consultations in 2003. Three years later, in 2006, business groups formed the KORUS FTA Industry Alliance, which "was a domestic policy network in which government officials, corporate managers, and economists participated together. . . . the main purpose of the alliance was to promote the interests of Korean businesses" (Kim 2011, 487).

Despite state-capital support, the KORUS FTA was extremely controversial in Korea. Indeed, it was almost derailed at a number of stages. Negotiations were opened in 2006, a treaty was signed in 2007, then renegotiated (at U.S. insistence) in 2010, and finally ratified in 2011. The KORUS FTA was clearly politically touch and go throughout the process.

Two veto players in Korea stand out: anti-American forces and agricultural protectionist forces. Agriculture is always a major actor in trade politics, and anti-Americanism is a major force in Korean policies, such that their conjunction led to some bitter opposition to the KORUS FTA. "Anti-American forces on the left of Korea's political spectrum allied with traditional anti-liberalization groups such as farmers and unions, leading to a formidable campaign against the KORUS FTA" (Sohn and Koo 2011, 448).[1] In all, the KORUS FTA was highly contentious in Korea:

> Widespread, sometimes violent, often highly disruptive demonstrations erupted at the height of Korean opposition to the KORUS FTA. Writing in April 2007, a South Korean English-language daily, the *Korea Herald*, noted that Seoul had experienced nearly one public anti-FTA demonstration every day since negotiations were announced in February 2006. The demonstrations also took on more extreme forms, including a highly publicized incident of self-immolation by a taxi-driver surnamed Heo. The incident received widespread coverage and drew attention to public opposition to the FTA. While anti-trade demonstrations are an accepted component of contemporary trade negotiations in both the bilateral and multilateral context, South Korean demonstrators are notable for being vocal and active. (Robertson 2012, 476)

The KORUS FTA then stalled in the U.S. Congress, making the problem more difficult for South Korea. In an attempt to sway the balance in the U.S. Congress, the Korean president unilaterally changed policy as a gesture

of international goodwill and opened up U.S. access to domestic beef markets. The domestic backlash on the part of Korean society was considerable.

> The conservative Lee Myung-bak administration, which took office
> in February 2008, has made a dramatic break with the progressive
> policies of the preceding 10 years. The FTA strategy is one of the few
> areas in which the Lee administration has followed in the footsteps of
> its predecessors. **Despite huge political adjustment costs due to the
> U.S. beef imports controversy in the first half of 2008**, the Lee ad-
> ministration has remained committed to the multitrack FTA strategy.
> (Koo 2010, 16; emphasis added)

Given widespread and vehement protest in Korea, why was the KORUS
FTA signed? The answer was largely already given in chapter 5, namely, that
the economic environment facing Korea made the FTA strategy rational. In
addition, politically, the Korean state had sufficient desire, autonomy, capacity, and so forth to push the FTA project forward for well over a decade.
When the critical fight came on the KORUS FTA, the development strategy
once again won out, albeit narrowly. Such critical historical moments, perhaps, are symbolically what separate development strategies from economic
policies.

Two factors facilitated the state's critical KORUS FTA victory. First, note
that the primary institutional veto player on executive trade policy is the
legislative branch. The U.S. Congress wields considerable power over trade
unless it specifically abdicates this power by granting executives "fast-track
authority" to negotiate freely, followed by a legislative vote that is either yes
or no.

The South Korean legislature, however, does not have power over FTA negotiation. Lee (2010) notes that it might be constitutionally unclear whether
the legislature technically has these powers, but de facto in democratic Korea
the legislature is restricted to an up-down vote on trade. Lee notes a variety
of informal imbalances between Korea's historically strong executive versus
its (newly awakening) legislature. A particularly telling anecdote concerns
the executive branch's dissemination of the KORUS FTA information to the
Korean legislature:

> About 20 days after FTA negotiations were completed, a dispute
> emerged regarding the release of the 500-page draft agreement to the
> National Assembly. The government decided to allow just one copy
> on a computer monitor inside the National Assembly. Copying was

not permitted and the available version was written in English. Access was also limited to just 20 members of the Korea-USA FTA Special Committee, accompanied by only one aide. The government tried to rationalise such restrictive measures, saying that the FTA was the community property of Korea and the USA, and that the disclosure of the details was not proper protocol. (Lee 2010, 298)

As Lee notes, in the United States "there was considerable legislation that allowed Congress and others to view the agreement. . . . But, in Korea's case, the difference is that no disclosure law existed at all" (2010, 298). It is not that these points are necessarily decisive, but they do illustrate that the executive branch held a strong hand in trade negotiations more generally (Lee 2010).

The second point to keep in mind when analyzing why the KORUS FTA passed is that South Korea has always been free trade and that the main opposition to the KORUS FTA was probably anti-Americanism, which explains why this agreement was more problematic than any other. As a political tactical matter, however, Park (2009, 462) argues that this very motivation was part of the weakness of the movement: "the key weakness of the ANGM [anti-neoliberal globalization movement] has been that its leading organizations strategically prioritize the anti-US imperialist struggle at the expense of a class analysis of the global economy and the role of the Korean state within it." Putting aside the high emphasis on class in this analysis, the underlying point is a valid one, namely, that the opposition's focus on anti-Americanism probably inhibited some more powerful narrative to mobilize anti–KORUS FTA activity.

In the end, the KORUS FTA was signed and ratified. The fact that this was such a political struggle is yet another testimony to the extent to which the Korean FTA strategy can be viewed as a long-term development strategy. This was no mere policy decision but rather a central part of a presidential administration's use of (necessarily limited) political power.

Conclusions

This quick tour of the KORUS FTA exemplifies the geopolitical approach. Concerning the action of the world's most important political economy, the United States of America, FTA policy has been overwhelmingly driven by security concerns, with only marginal attention to economic concerns. Although NAFTA and a handful of Western FTAs nicely flow from the gravity model approach, most other U.S. FTAs are inconsistent with the gravity model but are well explained by geopolitical concerns.

A second general conclusion from this chapter concerns the complex two-level game at play leading to the KORUS FTA. With two actors, the United States and South Korea, and two levels, the international and the domestic, this game includes four moving parts at a minimum. With respect to the international dimensions, both the United States and South Korea (see chapter 8) were motivated by geopolitical concerns, while South Korea was also motivated by economic concerns (see chapter 5). With respect to the domestic dimensions, the most relevant point is that FTAs do require agreement at each level of Putnam's game in both nations.

CHAPTER 8

China, the European Union, and Japan

The US-ROK alliance has permitted Seoul to expand its economic ties [with China] without being paranoid about China's growing military power. (Kim 2016, 720)

South Korean FTA policy is peerless in its trifecta with the United States, the EU, and China. Having examined the KORUS FTA in chapter 7, this chapter provides an understanding of the rest of the trifecta. Two points vividly emerge.

First, as introduced in the opening quotation above, the Chinese case is an irony for the trade and alliance literature: the U.S.-Korea alliance is so effective that it actually *overcomes* South Korea's otherwise natural fear of becoming overly trade dependent on its potential adversary, China. The U.S. security guarantee is perceived as strong enough that South Korea has been willing to increase its vulnerability to a worrisome China.

Second, turning to the EU-Korea FTA, we find that the traditional alliance politics and even geopolitical concerns are largely absent. The EU and South Korea, rather, both made a very important statement concerning service sector reforms. For the EU, this FTA was the first of a new wave of FTAs that would emphasize service sector reform. For South Korea, this FTA reinforced the substantial service sector liberalization of the KORUS FTA.

Lastly, this chapter examines the interesting puzzle of Japan, by far the largest economy not yet linked to Korea through an FTA.

I. China's FTA Policy

In the two-level game, the domestic game in China is simple. The combination of an authoritarian state and a centralized state bureaucracy allows state actors to utilize FTAs for security and diplomatic purposes:

> Lee's analysis of China's FTA strategy suggests that compared to other states, because of domestic policymaking centralization, China is able to systematically pursue clear foreign and security goals. In particular, the dominance of the Ministry of Foreign Affairs means that China could provide unilateral concessions to entice other countries to sign accords. (Aggarwal and Govella 2013)

The geographic focus of Chinese FTA policy can be seen in figure 8.1.[1] This map shows that China's FTA partners are strongly clustered geographically. Why?

There are two ways to think about the close proximity of China's FTA partners. The first way is to note that the gravity model clearly suggests that proximate trade partners are preferable, and this prediction corresponds with the facts.

A second explanation for the regional proximity of Chinese FTAs is that these FTAs are part of China's regional geopolitical strategy. While China's long-term goals are difficult to discern, in the medium run China has pursued what it calls a "good neighbor" policy. China is now clearly the rising power in our anarchic world and has at least tried to signal that it is a good neighbor, happy to work together toward cooperative regional goals, to help provide regional public goods, to strengthen regional institutions, and so forth.

In this second view China's economic policy exhibits "clear linkages being established between seemingly conventional trade interests and China's interests in wider economic, diplomatic and strategic relationships" (Antkiewicz and Whalley 2005, 1554). Concerning FTAs specifically, "China's diplomatic efforts to cultivate good relations with its neighbors are indivisible from its present strategy of entering FTAs with them" (Zhao and Webster 2011, 78).

A good example of China using FTAs to enhance its soft power is its FTA with ASEAN. China unilaterally opened its vast market to the ten countries in ASEAN before the agreement had formally taken effect, in a gesture of economic cooperation and goodwill. This was clearly not an economic decision but rather a politically motivated one, and China gained soft power through this so-called early harvest opening.

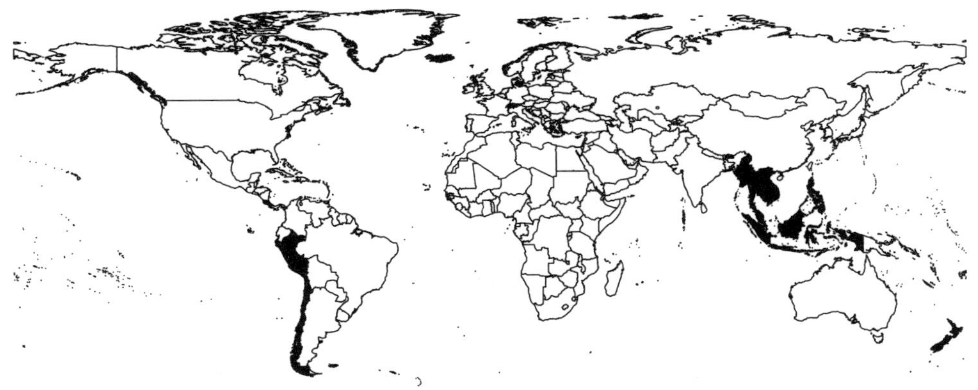

Figure 8.1. Chinese FTAs
Shaded areas show China's regional presence in Asia's FTA formation and relative lack of FTAs with other regions.

The implications for Korea are clear. China would be happy to sign an FTA with South Korea, consistent with figure 8.1 and with China's willingness to sign FTAs with most regional actors. China wanted to integrate itself as the regional institutional power. My point is that what prevented the Chinese FTA for such a long time was *Korean reluctance*, not Chinese reluctance. So why was the FTA between China and Korea, first proposed in 2004, only signed in 2015? Of all the Korean FTAs, this was the only one that was predicted in chapter 3 in global statistical models, and it was predicted strongly. What took so long? Why did not the strong gravity between China and Korea lead to an FTA much earlier?

"The real problem blocking the process of a China-Korea FTA is **geopolitical**. Deciding on a China-Korea FTA is dependent on the Korean government and experts in different fields changing their worrying minds about China" (Jianping 2006, 3; emphasis added).[2]

II. Active Hedging

The intuition that motivates security approaches to FTAs is that countries with alliances are more likely to form FTAs to reap the benefits of trade, but more likely to exclude their enemies to prevent them from gaining said benefits.

Seemingly counterintuitively, however, the alliance with the United States had a very different effect, namely, freeing South Korea to pursue economic trade with China. In the end, the U.S.-Korea alliance was so strong that South Korea was willing to go so far as to sign an FTA with China. In terms of causality, the U.S. alliance with South Korea might have been a necessary condition for the South Korean FTA with China, a country that has historically been an adversary of South Korea and remains a potentially serious military threat.

This analysis suggests that alliance effects on FTAs are complicated and can even seem prima facie counterintuitive, as with the Korea-China FTA. Ultimately, though, the Korea-U.S. alliance provided Korea not merely access to U.S. markets through the KORUS FTA, but additionally enough implicit security guarantee to pursue China's markets without worrying so much about trade dependency.

China's economic rise certainly has massive implications for Korea's trade policy. Whereas the United States once dominated South Korean trade, the United States is now dwarfed by China. In fact, 32 percent of all Korean exports go to China. Given that Korea is the world's seventh largest exporter, on par with Britain and Japan, the China-Korea economic relationship is an enormously significant one.

For Korea it is disconcerting to be so tightly tied to Asia's rising Great Power, especially given ongoing tensions between North Korea and South Korea. At least as early as Hirschman's work (1945) we have known that trade asymmetry is a source of political power, in wartime and in peacetime. Indeed, during the writing of this book, the Hirschman thesis was put to the test. North Korea's increasing nuclear belligerence in the last decade led the United States to propose the Terminal High Altitude Area Defense (THAAD), an anti-missile defense system installed in South Korea with U.S. technology. China unsurprisingly viewed this potential deployment as a threat and publicly threatened South Korea with economic sanctions if it were to deploy.

In January 2017 Seoul announced it would deploy the THAAD, and China immediately imposed a wide range of sanctions on South Korea. Though not economically substantial, the sanctions were highly public, including airline restrictions for travel from South Korea to China, sudden regulatory investigations of major Korean firms, and general harassment of Korean exporters. Indeed, South Korea felt obliged to formally raise the matter in international talks, and it remains to be seen how the THAAD deployment will play out, meaning it is still an open question whether China is willing to utilize meaningful sanctions and whether South Korea will reconsider deployment.

South Korea, in short, is in a geopolitically fascinating situation. The pessimistic view would say that Korea is caught between a rock and a hard place. The huge and proximate Chinese economy must be engaged, yet political independence from dominant China must be maintained. This is South Korea's challenge.

South Korea has a geopolitical strategy for addressing this difficult situation with China. Chung (2009) calls this strategy "active hedging." Hedging in IR theory is when a nation does not commit to either side of a bipolar alliance system but instead hedges its bets by attempting to maintain good relations with both sides of the conflict. *Active* hedging is a particularly engaged form of hedging in which a nation tries to engage constructively *both* alliance systems without overtly cutting ties with either.

South Korea is clearly an active hedger and, equally clearly, has reaped substantial benefits from this active hedging strategy. South Korea is allied with the United States against North Korea and therefore is in opposition to China. Given the ongoing threat from North Korea, maintaining this alliance seems imperative for South Korea for the foreseeable future.

Precisely because the U.S.-Korean military alliance is so deeply grounded in the historical geopolitics of the Korean peninsula, it provides a powerful political foundation for South Korea to economically engage its potential adversary, China, as well as its ally the United States. As Kim perceptively notes:

> South Korea's behavior can be fully understood only when the US role in East Asian security is also taken into account. Since World War II, the US has played a key balancing role in East Asia through the US centered hub-and-spoke system. Thanks to US security commitments to the region as well as the Korean Peninsula, South Korea has been able to engage China and deepen economic ties with Beijing without excessive fear for its own security. (2016, 722)

So long as it can rely on the United States as a military ally, Korea can increase its economic entwinement with China and benefit enormously. This is geopolitical hedging at its best. Korea has achieved deep economic relationships with both global superpowers and simultaneously maintains viable political relations with each.

III. The Japanese Exception

Although the Japanese economy is not as large as those of the EU, the United States, and China, especially given recent decades of Japanese economic stagnation, it is nonetheless the fourth largest economy in the world. Moreover, Japan is immediately to the east of South Korea, making it just as geographically proximate as China and thereby making trade likely. Finally, geopolitically, Japanese colonial control over Korea (1905–45) is a fact that bears upon trade politics.

We have already noted that Japan stands out as being the largest trading partner with which South Korea does not have an FTA. Prima facie, there is a puzzle here to be solved, but not all prima facie puzzles are true puzzles. So, upon what grounds might one believe that the absence of an FTA with Japan is something worth exploring?

A Puzzle?

The statistical evidence, on net, suggests that the prima facie conclusion is correct. These form good reason to suspect that a South Korea–Japan FTA should exist, and yet does not. There is a puzzle here.

The first evidence we have already noted in chapter 5. A logit analysis of South Korea's trading partners revealed that the model conformed well to theory successfully predicting most of South Korea's partners. Even most of the outliers were easily explained. The conspicuous exception, as noted, was Japan. My model suggested a 99 percent chance of a Korea-Japan FTA.

On the other hand, my global BTSCS in chapter 3 did not predict a Korea-Japan FTA. That said, however, I have seen another FTA analysis that reports outliers (Baier and Bergstrand 2004). In that global analysis, the Japan-Korea dyad was so markedly mis-predicted that it showed up in their short table of mis-predicted dyads. The evidence, on net, does suggest that there is a puzzle here to be explained.

Explaining the Puzzle

Explaining a nonevent is a notoriously difficult undertaking, so my reflections on why South Korea has no FTA with Japan are more directed toward creating a plausible set of explanations rather than attempting to adjudicate between these explanations.

One geopolitical explanation is straightforward. The Japanese colonized Korea during the first half of the twentieth century, and their rule was brutal and inhumane. A particularly controversial issue is the so-called comfort women, namely, South Korean women whom the Japanese forced into sexual servitude. South Koreans and Japanese have been suspicious of each other and remained so through the post-colonial decades. From a geopolitical perspective, it is perhaps no surprise that Korea has been loathe to sign an FTA with its former colonial ruler.

On the other hand, there are two alternative explanations, both economic in nature, that would also explain why South Korea did not conclude an FTA with Japan. First, I am intrigued by the CGE findings in chapter 6. Most studies show that Japan did not add much to the Korean economy even under conventional trade approaches, and this in itself might be something of a deterrent to a rational technocrat.

Second, South Korea has long run a trade deficit with Japan. Just as South Korea historically provided intermediate goods to China for production there and export to the United States, so too does South Korea import high-technology goods from Japan in order to run its own vast export machine. To my knowledge economic theory does not provide any particular reason to believe that trade will asymmetrically grow under an FTA, but the United States faced deficits with both Mexico and Korea in the early years of the FTAs, so it is not unreasonable to think this might happen. Unlike all the other FTAs, the one with Japan had some potential for driving up trade deficits.

If one does an informal cost-benefit analysis, in short, it seems the Japanese FTA had little benefit in terms of CGE predictions but did have some potential cost in terms of a deficit surge. The uneasy geopolitical history may have played a role in the lack of a Japanese FTA but the economics point to a similar conclusion.

IV. The European Union: Setting Standards in Services

The South Korean perspective has been that an FTA with most major economies, including the EU, is desirable. What motivated the EU? Reacting to the rest of the world, the EU launched its own *Global Europe* FTA initiative in 2006. Of all the countries on the planet to pursue, the EU chose South Korea as its first FTA partner. This sharpens the question. Why?

For an answer we can turn to Horng's (2012) analysis of the EU's Global Europe initiative, in which he focuses especially on South Korea as the first nation selected under this new initiative. Two points emerge. First, in stark contrast with U.S. policy, the EU was looking for meaningful economic markets. In Horng's words, "The key criteria for new FTA partners should be market potential (economic size and growth) and the level of protection against EU exporters (tariff and non-tariff barriers)" (309). Europe was looking for markets, not security leverage.

Second, and what made the 2006 Global Initiative new, is that "in terms of content, the new generation of FTAs needs to be comprehensive in scope and to aim at the highest possible degree of trade liberalization—*including far-reaching liberalization of services and investment*" (Horng 2012, 309; emphasis added). As was documented in chapter 6, South Korea's FTAs with the United States and the EU were bold attempts to liberalize services, making the nation unusual and hence explaining the EU's interest.

Indeed, "the EU took a lot of interest in negotiations in trade in services because it saw gains accruing to it by expansion of trade in services" (Das 2012, 10). Even more generally, Horng (2012, 314) underlines the significance of the EU-Korea FTA for future EU standards, in which "the EU-Korea FTA will be by far the most ambitious services-type FTA ever concluded by the EU."[3] For South Korea, setting the EU precedent meant agreeing to competition in banking, insurance, and legal services. The EU and KORUS agreements likely complement each other by providing for robust competition within the service sector rather than dominance by either the United States or the EU alone.

Conclusions

We can learn two lessons from this exploration of South Korea's FTA trifecta. The Korea-U.S. alliance played a particularly important role in the South Korean FTA strategy. This alliance was the foundation for the KORUS agreement but it also had important second-order effects. Somewhat ironically, the U.S. alliance and the KORUS FTA encouraged South Korea to sign an FTA with a large potential threat, China.

The second lesson of the chapter concerns the FTA with the EU. Whereas military security was a central part of South Korean economic policy, especially concerning China and the United States, the relationship with Europe was more economic in nature. For differing reasons, both the EU and South Korea wanted to sign an FTA with high service sector liberalization built in. The result is an exemplar FTA for services. Whereas the KORUS reflected hard power, rooted in the U.S.-Korean alliance, the FTA with the EU reflected soft power, in which South Korea further bolstered its reputation as the world's FTA exemplar.

CHAPTER 9

The Emerging Geopolitical Economy

Many observers say that Korea is the number one priority in contemporary geopolitics—that is, North Korea, not South Korea. Kim Jung Un's pursuit of rockets able to land nuclear devices on U.S. and allied soils is arguably the first credible nuclear threat to U.S. hegemony from a "rogue state." U.S. policymakers are following these events closely, with outgoing president Obama informing incoming president Trump that the Korean peninsula is the biggest geopolitical challenge on the horizon. Indeed, Jim Mattis's first foreign diplomatic step as secretary of defense was on South Korean soil. The two nations are and remain close allies, politically and economically. But what is the relationship between "politically" and "economically"? That has been our question all along.

I. Geopolitics and FTAs

At a conceptual level, the fact that we have such a thing as an FTA is testimony to the prevailing state-centric system of international relations. It is taken as axiomatic that different states exist and that they have control over their geographic domain, domestic populations, and economic processes. In stark contrast to the classic liberal *theoretical* idea of a state of nature, with its free markets in labor, goods, and capital, historically international trade has in fact been political, with national states controlling trade relations under the mercantilist system, under the colonial system, and—despite many FTAs—in the modern, and contemporary, world as well. FTAs must be understood as a limited liberalization of what is usually politically regulated international trade.

As we discussed in chapter 2, from the end of World War II to the fall of the Berlin Wall, the nature of interstate relations globally was thoroughly infused by the political struggle between the United States and the USSR. Each had its set of supporting states, all facing off in yet another historical world-as-chessboard "great game." Indeed, the modern system of close trade relations between Europe and the United States, and Japan's inclusion in that liberal order, was predicated upon this geopolitical struggle between these superpowers. Trade with Europe and Asia was not merely a matter of enjoying comparative advantage à la Ricardo. Trade was also a powerful security measure to contain communism.

The Korean case study and related evidence provided in this book indicate that geopolitics continues to shape trade policy. The rest of this chapter examines how South Korean exemplifies geopolitical economy more generally, such as the increasingly geographic diffusion of production and the ongoing geopolitics of major trade negotiations, such as the TPP and RCEP.

II. FTAs as Development Strategy

A "free trade" agreement seems like a liberal economic policy, designed to reduce the state's role in trade. Politically, however, an FTA strategy is an ambitious *statist* project. To pursue, negotiate, and conclude a large number of FTAs is a very complex policymaking process that in many ways resembles industrial policy. The state has to decide whether and when to pursue FTAs. In addition, the state must decide which potential partners to pursue.

I have argued that FTAs in South Korea were not merely an economic policy but rather a full-fledged economic development strategy that has been at the forefront of South Korean foreign economic policy. Specifically, FTAs were not just one policy measure among many, but rather they constituted Korea's core strategy for pursuing long-run growth through industrial exports. Moreover, and for precisely this reason, FTA policy was a major economic foreign policy goal of three different presidential administrations.

The Korean strategy, furthermore, was arguably a *smart trade strategy*. Most studies suggest that the FTAs increased the value of exports, FDI, and overall GDP. Moreover, in today's hostile trade climate, it is possible that Korea has locked in some important long-run gains from trade. Following President Trump's decision to pull out of the TPP and his critical comments concerning NAFTA and other trade agreements, other countries may not be so fortunate. In this sense, Korea has been successful in hedging against what it (apparently correctly) perceived as rather uncertain prospects for multilateral and semi-multilateral agreements.

States, for good or for ill, seek to enhance their international economic competitiveness. As Gilpin (2011, 130) notes, building upon Krugman's work on the geography of trade theory and other theories of constructed comparative advantage:

> In a world where economic growth, the geographic location of industry, and comparative advantage are frequently produced by arbitrary decisions and cumulative processes, national governments have an almost overwhelming incentive to intervene in their domestic economies. *Through industrial, strategic, and other interventionist policies, every nation, to one degree or another, does attempt to affect the international division of labor.* There is growing concern within nation-states about which countries produce what and about the location of high-tech jobs and industries; this makes it unlikely that such crucial matters will be left solely to the interplay of market forces. National governments repeatedly attempt to use their political power and their position in the international political system to influence the international division of economic specialization as much as possible. (emphasis added)

FTA strategy in South Korea exemplifies such a development strategy to improve Korea's future position in the international division of labor. Specifically, I have argued that FTAs were not merely one policy measure among many but rather constituted South Korea's core strategy for pursuing long-run economic growth, including service sector liberalization.

III. The Emerging Geopolitical Economy

In executing its ambitious FTA strategy, South Korea has become an exemplar of the emerging geopolitical economy. Two global trends are sweeping the world. The first, well advanced, is global supply chains, and the second, less well advanced but with strong future growth potential, is the service sector.

South Korea in many ways exemplifies what Baldwin (2013) dubbed the "second unbundling," the extension of the traditional two-country trade model to a three-country trade model, wherein there are two stages of production rather than just one stage of production. As I discussed in chapter 6, South Korea is a good illustration of this two-stage production process. These "global supply chains" (Baldwin 2013) capture an important intuition. The world has further specialized, with clear geographic consequences: firms have diversified beyond the traditional *two*-country comparative advantage model, as in the Britain-Portugal story, and instead operate increasingly in a *three*-country comparative advantage model, such as the Korea-Vietnam--U.S. global supply chain described in detail in chapter 6.

While global supply chains are already an established fact in the contemporary global economy, service sector liberalization is still in its infancy. This seems somewhat of an economic disequilibrium, given that services are an increasingly large portion of richer countries' GDP.

[Some] service industries, including finance, telecommunications, education and health care, are increasingly tradable thanks to advances in information technology. Such services account for an enormous share of GDP and employment in most rich countries, but only a tiny sliver of trade. Liberalisation could open them up to global competition. (*Economist* 2015)

Despite the growing importance of the service sector, international negotiations covering trade in this sector have not progressed. A service provision in the Doha Round of WTO talks addresses this topic, but the Doha Round does not look likely to be completed. Likewise, the TPP had a strong service sector component, but the United States pulled out of it. *The Economist*, in a discussion of the now defunct TPP, noted the importance of the service sector more generally for long-run globalization:

A ten-year horizon misses the point. . . . TPP's real promise lies in the liberalisation of trade in services. Just as it took decades for supply-chain integration to flower into the rapid goods-trade growth of the 1990s and 2000s, the pay-off from TPP, and deals like it, is further off. . . . One day service industries may be as efficient and as globally integrated as manufacturing is today. (*Economist*, November 12, 2015)

China is already a boom market for South Korean service sector exports. According to Schott (2015, 6), in 2000 Korean service exports were worth a paltry $4.6 billion, whereas by 2014 they had multiplied sevenfold, to $36.1 billion. Moreover, while services were 7 percent of Korean exports to China in 2000, by 2014 they made up 16 percent of all Korean exports to China, suggesting that services are clearly the most rapidly growing market for Korea in China. Given the vast potential of the Chinese market, this bodes well for future Korean service exports to China.[1]

With the TPP dead or at least seriously stalled, South Korea will have FTA first-mover advantages for a longer period than previously thought. Korea will nonetheless struggle with U.S. and EU competition, and to date Singapore has dominated services in Asia (e.g., Alvstam et al. 2016).

In the competitive struggle for efficiency in global services, however, South Korea has been notable in signing "high-quality FTAs" that liberalize the service sectors and protect investment. Williams et al. (2014, 15) note that the KORUS FTA will be emulated by other countries, and Zhuang, Hong, and Bai (2014) note that the China-Korea FTA will put pressure on Japan to join with these two nations. These two FTAs further increase South Korea's visibility as a force for trade liberalization.

IV. Future Trade Negotiations

In this book's final section, I turn from history to future, and from Korea specifically to the world generally, especially in the Pacific and the Atlantic.

The Pacific

If China is indisputably a rising power, with its share of global GDP steadily increasing, it is also the case that the United States still maintains a stronger military and diplomatic hand globally. Partially due to the Atlantic's more advanced military technologies and partially due to the ideological alliance of Western democracies against authoritarianism, China has never held much sway there. In the Pacific, the United States and China are regional powers. As the primary balancing power to China in all of Asia, the United States is more inclined to "contain" China than "bandwagon" with China.

This was one major motivation for the KORUS FTA, as noted in previous chapters. The United States signed the KORUS FTA partially to cement its role in Asia, knowing that South Korea is a major political economy and that the FTA would strengthen not merely trade but also FDI, sectoral transformation, information exchange, and overall relationships.

The TPP was similarly inspired as a way to bind the United States to Asia and reap some benefits from the competitive U.S. service sector. There was also, of course, a large geopolitical element, in which the TPP was part of a post-Cold War attempt to contain China through economics (Lee,2015). Aggarwal (2016) argues that the rise of China is overly emphasized in contemporary policy discourse, and that this discourse is a thinly veiled sales ploy for liberal trade policies in the U.S. when voters are wary of free trade. In either case, as Aggarwal himself notes (2016: 4), the TPP discourse was heavily influenced by geopolitical rhetoric: "Secretary of Defense Ashton Carter has also emphasized this strategic theme. As he put it: [Y]ou may not expect to hear this from a Secretary of Defense, but in terms of our rebalance in the broadest sense, passing TPP is as important to me as another aircraft carrier."

In the TPP, geopolitics and standard trade theory were on the same side; however, domestic politics were stronger. The U.S. debate over the TPP was a classic instance of low politics defeating high politics. The bipartisan geopolitical desire to write the rules of the Pacific economy was pitted against the powerful domestic reality that U.S. economic inequality had grown massively. Despite the fact that the TPP actually excluded China, Donald Trump rode an anti-trade sentiment, scapegoating Mexico and China for American economic difficulties.

Given that both traditional trade theory and geopolitical theory support the U.S. TPP interest, President Trump's actions hinder the United States economically and politically. "Trump's opposition to the Trans-Pacific Partnership, which would have created a strong trading—and, implicitly, security—bulwark against China, was particularly misguided. With American markets restricted, countries such as Taiwan, Vietnam, and Myanmar will more easily succumb to Chinese economic hegemony" (Bloomberg, June 15, 2017).

It is highly doubtful, however, that the United States will forever stay out of Asian trade negotiations. The Regional Comprehensive Economic Partnership (RCEP) will bind most countries *except* the United States. Presumably gains from trade will accrue to these nations while U.S. exporters and U.S. consumers will lose out on them, leading to a geopolitical shift in corresponding economic and military power in the East. That is, there are strong geopolitical and economic motivations for American policymakers to revisit the topic of trade with Asia.[2]

The Atlantic

It is remarkable how Russia continues to be such a major geopolitical player. Despite Russia's considerable political, social, and economic turmoil after the end of communism, Vladimir Putin has used Russia's authoritarian state and military might to pursue strongman-style geopolitics. Putin seized Crimea, a valuable port, violating all international law and norms, without a major reprisal. He then seized large parts of the Ukraine, again without major reprisals. In the Middle East, Putin is closely allied with Syria's reviled leader Bashar Al-Assad. And most brazenly, Putin launched coordinated cyber attacks in 2016 and 2017 on the United States and France, the intent of which was to alter the outcome of these two countries' presidential elections. Russia, in recent years, has become a major threat to a variety of nations' interests, and thus once again is a major geopolitical player.

Realist trade theory suggests that Putin's clear and serious threats should generate increased incentive for the EU and the United States to finalize the Transatlantic Trade and Investment Partnership (TTIP), the major proposed FTA between the EU and the United States. Yet the predicted geopolitical result did *not* occur. This is a clear instance where, in Putnam's (1988) two-level game, the *domestic* level is prevailing. With both Bernie Sanders on the left and Donald Trump on the right running against the TPP, trade is not a popular domestic agenda item in the United States. On the other side of the Atlantic, moreover, Trump's counterparts are cautious due to Brexit and ambiguities surrounding Trump's commitment to the North Atlantic Treaty Organization. Russia is currently a geopolitical aggressor. Trade policy coordination amongst its rivals, obviously, does not automatically follow suit.

Nonetheless, the TTIP is important because the more advanced economies of the Atlantic have a higher proportion of their GDPs involved in the service sector than do those of the Pacific. Indeed:

> The services industry accounts for more than 60% of economic activity in both the European Union and the United States, and they are the world's largest exporters of services. Both sides therefore are keen to obtain greater access to each other's services sectors, irrespective of the fact that services already account for a considerable share of transatlantic trade, with the European Union being the main services exporter to the United States and vice versa. (Pitschas 2016, 327)

Moreover, both the United States and the EU are internationally competitive in services, making both active proponents of global service sector trade. The TIPP was to be the ultimate liberalization of the service sector, but its fate is unclear. What does seem clear though, is that the future of the world economy lies with service sector liberalization and South Korea remains an exemplar.

Appendix

*Documentation of Chapter 3 and Chapter 5
Data and Variables*

Overview

Original data sources are given separately for chapter 3 and chapter 5 data and variables. The data for chapter 3 was compiled and shared by Yamamoto (2016) with the addition of alternative variables. The data for chapter 5 was compiled by Rosenbaum and Krieckhaus (2016).

Data Requests

For requests to use the data set for chapter 3 and/or chapter 5, please contact the author at KrieckhausJ@missouri.edu.

Citation

In any papers or publications that utilize the data set for chapter 3, users are asked to cite the data set as follows:

Krieckhaus, Jonathan. 2018. *Geopolitical Economy: The South Korean FTA Strategy*. Ann Arbor: University of Michigan Press.

and

Yamamoto Rosenbaum, Chika. 2016. "Free Trade Agreements in Japan and East Asian Regionalism: Sino-Japanese Rivalry and Beyond." PhD diss., University of Missouri.

In any papers or publications that utilize the data set for chapter 5, users are asked to cite the data set as follows:

Krieckhaus, Jonathan. 2018. *Geopolitical Economy: The South Korean FTA Strategy*. Ann Arbor: University of Michigan Press.

and

Drury, A. Cooper, Jonathan Krieckhaus, and Chika Yamamoto. 2014. "How Democracy Facilitates South Korean Interest in Free Trade Agreements." *Korea Observer* 45 (1): 39–60.

and

Yamamoto Rosenbaum, Chika, and Jonathan Krieckhaus. 2016. "What Explains South Korean Interest in FTA Partners? An Empirical Analysis." *Asian Survey* 56 (5): 982–1004.

Chapter 3 Data and Variables

Overview

The data set to conduct the logistic regressions and marginal effects in chapter 3 has 396,292 total observations with a temporal domain of 1992–2013 and a global sample of 160 countries.

TABLE A.1. Variables Used In Chapter Three

Variable	Variable label	Variable description	Data source
ccode1	COW Country Code 1	Country Designated Number	EUGene Data
ccode2	COW Country Code 2	Country Designated Number	EUGene Data
year	Year	Years 1992–2013	EUGene Data
abbrev1	COW Country 1 Abbr.	3-Letter Abbreviation	EUGene Data
abbrev2	COW Country 2 Abbr.	3-Letter Abbreviation	EUGene Data
region1	Region 1	Home Region Defined by the COW Interstate System Member List: 1 = Europe 2 = Middle East 3 = Africa 4 = Asia 5 = North and South America	EUGene Data
region2	Region 2	See Region 1 Description	EUGene Data
region	Region	Dummy variable; 1 = Shared Region (region1 = region2)	EUGene Data
distance	Distance	Distance Between Country Capitols	EUGene Data
distance1	Distance 1	Distance / 1000	EUGene Data
conttype	Contiguity	Dummy Variable Coded as 1 if Country 1 and Country 2 Share a Common Border	COW
gdp1	Country 1 GDP	GDP in Current U.S. Dollars	World Bank
gdp2	Country 2 GDP	GDP in Current U.S. Dollars	World Bank
gdpgrow1	Country 1 GDP Growth	GDP Growth Annual %	World Bank
gdpgrow2	Country 2 GDP Growth	GDP Growth Annual %	World Bank
pc1	Country 1 Per Capita GDP	GDP Per Capita in Current U.S. Dollars	World Bank
pc2	Country 2 Per Capita GDP	GDP Per Capita in Current U.S. Dollars	World Bank
pcgrow1	Country 1 Per Capita Growth	GDP Per Capita Growth Annual %	World Bank
pcgrow2	Country 2 Per Capita Growth	GDP Per Capita Growth Annual %	World Bank
fact	Difference (Per Capita Income)	Absolute Value of (pc2-pc1)	World Bank
gravity	Gravity	Country 1 GDP * Country 2 GDP	World Bank
diff	GDP Difference	Difference Between Country 1 GDP and Country 2 GDP	World Bank
diff_pc	GDP Per Capita Difference	Difference of GDP Per Capita in Current U.S. Dollars Between Countries, Proxies as a Difference Of Market Sizes	World Bank

Variable	Variable label	Variable description	Data source
import	Imports	Import of Country 1 from Country 2 (until 2009)	COW
export	Exports	Export of Country 2 from Country 1 (until 2009)	COW
polity1	Country 1 Democracy Score	Democracy Score (-10 to 10)	Polity IV Project
polity2	Country 2 Democracy Score	Democracy Score (-10 to 10)	Polity IV Project
defense	Defense	Dummy Variable Coded as 1 if a Defense Alliance Exists Between Countries; Otherwise 0	COW
entente	Entente	Dummy Variable Coded as 1 if an Entente Alliance Exists Between Countries; Otherwise 0	COW
neutrality	Neutrality	Dummy Variable Coded as 1 if a Neutrality Alliance Exists Between Countries; Otherwise 0.	COW
nonaggression	Nonaggression	Dummy Variable Coded as 1 if a Nonaggression Alliance Exists Between Countries; Otherwise 0.	COW
alliance	Alliance	Dummy Variable Coded as 1 if: Defense = 1 Entente = 1 Neutrality = 1 Nonaggression = 1 Otherwise = 0	COW
wto	World Trade Org.	Dummy Variable Coded as 1 if Both States Are Members of WTO	WTO Website
ro1	Reg. Org. 1	Regional Organization as Single FTA Pursuers: 1 = NAFTA 2 = MERCOSUR 3 = ASEAN 4 = GCC 5 = SACU 6 = EFTA 7 = EU 8 = CACM 9 = CAN	See Reg. Org. Websites
ro2	Reg. Org. 2	See Description of Reg. Org. 1	See Reg. Org. Websites
ros	Shared Association 1	Dummy Variable Coded as 1 if Dyad Has a Shared Association in Reg. Org. (ro1 = ro2)	See Reg. Org. Websites

TABLE A.1. *Continued*

Variable	Variable label	Variable description	Data source
eu	European Union Member	Dummy Variable Coded as 1 if a State Belongs to the EU (1 if ro1 = 7) (1992–2005)	See Reg. Org. Websites
sig	FTA Signed	Dummy Variable Coded as 1 if an FTA is at least Signed	JETRO: Molders 2012
sigb2	Bilateral or Semi-Bilateral FTA Signed	Dummy Variable Coded as 1 if a Bilateral or Semi-Bilateral FTA is at least Signed	JETRO: Molders 2012
sigm2	Multilateral FTA Signed	Dummy Variable Coded as 1 if a Multilateral FTA is at Least Signed	JETRO: Molders 2012
sum_sig	Sum of Signed FTAs	Summary of Signed FTAs by Country in 2013	JETRO: Molders 2012
polconv_1	Veto Player 1	Veto Player Associated with Country 1	Henisz 2000
polconv_2	Veto Player 2	Veto Player Associated with Country 2	Henisz 2000
t1	Time 1	Time Since Last FTA Signed—BTSCS	Carter and Signorino 2010
t2	Time 2	Time 2 Since Last FTA Signed—BTSCS	Carter and Signorino 2010
t3	Time 3	Time 3 Since Last FTA Signed—BTSCS	Carter and Signorino 2010

Notes about FTA variables:

1. JETRO database (in Japanese) is used as the basic data set, which records 314 FTAs, including proposed, negotiated, signed, and implemented FTAs as well as both bilateral and multilateral FTAs. Molders's (2012) attached list of FTAs was used to supplement missing years of proposal, negotiation, signature, or implementation of 291 FTAs plus twenty-four economic partnership agreements as well as custom unions. The total number of trade agreements included is 315 (Yamamoto 2016).

2. Bilateral FTA refers to an FTA between individual states; semi-bilateral FTA refers to an FTA between an individual state and some kind of regional organization or group, such as the EU,

ASEAN, or the Gulf Cooperation Council; multilateral FTA refers to an FTA between regional organizations (Yamamoto 2016).

3. If state A has FTAs with state B in both bilateral and multilateral manners, the earlier dates, regardless of the types, are used to code the signature variable (Yamamoto 2016).

4. To ensure the accuracy of FTA count variables in the data set from 1992 to 2013, I confirmed with several government websites, including South Korea (8), Japan (13), the United States (14), Canada (9, excluding the Canada-U.S. Free Trade Agreement, which is the precursor of NAFTA), and Singapore (19). All of these FTAs are correctly reflected in the data set (Yamamoto 2016).

Chapter 5 Data and Variables

Overview

These variables are used for table 5.3 and table 5.5. Table 5.3 is a cross-sectional logistic analysis of South Korean FTA signatures with its trading partners. Table 5.5 utilizes a survival analysis using a time-series cross-sectional dyadic data set for South Korea and its trading partners from 2000 to 2011.

TABLE A.2. Variables Used in Chapter Five

Variable Label	Variable Description	Data Source
Signed FTAs	Length of Time until a Dyad (South Korea and a Trading Partner Country) Signs an FTA in any Given Year since 2000 until 2011.	JETRO: Molders 2012
Proposed FTAs	Length of Time until a Dyad (South Korea and a Trading Partner Country) Proposes an FTA in any Given Year since 2000 until 2011.	JETRO: Molders 2012
Distance	Distance between Seoul and the Capital City of a Trading Partner in miles. Serves as a Proxy for Transportation Costs.	EUGene Data
Logged Distance	Logged Distance between Seoul and the Capital City of a Trading Partner in miles. Serves as a Proxy for Transportation Costs.	EUGene Data
GDP	Total GDP of South Korea and its Trading Partners in U.S. Millions of Dollars.	World Bank
Logged GDP	Logged Total GDP of South Korea And its Trading Partners in U.S. Millions of Dollars.	World Bank
GDP Per Capita	The Income Per Capita of Korea's Trading Partners.	World Bank
Logged GDP Per Capita	Logged GDP Per Capita of Korea's Trading Partners	World Bank
Democracy	The Levels of Democracy Among South Korean Trading Partners. Scores Range from -10 to 10.	Polity IV Project
Prior FTAs (#)	Total Number of FTAs Each Nation Has Signed. Serves as a Proxy for Trade Diversion Incentive Effects.	JETRO: Molders 2012
Japan	Japan Effect—Dummy Variable Coded as 1 if a Trading Partner of South Korea has Engaged in the Consideration of an FTA with Japan.	JETRO: Molders 2012
China	China Effect—Dummy Variable Coded as 1 if a Trading Partner of South Korea has Engaged in the Consideration of an FTA with China.	JETRO: Molders 2012
(ln)GDP per capita*t	Interaction term between the Logged Per Capita of Korea's Trading Partners and Time (t). Corrects for the Violation of Logged GDP Per Capita Not Being Proportional Across Time in the Cox Proportional Hazards Model.	World Bank

Notes

Chapter 1

1. The quote from Chung 2003 refers to the size of GDP, where South Korea ranked twelfth in 2003. My claim refers to the size of exports, where South Korea ranks sixth in 2015 according to the online World Bank World Development Indicators.

2. As Mansfield and Milner (2012, 13) note, FTAs are simply the second step on a continuum of increasingly strong trade agreements: (1) preferential agreements giving a country lower tariffs on a specific trading sector or sectors, (2) FTAs that eliminate most trade barriers, (3) custom unions that have no internal trade barriers but have a common external tariff, (4) a common market that additionally has free flow of factors of production, and (5) an economic union where nations also coordinate economic and fiscal policy (i.e., the EU).

3. Forty-nine was the count as of January 26, 2016.

4. The only important country Korea has not yet signed with is Japan, where an FTA has been proposed but negotiations have long stagnated.

5. I put the word "privileged" in quotes because the point is that these regions are highly salient but not *necessarily* beneficiaries of this salience. At times this meant that the U.S. militarized nation-states on the rim, such as Iran, and this obviously had deeply harmful consequences. My point is not a normative one, in short, but rather meant to notice that causal effects fall heavily on the rim nations.

Chapter 2

1. There are, of course, other barriers to trade, including language and cultural differences.

2. I state these hypotheses explicitly for three related reasons. First, a precise statement of the hypotheses shapes my analytic narrative, and I utilize the hypotheses to structure my historical account of Korean FTAs as well as FTAs in other countries. Second, I test these hypotheses in chapters 3 and 5. Third, when conducting a global model I examine each of these variables in the Korean case to gain insight into how

each of the hypotheses explains (or does not) the statistical predictions for the Korean case.

3. Liberals also accept that anarchy matters, but they also argue that these real effects can be substantially influenced by institutions, trade, and culture.

4. This is not to deny that the USSR and the United States fought many proxy wars in Africa and Latin America, but the stakes were lower than direct containment policy.

Chapter 3

1. The cubic polynomials provide the same function as splines, meaning that they correct for temporal dependence, but they have two additional advantages. First, they are easy to implement. Second, they prevent the common but unintentional user error of using an overly mechanistic interpretation of Beck, Katz, and Tucker 1998.

2. Mansfield and Milner (2012) emphasize that their veto player argument holds for FTA ratification, while my analyses focus on FTA signatures. I ran the models with FTA ratification as a dependent variable, however, and the sign remains positive as in Table 3.1.

3. We usually use trade as a dependent variable in a gravity model. Including it in model 2 seems to inherently introduce endogeneity, in that we are essentially sucking the trade-seeking impulse out of the model by introducing trade itself as another independent variable. In the extreme case, if the causal variables influence trade and FTAs in equal portion, including trade as a control variable would essentially be reintroducing the dependent variable a second time into the model. Trade is perhaps an independent variable, as per model 3, but it is perhaps an intervening variable, which makes model 2 the correct specification. See King, Keohane, and Verba (1994, 78) on the crucial point that intervening process should not be control variables.

4. As an additional robustness check I utilized rare-events logit for all five models, and obtained substantively the same results.

Chapter 4

1. Unless otherwise noted, all data in this book comes from the online World Bank World Development Indicators.

Chapter 5

1. See Haggard (1990) for a classic comparison of EOI in Asia and ISI in Latin America.

2. Lim (1998) is an exception to the rule and notes that the state was at least tacitly depending upon business willingness to invest, and hence was not entirely autonomous.

3. The y axis data is from the online World Bank World Development Indicators from 2015. Figure 5.1 excludes countries below ten million people because they tend to

be idiosyncratic trade outliers. Particularly concerning are island states, since most are dominated by trade but nonetheless operate under fundamentally different economic processes than normal nation-states. See, for instance, Bertram 2003. Lowering the cutoff below ten million does not make much difference to the following story, with the important exception of Singapore, as discussed below.

4. I thank Mölders (2012) for publishing this comprehensive list of FTAs. I thank Gayeon Ryu for accurately transcribing Mölders 2012 (41–47) into Excel. I thank Rebecca Miller for overseeing the data set generation process, including writing most of the Stata code. The x axis in figure 5.1 is then generated from the resulting data set. I utilize the Mölders 2012 data set to create a dyadic BTSCS data set of FTA existence between all country dyads and then merge dyadic trade data from EUGene. By multiplying the FTA dyadic dummy variable with each dyad's trade volume, it is easy to aggregate and provide an overall measure of the percentage of each country's total trade conducted under the auspices of FTAs.

5. About 80 percent of Mexican exports go to the United States, and another 6 percent go to Canada. NAFTA, in short, single-handedly places Mexico on the far right of Figure 5.1. Mexico, however, also signed an important FTA with the EU such that its other major trading partners are also FTA covered.

6. With respect to the Netherlands, for instance, its top twenty trading partners equal more than 87 percent of all exports, and these are entirely European with only two exceptions (United States at 4.3 percent of trade and China at 1.1 percent of trade). This strong EU trade orientation obviously explains why the Netherlands has such a high FTA coverage score. Exports from the small populations of Belgium and the Czech Republic are also overwhelmingly internal to the EU, giving them high FTA coverage as well.

7. For instance, Bolivia exports 40 percent of its trade to Brazil and additional amounts to its other Mercosur partners, such that the Mercosur FTA largely explains Bolivia's high FTA coverage. (Mercosur is an FTA between a number of South American countries.) Tunisia, on the other hand, is dominated by EU trade, especially with France and Italy.

8. Again, note that island states have much higher levels of trade than anything shown in Figure 5.1, although these islands are not comparable in terms of development strategy.

9. The scores range from -10 to 10. The highest score of 10 indicates the highest level of democratization to be achieved in a country, whereas -10 reflects autocratic states, as the furthest from democratic.

10. Recall that this somewhat unusual specification is purposeful, namely, to model comparative advantage, as discussed above. Given that a simpler measure, namely, GDP per capita (*without* taking the difference from Korea), is a common control variable in political economy studies, I tried that variable as an alternative, but it, too, was insignificant.

11. See Park and Koo's (2007) comment that "the South Korean government had difficulty in choosing its FTA partners. It contacted a number of countries, but only a few of them showed explicit interest in discussing FTAs with South Korea, which had yet to recover from the effects of the Asian financial crisis. As of mid-1998, South Korea received positive responses from only six countries: Turkey, South America [sic], Thailand, New Zealand, Israel and Chile" (267).

12. Diagnostic tests suggest that column 2 is better specified than column 1, which does not include the interaction between GDP per capita and a time trend variable, and thereby misses a degree of nonlinearity in the effect of GDP per capita on South Korean FTA policy. Cox proportional hazards models assume that the effects of the covariates are consistent over time or change only by a factor of proportionality (Box-Steffensmeier and Jones 2004). This assumption can be tested with the Grambsch and Therneau non-proportionality test. This residual-based test detects independent variables that violate the proportional hazards assumption necessary to properly run the Cox proportional hazards model. The failure to assume the assumption then leads to incorrect estimates of all independent variables (Box-Steffensmeier and Jones 2004). The diagnostic suggests that the logged value of South Korea's trading partner's GDP per capita violates the proportional hazards assumption (the null hypothesis is rejected), meaning that the effect of this explanatory variable is non-proportional. Thus, this variable is interacted with the natural log of time in order to take into account the non-proportionality of the covariates (Box-Steffensmeier and Zorn 2001).

Chapter 6

1. Author's calculations are based on the online World Bank *World Development Indicators*.

2. This is the so-called conditional convergence effect. See, for instance, Barro and Sala-i-Martin (1995).

3. One can question the empirical accuracy of CGE models. In fact, a recent paper (Rosnick and Baker 2016) critiques CGE models in general and the KORUS FTA in particular, as discussed later.

4. For those with no prior experience with "static" and "dynamic" CGE models, or even the "gravity" model approach in trade theory, can find a non-technical introduction in Piermartini and Teh (2005)'s useful "Demystifying modelling methods for trade policy."

5. Cheong (2014), however, notes that previous analyses of the Korea-China FTA had not taken into account the extent to which trade runs through special economic zones as intermediate goods without tariffs, consistent with the more general vision of production networks. As such, the formal tariff reduction will have less effect.

Schott (2015) also provides an evaluation of the China FTA with Korea and found it limited.

6. The dynamic effects are much harder to get at. Some studies provide dynamic models, but the models are fairly simple. Kyoto and Stern (2007), for instance, use increased FDI to measure efficiency, and model (arbitrarily) effects from a 1 percent increase in FDI and a 5 percent increase in FDI, which resulted in reasonably large GDP increases.

7. This statement is based on author calculations by filling in a missing GDP growth rate datum for 2014.

8. See the annual Going for Growth reports from the OECD from 2007 to 2014.

Chapter 7

1. Indeed, the United States had earlier assumed that South Korea could <u>not</u> quell its agriculture sector politically, so it just assumed there would be no U.S. FTA with Korea. "When asked why at an Institute conference in May 2004, then USTR Robert Zoellick answered, 'They're not ready to talk about agriculture'" (Schott, Bradford, and Moll 2006, 1).

Chapter 8

1. China also has FTAs with Peru and Chile.
2. For recent discussions of the Chinese view, see Xiaotong 2015 and Xiaotong et al. 2014.
3. "**Overall assessment of the services sector.** Korea agreed to open its market substantively in the areas of professional services, telecommunications, audiovisual services, and financial services. In the area of financial services, all financial firms from the United States and the EU will be able to freely transfer data from their branches and affiliates to their headquarters" (Song 2011, 9; emphasis in original).

Chapter 9

1. That said, the actual Korea-China agreement was seen as something of a disappointment by some trade observers (e.g., Schott et al. 2015). Liberalization was delayed and not very deep. In manufacturing, services, and agriculture, there are clear limitations on the extent of liberalization. Nonetheless, China will remain a large and important market for Korea, and there will be many opportunities in the future for further liberalization between the two countries.
2. As a final geopolitical economy point, note that both the TPP and the RCEP put into the hands of geographic fate a substantial amount of third-party trade effects. "But many 'global integrators' are excluded in the RCEP and TPP negotiations as a result of geography (they are not Pacific countries)" (Hoekman 2014, 247).

Bibliography

Acharya, Amitav. 2014. *Constructing a Security Community in Southeast Asia: ASEAN and the Problem of Regional Order*. New York: Routledge.

Aggarwal, Vinod. K. 2013a. "U.S. Free Trade Agreements and Linkages." International Negotiation 18 (1): 89–110. doi: 10.1163/15718069-12341246.

Aggarwal, Vinod K. 2013b. "Linking Traditional and Non-traditional Security in Bilateral Free Trade Agreements: The US Approach." In *Linking Trade and Security*, 175–99. Springer.

Aggarwal, Vinod K. 2016. "Mega-FTAs and the Trade-Security Nexus: The Trans-Pacific Partnership (TPP) and Regional Comprehensive Economic Partnership (RCEP)." *Asia Pacific Issues* no. 123 (March):1–8.

Aggarwal, Vinod K, and Kristi Govella. 2013. *Linking Trade and Security: Evolving Institutions and Strategies in Asia, Europe, and the United States*. Vol. 1: Springer Science & Business Media.

Aggarwal, Vinod K., and Min Gyo Koo. 2005. "Beyond Network Power? The Dynamics of Formal Economic Integration in Northeast Asia." *Pacific Review* 18 (2): 189–216.

Agnew, John, and Luca Muscarà. 2012. *Making Political Geography*. Lanham: Rowman and Littlefield.

Ahn, Se-Young, and JeongGon Kim. 2012. "The Economic and Geopolitical Implications of the Ongoing China-Korea FTA Negotiations." *Sogang IIAS Research Series on International Affairs* 12:57–80.

Alba, Joseph, Jung Hur, and Donghyun Park. 2010. "Do Hub-and-Spoke Free Trade Agreements Increase Trade? A Panel Data Analysis." ADB Working Paper Series on Regional Economic Integration No. 46. Manila: Asian Development Bank. http://hdl.handle.net/11540/1958

Alvstam, C. G., E. Kettunen, and P. Ström. 2016. "The Service Sector in the Free-trade Agreement between the EU and Singapore: Closing the Gap between Policy and Business Realities." *Asia Europe Journal*: 1–31. doi: 10.1007/s10308-016-0464-z.

Ameer, Rashid. 2007. "What Moves the Primary Stock and Bond Markets? Influence of Macroeconomic Factors on Bond and Equity Issues in Malaysia and Korea." *Asian Academy of Management Journal of Accounting and Finance* 3 (1): 93–116.

Amsden, Alice H. 1989. *Asia's Next Giant: South Korea and Late Industrialization*. New York: Oxford University Press.

Amsden, Alice H., and Yoon-Dae Euh. 1993. "South Korea's 1980s Financial Reforms: Good-bye Financial Repression (Maybe), Hello New Institutional Restraints." *World Development* 21 (3): 379–90.

An, Jiyoun, and Cheolbeom Park. 2012. *"Election Cycles and Stock Market Reaction: International Evidence."* *KIEP Working Paper* 12–04. Seoul: Korea Institute for International Economic Policy.

Ando, Mitsuyo, and Shujiro Urata. 2005. "The Impacts of East Asia FTA: A CGE Model Simulation Study." Keio University Market Quality Research Project (KUMQRP) Discussion Paper Series 21.

Andreosso-O'Callaghan, Bernadette. 2009. "Economic Structural Complementarity: How Viable Is the Korea-EU FTA?" *Journal of Economic Studies* 36 (2): 147–67.

Antkiewicz, Agata, and John Whalley. 2005. "China's New Regional Trade Agreements." *World Economy* 28 (10): 1539–57.

Armitage, Richard L., and Joseph S. Nye. 2007. *The US-Japan Alliance: Getting Asia Right through 2020*. Washington, DC: Center for Strategic and International Studies.

Bae, Chankwon, and Yong Joon Jang. 2013. "The Impact of Free Trade Agreements on Foreign Direct Investment: The Case of Korea." *Journal of East Asian Economic Integration* 17 (4): 417–44.

Baier, Scott L., and Jeffrey H. Bergstrand. 2004. "Economic Determinants of Free Trade Agreements." *Journal of International Economics* 64 (1): 29–63.

Balassa, Bela. 1978. "Exports and Economic Growth: Further Evidence." *Journal of Development Economics* 5:181–89.

Baldwin, David A. 1993. "Neoliberalism, Neorealism, and World Politics." *Neorealism and Neoliberalism: The Contemporary Debate* 3.

Baldwin, Richard. 1995. "A Domino Theory of Regionalism." In *Expanding Membership of the European Union*, edited by Richard Baldwin, Pertti Haaparanta and Jaakko Kiander, 25-53. New York: Cambridge University Press.

Baldwin, Richard. 2013. "Global Supply Chains: Why They Emerged, Why They Matter, and Where They Are Going." In *Global Value Chains in a Changing World*, edited by Deborah K. Elms and Patrick Low, 13–60. Geneva: World Trade Organization.

Baldwin, Richard, and Dany Jaimovich. 2012. "Are Free Trade Agreements Contagious?" *Journal of International Economics* 88 (1): 1–16.

Barnes, K. E., and P. F. Barker. 2012. *The U.S.-South Korea Free Trade Agreement, The U.S.-South Korea Free Trade Agreement*: Nova Science Publishers Book.

Barro, Robert J., and Xavier Sala-i-Martin. 1995. *Economic Growth*. New York: McGraw-Hill.

Bates, Robert. 1981. *States and Markets in Tropical Africa: The Political Basis of Agricultural Policy*. Series on Social Choice and Political Economy. Berkeley: University of California Press.

Bennett, D. Scott, and Allan Stam. 2000. "EUGene: A Conceptual Manual." *International Interactions* 26: 179–204.

Bennett, James, Andrew Ainslie, and John Davis. 2013. "Contested Institutions? Traditional Leaders and Land Access and Control in Communal Areas of Eastern Cape Province, South Africa." *Land Use Policy* 32: 27–38.

Bates, R. H. 2009. "From Case Studies to Social Science: A Strategy for Political Research." In *The Oxford Handbook of Comparative Politics*. edited by Carles Boix, Susan Carol Stokes, 172–85. New York.

Bates, Robert, Avner Greif, Margaret Levi, Jean-Laurent Rosenthal, and Barry Weingast. 2000. "Analytic Narratives Revisited." *Social Science History* 24 (4): 685–96.

Bates, Robert H., Avner Greif, Margaret Levi, Jean-Laurent Rosenthal, and Barry R. Weingast. 1998. *Analytical Narratives*. Princeton, NJ: Princeton University Press.

Baucus, Max. 2004. "Speech of US Senator Max Baucus at the First Annual Forum 'Toward a Strong Asia Trade Policy.'" U.S. Senate Committee on Finance, September 21.

Beck, Nathaniel, Jonathan N. Katz, and Richard Tucker. 1998. "Taking Time Seriously: Time-Series-Cross-Section Analysis with a Binary Dependent Variable." *American Journal of Political Science* 42 (4): 1260–88.

Bennett, D. Scott, and Allan C. Stam. 2000. "EUGene: A Conceptual Manual." *International Interactions* 26 (2): 179–204.

Bertram, Geoffrey. 2003. "On the Convergence of Small Island Economies with Their Metropolitan Patrons." *World Development* 32 (2):343-364.

Bhagwati, Jagdish N., and Arvind Panagariya. "The Economics of Preferential Trade Agreements." Washington, D.C.; College Park, 1996.

Bhagwati, Jagdish N., and Bank World. 1992. *Regionalism and Multilateralism: An Overview*. New York: Columbia University, Dept. of Economics.

Bhattacharyay, Biswa Nath. 2013. "Determinants of Bond Market Development in Asia." *Journal of Asian Economics* 24: 124–37.

Black, Jeremy M. 2016. *Geopolitics and the Quest for Dominance*. Bloomington: Indiana University Press.

Bliss, Harry, and Bruce Russett. 1999. "Democracy and Trade: Ties of Interest and Community." In *Democratic Peace in Europe: Myth or Reality*, edited by Gustaaf Geeraerts and Patrick Stouthuysen, 107–30. Brussels: VUB University Press.

Box-Steffensmeier, Janet M., and Bradford S. Jones. 2004. *Event History Modeling: A Guide for Social Scientists, Analytical Methods for Social Research*: Cambridge, NY: Cambridge University Press.

Boyer, Robert, Hiroyasu Uemura, and Akinori Isogai. 2013. *Diversity and Transformations of Asian Capitalisms*. New York: Routledge.

Brazinsky, G. A. 2009. *Nation Building in South Korea: Koreans, Americans, and the Making of a Democracy*. Chapel Hill: University of North Carolina Press.

Brzezinski, Zbigniew. 1997. *The Grand Chessboard: American Primacy and Its Geostrategic Imperatives*. New York: BasicBooks.

Bueno de Mesquita, Bruce, James D. Morrow, Randolph M. Siverson, and Alastair Smith. 2002. "Political Institutions, Policy Choice and the Survival of Leaders." *British Journal of Political Science* 32 (4): 559–90.

Bull, Hedley. 1977. *The Anarchical Society*. London: Macmillan, 1977.

Büthe, T., and H. V. Milner. 2008. "The Politics of Foreign Direct Investment into Developing Countries: Increasing FDI through International Trade Agreements?" *American Journal of Political Science* 52 (4): 741–62. doi: 10.1111/j.1540-5907.2008.00340.x.

Campbell, Kurt, and Brian Andrews. 2013. "Explaining the US 'Pivot' to Asia." The Asia Group, Americas 2013/01. Perceptions of the US Project. London: Chatham House.

Carmody, Pádraig. 2012. "Another BRIC in the Wall? South Africa's Developmental Impact and Contradictory Rise in Africa and Beyond." *European Journal of Development Research* 24 (2): 223–41.

Carter, David B., and Curtis, S. Signorino. 2010. "Back to the Future: Modeling Time Dependence in Binary Data." *Political Analysis* (3): 271.

Castley, R. J. 1996. "The Role of Japanese Foreign Investment in South Korea's Manufacturing Sector." *Development Policy Review* 14 (1): 69–88.

Chan, Kam C., Benton E. Gup, and Ming-Shiun Pan. 1992. "An Empirical Analysis of Stock Prices in Major Asian Markets and the United States." *Financial Review* 27 (2): 289–307.

Chan, Sarah, and Chun-Chien Kuo. 2005. "Trilateral Trade Relations among China, Japan and South Korea: Challenges and Prospects of Regional Economic Integration." *East Asia* 22 (1): 33–50.

Chang, Ha-Joon. 1998. "Korea: The Misunderstood Crisis." *World Development* 26 (8): 1555–61.

Chang, Ha-Joon. 2000. "The Hazard of Moral Hazard: Untangling the Asian Crisis." *World Development* 28 (4): 775–88.

Chang, Ha-Joon. 2002. *Kicking Away the Ladder: Development Strategy in Historical Perspective*. London: Anthem Press.

Chen, Maggie Xiaoyang, and Sumit Joshi. 2010. "Third-Country Effects on the Formation of Free Trade Agreements." *Journal of International Economics* 82 (2): 238–48.

Cheong, Inkyo. 2004. "East Asian Economic Integration: Implications for a US-Korea FTA." Rising Asian Regionalism and the Prospects of a U.S.-Korea FTA. American Enterprise Institute for Public Policy Research, Washington, DC: October 26. http://www. aei. org/docLib/20041026_Cheong. pdf

Cheong, Inkyo. 2007. "Evaluation of the Korea-US FTA and Implications for East Asian Economic Integration." *Journal of East Asian Affairs* 21 (2): 1–26.

Cheong, Inkyo. 2014. "An Analysis of the Effect of the China-Korea FTA with the Consideration of FTA Sequence and FTA Hub Gains." *Journal of Korea Trade* 18 (1): 63–84.

Cheong, Inkyo, and Yunjong Wang. 1999. "*Korea-U.S. FTA: Prospects and Analysis*." *KIEP Working Paper* 99–03. Seoul: Korea Institute for International Economic Policy.

Cherry, Judith. 2005. "'Big Deal' or Big Disappointment? The Continuing Evolution of the South Korean Developmental State." *Pacific Review* 18 (3): 327–54.

Cherry, Judith. 2006. "Killing Five Birds with One Stone: Inward Foreign Direct Investment in Post-Crisis Korea." *Pacific Affairs* 79 (1): 9–27.

Cherry, Judith. 2012. "Upgrading the 'Software': The EU-Korea Free Trade Agreement and Sociocultural Barriers to Trade and Investment." *Pacific Review* 25 (2): 247–68.

Chiang, Min-Hua. 2013. "The Potential of China-Japan-South Korea Free Trade Agreement." *East Asia* 30 (3): 199–216.

Chiu, Chien-Liang, Chun-Da Chen, and Wan-Wei Tang. 2005. "Political Elections and Foreign Investor Trading in South Korea's Financial Markets." *Applied Economics Letters* 12 (11): 673–77.

Choi, Byung-il, and Jennifer Sejin Oh. 2011. "Asymmetry in Japan and Korea's Agricultural Liberalization in FTA: Domestic Trade Governance Perspective." *Pacific Review* 24 (5): 505–27.

Choi, Inbom, and Jeffrey J. Schott. 2001. *Free Trade between Korea and the United States?* Washington, DC: Institute for International Economics.

Choi, Inbom, and Jeffrey J. Schott. 2004. "Korea-US Free Trade Revisited." In *Free Trade Agreements: US Strategies and Priorities*, edited by Jeffrey J Schott, 173–96. Washington, DC: Institute for International Economics.

Choi, Nakgyoon. 2011. "Determinants of Staging Categories for Tariff Elimination in Chinese, Japanese, and Korean Negotiations of Free Trade Agreements." *Asian Economic Papers* 10 (2): 1–17.

Choi, Won-Mog. 2009. "Aggressive Regionalism in Korea-U.S. FTA: The Present and Future of Korea's FTA Policy." *Journal of International Economic Law* 12 (3): 595–615.

Chu, Yin-wah. 2009. "Eclipse or Reconfigured? South Korea's Developmental State and Challenges of the Global Knowledge Economy." *Economy and Society* 38 (2): 278–303.

Chuang, I., Jin-Ray Lu, and Keshin Tswei. 2007. "Interdependence of International Equity Variances: Evidence from East Asian Markets." *Emerging Markets Review* 8 (4): 311–27.

Chung, Hae-kwan. 2003. "The Korea-Chile FTA: Significance and Implications." *East Asian Review* 15 (1): 71–86.

Chung, Jae Ho. 2009. "East Asia Responds to the Rise of China: Patterns and Variations." *Pacific Affairs* 82 (4): 657–75.

Clark, Barry Stewart. 1998. *Political Economy: A Comparative Approach*. New York: Praeger.

Cole, David Chamberlin, and Princeton N. Lyman. 1971. *Korean Development: The Interplay of Politics and Economics*. Cambridge, MA: Harvard University Press.

Cooper, William H., Mark E. Manyin, Remy Jurenas, and Michaela D. Platzer. 2010. *The Proposed U.S.-South Korea Free Trade Agreement (KORUS FTA): Provisions and Implications*. Washington, DC: Congressional Research Service.

Corning, Gregory P. 2014. "CJK Investment Agreements in East Asia: Building a Bifurcated Investment Regime." *Asian Politics and Policy* 6 (2): 285–306.

Crotty, James, and Kang-Kook Lee. 2006. "The Effects of Neoliberal 'Reforms' on the Post-Crisis Korean Economy." *Review of Radical Political Economics* 38 (4): 669–75.

Cumings, Bruce. 1981. *The Origins of the Korean War: Liberation and the Emergence of Separate Regimes, 1945–1947*. Princeton, NJ: Princeton University Press.

Davis, Christina L. 2010. "Cashing in on Cooperation: Democracy, Free Trade, and International Rules." *Harvard International Review* 31 (4): 56–60.

Davis, Christina L. 2012. *Why Adjudicate? Enforcing Trade Rules in the WTO*. Princeton, NJ: Princeton University Press.

Debaere, Peter, Joonhyung Lee, and Myungho Paik. 2010. "Agglomeration, Backward and Forward Linkages: Evidence from South Korean Investment in China." *Canadian Journal of Economics/Revue canadienne d'économique* 43 (2): 520–46.

Decreux, Yvan, Chris Milner, and Nicolas Péridy. 2010. "The Economic Impact of the Free Trade Agreement (FTA) between the European Union and Korea." *Report for the European commission, DG Trade.* http://trade. ec. europa. eu/doclib/docs/2007/ may/tradoc_134706. pdf.

Decreux, Yvan, Chris Milner, and Nicolas Péridy. 2010. "Some New Insights into the Effects of the EU-South Korea Free Trade Area: The Role of Non Tariff Barriers." *Journal of Economic Integration* 25 (4): 783–817.

Deltas, George, Klaus Desmet, and Giovanni Facchini. 2012. "Hub-and-Spoke Free Trade Areas: Theory and Evidence from Israel." *The Canadian Journal of Economics / Revue canadienne d'Economique* 45 (3): 942–77.

Dent, Christopher M. 2005. "Bilateral Free Trade Agreements: Boon or Bane for Regionalism in East Asia and the Asia-Pacific?" *European Journal of East Asian Studies* 4 (2): 287–314.

Dent, Christopher M., and Claire Randerson. 1996. "Korean Foreign Direct Investment in Europe: The Determining Forces." *Pacific Review* 9 (4): 531–52.

Deyo, Frederick. 1987. "State and Labor: Modes of Political Exclusion in East Asian Development." In *The Political Economy of the New Asian Industrialism*, edited by Frederick Deyo. Cornell.

Dittmer, Lowell. 2007. "The Asian Financial Crisis and the Asian Developmental State: Ten Years After." *Asian Survey* 47 (6): 829–33.

Dolowitz, David, and David Marsh. 1996. "Who Learns What from Whom: A Review of the Policy Transfer Literature." *Political Studies* 44 (2): 343–57.

Dolowitz, David P., and David Marsh. 2000. "Learning from Abroad: The Role of Policy Transfer in Contemporary Policy-Making." *Governance* 13 (1): 5–23.

Downs, Anthony. 1957. *An Economic Theory of Democracy*. New York: Harper.

Drury, A. C., J. Krieckhaus, and C. Yamamoto. 2014. "How Democracy Facilitates South Korean Interest in Free Trade Agreements." *Korea Observer* 45 (1): 39–60.

Economist, The. 2007. "The Great Unbundling: Does Economics Need a New Theory of Offshoring?" Vol. 382 (8512): 86.

European Union. 2011. *The EU-Korea Free Trade Agreement in Practice*. Luxembourg: Publications Office of the European Union.

Evans, Mark. 2009. "New Directions in the Study of Policy Transfer." *Policy Studies* 30 (3): 237–41.

Evans, Peter. 1979. *Dependent Development: The Alliance of Multinational, State, and Local Capital in Brazil*. Princeton: Princeton University Press.

Evans, Peter. 1995. *Embedded Autonomy: States and Industrial Transformation*. Princeton: Princeton University Press.

Evans, Peter B., Dietrich Rueschemeyer, and Theda Skocpol, eds. 1985. *Bringing the State Back In*. Cambridge: Cambridge University Press.

Evenett, Simon. 2003. "Study on Issues Relating to a Possible Multilateral Framework on Competition Policy." *Working Group on the Interaction between Trade and Competition Policy.*WT/WGTCP/W/152, Geneva: *World Trade Organization.*

Feng, Yi. 2001. "Political Freedom, Political Instability, and Policy Uncertainty: A Study of Political Institutions and Private Investment in Developing Countries." *International Studies Quarterly* 45 (2): 271–94.

Francis, Joseph, Hanna Norberg, and Martin Thelle. 2007. *Economic Impact of a Potential Free Trade Agreement (FTA) between the European Union and South Korea.* Institute for International and Development Economics.

Frankel, Jeffrey A. 1997. *Regional Trading Blocs in the World Economic System*: Washington, DC: Institute for International Economics.

Frankel, Jeffrey A., Ernesto Stein, and Shang-Jin Wei. 1997. "The Gravity Model of Bilateral Trade." In *Regional Trading Blocs in the World Economic System*, 49–76. Washington, DC: Institute for International Economics.

Frieden, Jeff. 1981. "Third World Indebted Industrialization: International Finance and State Capitalism in Mexico, Brazil, Algeria, and South Korea." *International Organization* 35 (3): 407–31.

Fukagawa, Yukiko. 2005. "East Asia's New Economic Integration Strategy: Moving Beyond the FTA." *Asia-Pacific Review* 12 (2): 10–29.

Fukuyama, Francis. 1989. "The End of History?" *National Interest* 16:3-18.

Fukuyama, Francis. 2012. "The End of History and the Last Man." London: Penguin.

Gaddis, John Lewis. 2011. *George F. Kennan: An American Life*. New York: Penguin.

Gerring, John. 2004. "What Is a Case Study and What Is It Good For?" *American Political Science Review* 98 (2): 341–54.

Gibbs, David. 1996. "Review of *Economic Development and Industrial Policy: Korea, Brazil, Mexico, India and China* by R. M. Auty." *Transactions of the Institute of British Geographers, New Series* 21 (1): 304–5.

Gilpin, Robert. 1987. *The Political Economy of International Relations*. Princeton: Princeton University Press.

Gilpin, Robert. 2011. *Global Political Economy: Understanding the International Economic Order*: Princeton University Press.

Gökmen, Semra Ranâ. 2010. "Geopolitics and the Study of International Relations." PhD diss., Middle East Technical University.

Goldstein, Judith. 1988. "Ideas, Institutions, and American Trade Policy." *International Organization* 42 (1): 179–217.

Gourevitch, Peter. 1986. *Politics in Hard Times: Comparative Responses to International Economic Crises*. Ithica: Cornell University Press.

Gowa, Joanne. 1995. *Allies, Adversaries, and International Trade*: Princeton University Press.

Gowa, Joanne, and Edward D Mansfield. 1993. "Power Politics and International Trade." *American Political Science Review* 87 (02): 408–20.

Groth, Alexander J. 2006. "Regimes and Economic Development: China, India and Some Others." *Journal of East Asian Affairs* 20 (01): 181–202.

Ha, Yong-Chool, and Wang Hwi Lee. 2007. "The Politics of Economic Reform in South Korea: Crony Capitalism after Ten Years." *Asian Survey* 47 (6): 894–914.

Haggard, Stephan. 1990. "The Political Economy of the Philippine Debt Crisis." In

Economic Crisis and Policy Choice: The Politics of Adjustment in the Third World, edited by Joan Nelson, 215–55. Princeton, NJ: Princeton University Press.

Haggard, Stephan, and Jongryn Mo. 2000. "The Political Economy of the Korean Financial Crisis." *Review of International Political Economy* 7 (2): 197–218.

Haggard, Stephan, and Robert R. Kaufman. 1992. *The Politics of Economic Adjustment: International Constraints, Distributive Conflicts, and the State*: Princeton, NJ: Princeton University Press.

Haggard, Stephan, Daniel Pinkston, and Jungkun Seo. 1999. "Reforming Korea Inc.: The Politics of Structural Adjustment under Kim Dae Jung." *Asian Perspective* 23 (3): 201–35.

Han, C. Min. 2002. "Korea's Direct Investments in China: Technology, Experience, and Ownership Factors in Performance." *Asia Pacific Journal of Management* 19 (1): 109–26.

Hart-Landsberg, Martin. 2011. "Capitalism, the Korea-US Free Trade Agreement, and Resistance." *Critical Asian Studies* 43 (3): 319–48.

Henisz, Witold Jerzy. 2000. "The Institutional Environment for Economic Growth." *Economics and Politics* 12 (1): 1–31.

Higgott, Richard. 2004. "After Neoliberal Globalization: The 'Securitization' of US Foreign Economic Policy in East Asia." *Critical Asian Studies* 36 (3): 425–44.

Hill, Hal. 2012. "Comment on 'Chaebol and Industrial Policy in Korea.'" *Asian Economic Policy Review* 7 (1): 89–90.

Hirschman, Albert O. 1958. *The Strategy of Economic Development*. New Haven: Yale University Press.

Hirschman, Albert O. 1980. *National Power and the Structure of Foreign Trade*. Vol. 105: University of California Press.

Ho, Catherine S. F. 2011. "Domestic Macroeconomic Fundamentals and World Stock Market Effects on ASEAN Emerging Markets." *International Journal of Economics and Management* 5 (1): 1–18.

Hoadley, S., and J. Yang. 2007. "China's Cross-Regional FTA Initiatives: Towards Comprehensive National Power." *Pacific Affairs* 80 (2): 327–48.

Hoekman, Bernard. 2014. "Sustaining Multilateral Trade Cooperation in a Multipolar World Economy." *The Review of International Organizations* 9 (2): 241–60.

Holcombe, Randall G. 2013. "South Korea's Economic Future: Industrial Policy or Economic Democracy?" *Journal of Economic Behavior and Organization* 88: 3–13.

Horng, Der-Chin. 2012. "Reshaping the EU's FTA Policy in a Globalizing Economy: The Case of the EU-Korea FTA." *Journal of World Trade* 46 (2): 301–26.

Huang, Yasheng. 2002. "Between Two Coordination Failures: Automotive Industrial Policy in China with a Comparison to Korea." *Review of International Political Economy* 9 (3): 538–73.

Hundt, David. 2008. *Korea's Developmental Alliance: State, Capital and the Politics of Rapid Development*: New York: Routledge.

Huntington, Samuel P. 1999. "The Lonely Superpower." *Foreign Affairs* 78 (2): 35–49.

Hwang, Ki-Sik. 2010. "Korea, China, and Japan's FTA Policy towards ASEAN: With Special Focus on Agricultural Sectors." *Journal of East Asian Affairs* 39–81.

Hyun, Jung Taik. 2003. "Free Trade Agreements and Korea's Trade Policy." *Journal of International and Area Studies* 10 (2): 21–37.

Hyun-Chin, Lim, and Jang Jin-Ho. 2006. "Between Neoliberalism and Democracy: The Transformation of the Developmental State in South Korea." *Development and Society* 35 (1): 1–28.

Im, K. 2015. "Korean Exchange Rate and FTAs under the Roh Moo-hyun Administration." *International Relations of the Asia-Pacific* 15 (2): 367–96. doi: 10.1093/irap/lcu022.

Im, Tobin. 2013. "Bureaucracy in Three Different Worlds: The Assumptions of Failed Public Sector Reforms in Korea." *Public Organization Review* 14 (4): 577–96.

Jaung, Hoon. 2005. "Foreign Policy and South Korean Democracy: The Failure of Party Politics." *Taiwan Journal of Democracy* 1 (2): 49–68.

Jayasuriya, Kanishka. 2001. "Globalization and the Changing Architecture of the State: The Regulatory State and the Politics of Negative Co-ordination." *Journal of European Public Policy* 8 (1): 101–23.

Jeon, Bang Nam, and Sung Sup Rhee. 2008. "The Determinants of Korea's Foreign Direct Investment from the United States, 1980–2001: An Empirical Investigation of Firm-Level Data." *Contemporary Economic Policy* 26 (1): 118–31.

Jeong, Hyung-Gon. 2012. "South Korea: Which Way Will It Go on Asian Integration?" In *Joint US-Korea Academic Studies*, edited by Gilbert Rozman, 207–26. Washington, DC: Korea Economic Institute.

Jeon, Jei Guk. 1994. "The Political Economy of Crisis Management in the Third World: A Comparative Study of South Korea and Taiwan (1970s)." *Pacific Affairs* 67 (4): 565–85. doi: 10.2307/2759574.

Jiang, Y. 2008. "Australia-China FTA: China's Domestic Politics and the Roots of Different National Approaches to FTAs." *Australian Journal of International Affairs* 62 (2): 179–95. doi: 10.1080/10357710802060543.

Jiang, Y. 2010. "China's Pursuit of Free Trade Agreements: Is China Exceptional?" *Review of International Political Economy* 17 (2): 238–61. doi: 10.1080/09692290903337799.

Jianping, Zhang. 2006. *"Analysis on the Issues of and Prospects for a China-Korea FTA."* *Center for Northeast Asia Economic Cooperation Research Series* 06–04. Seoul: Korea Institute for International Economic Policy.

Johnson, Chalmers. 1982. *MITI and the Japanese Miracle: The Growth of Industrial Policy: 1925–1975.* Stanford, CA: Stanford University Press.

Jones, Leroy P., and Il Sakong. 1980. *Government, Business, and Entrepreneurship in Economic Development: The Korean Case.* Cambridge, MA: Harvard University Press.

Jordaan, Eduard. 2003. "The Concept of a Middle Power in International Relations: Distinguishing between Emerging and Traditional Middle Powers." *Politikon* 30 (1): 165–81.

Jung, Chang Lyul, and Alan Walker. 2009. "The Impact of Neo-liberalism on South Korea's Public Pension: A Political Economy of Pension Reform." *Social Policy and Administration* 43 (5): 425–44.

Kalinowski, Thomas. 2009. "The Politics of Market Reforms: Korea's Path from Chaebol Republic to Market Democracy and Back." *Contemporary Politics* 15 (3): 287–304.

Kalinowski, Thomas, and Hyekyung Cho. 2012. "Korea's Search for a Global Role between Hard Economic Interests and Soft Power." *European Journal of Development Research* 24 (2): 242–60.

Kang, David C. 1995. "South Korean and Taiwanese Development and the New Institutional Economics." *International Organization* 49 (3): 555–87.

Kang, David C. 2002. "Bad Loans to Good Friends: Money Politics and the Developmental State in South Korea." *International Organization* 56 (1): 177–207.

Kang, Kichun. 2012. "Is the Relationship between Foreign Direct Investment and Trade Different across Developed and Developing Countries? Evidence from Korea." *Asian-Pacific Economic Literature* 26 (2): 144–54.

Kaplinsky, Raphael, and Mike Morris. 2009. "Chinese FDI in Sub-Saharan Africa: Engaging with Large Dragons." *European Journal of Development Research* 21 (4): 551–69.

Kassimatis, Konstantinos. 2002. "Financial Liberalization and Stock Market Volatility in Selected Developing Countries." *Applied Financial Economics* 12 (6): 389–94.

Katzman, Kenneth. 2016a. "Bahrain: Reform, Security, and U.S. Policy." *CRS Report.* Washington, DC: Congressional Research Service.

Katzman, Kenneth. 2016b. *Oman: Reform, Security, and U.S. Policy.* Congressional Research Service. https://fas.org/sgp/crs/mideast/RS21534.pdf.

Kawai, Masahiro. 2005. "East Asian Economic Regionalism: Progress and Challenges." *Journal of Asian Economics* 16 (1): 29–55.

Kawai, Masahiro, and Ganeshan Wignaraja. 2011. "Asian FTAs: Trends, Prospects and Challenges." *Journal of Asian Economics* 22 (1): 1–22.

Kelsey, Jane. 2008. *Serving Whose Interests? The Political Economy of Trade in Services Agreements.* New York: Routledge-Cavendish.

Kennan, George F. 1947. "The Sources of Soviet Conduct." *Foreign Affairs* 25 (4): 566–82.

Kepaptsoglou, Konstantinos, Matthew G. Karlaftis, and Dimitrios Tsamboulas. 2010. "The Gravity Model Specification for Modeling International Trade Flows and Free Trade Agreement Effects: A 10-Year Review of Empirical Studies." *Open Economics Journal* 3: 1–13.

KIEP. 2014. "A Study on the Decade of Korea's FTAs: Evaluation and Policy Implications" (Korean), Research Report 14-15. KIEP.

Kim, Chi-Wook. 2011. "Toward a multistakeholder model of foreign policy making in Korea? Big business and Korea-US relations." *Asian Perspective* 35 (3): 471–95.

Kim, Chuk. 2005. "An Industrial Development Strategy for Indonesia: Lessons from the South Korean Experience." *Journal of the Asia Pacific Economy* 10 (3): 312–38.

Kim, Eun Mee, and Jai S Mah. 2006. "Patterns of South Korea's Foreign Direct Investment Flows into China." *Asian Survey* 46 (6): 881–97.

Kim, Gyu Pan, Hyong Kun Lee, and Eun Ji Kim. 2015. "Japan's FTA Strategy and Its Implications for Korea." *KIEP World Economy Update* 5 (6).

Kim, Jong Duk, Seungrae Lee, Jun-Gu Kang, and Hyuk Kim Kim. 2014. "The Effects of Trade and Investment Liberalization on Korea's FDI." *KIEP World Economy Update* 4 (36).

Kim, Min-Hyung. 2016. "South Korea's Strategy toward a Rising China, Security Dynamics in East Asia, and International Relations Theory." *Asian Survey* 56 (4): 707–30. doi: 10.1525/AS.2016.56.4.707.

Kim, Seokwoo. 2008. "Theories and Realities of FTA Formation between Korea and Canada." *Korean Social Science Journal* 35 (4): 55–78.

Kim, Sung-Young. 2012. "Transitioning from Fast-Follower to Innovator: The Institutional Foundations of the Korean Telecommunications Sector." *Review of International Political Economy* 19 (1): 140–68.

Kim, Taeho. 2002. "South Korea and a Rising China: Perceptions, Policies and Prospects " In *The China Threat: Perceptions, Myths and Reality*, edited by Herbert Yee and Ian Storey, 166–80. New York: Routledge.

Kim, Wan-Soon, and You-Il Lee. 2007. "Challenges of Korea's Foreign Direct Investment-Led Globalization: Multinational Corporations' Perceptions." *Asia Pacific Business Review* 13 (2): 163–81.

Kim, Young Gui. 2015. "Evaluation of a Decade of Korea's FTA Policy." *KIEP World Economy Update* 5 (22).

Kim, Young Gui, Jun Hyun Eom, Kim Hyuk-Hwang, and Do Hee Kim. 2015. "Korea--U.S. FTA in Its Third Year: Current Status of Implementation and Issues." *KIEP World Economy Update* 5 (18).

Kim, Young Gui, Keum, Hyeyoon, Yoo, Saebyul, Kim, Yang-Hee, and Kim, Han Sung. 2014. "A Study on the Decade of Korea's FTAs: Evaluation and Policy Implications." KIEP Research Report 14-05. Sejong-Si, Korea: Korea Institute for International Economic Policy.

Kim, Yun Tae. 2005. "DJnomics and the Transformation of the Developmental State." *Journal of Contemporary Asia* 35 (4): 471–84.

Kindleberger, Charles P. 1973. *The World in Depression, 1929–39*. Oakland: University of California Press.

King, Gary, Robert O. Keohane, and Sidney Verba. 1994. *Designing Social Inquiry: Scientific Inference in Qualitative Research*. Princeton: Princeton University Press.

Kiyota, Kōzō, and Robert Mitchell Stern. 2007. *Economic Effects of a Korea-US Free Trade Agreement*. Washington, DC: Korea Economic Institute of America.

Kohli, Atul. 2004. *State-Directed Development: Political Power and Industrialization in the Global Periphery*. New York: Cambridge University Press.

Koo, Min Gyo. 2006. "From Multilateralism to Bilateralism? A Shift in South Korea's Trade Strategy." In *Bilateral Trade Arrangements in the Asia-Pacific: Origins, Evolution, and Implications*, edited by Vinod K. Aggarwal and Shujiro Urata, 140–59. New York: Routledge.

Koo, Min Gyo. 2008. "South Korea's FTAs: Moving from an Emulative to a Competitive Strategy." *GIARI (Global Institute for Asian Regional Integration) Working Paper* 2008-E-13. Paper presented at the *International Symposium Competitive Regionalism*, Ibuka International Conference Hall, Waseda University, Tokyo, Japan, May 30–31, 2008.

Koo, Min Gyo. 2010. "Embracing Free Trade Agreements, Korean Style: From Developmental Mercantilism to Developmental Liberalism." *Korean Journal of Policy Studies* 25 (3): 101–23.

Koo, Min Gyo, and Whasun Jho. 2013. "Linking Domestic Decision-Making and International Bargaining Results: Beef and Automobile Negotiations between South Korea and the United States." *International Relations of the Asia-Pacific* 13 (1): 65–93.

Kotbee, Shin, and Bo-Young Choi. 2016. "The Impact of Chinese Economic Structural Changes on Korea's Export to China." *KIEP Research Paper No. Working Papers 16-04*. https://papers.ssrn.com/sol3/papers.cfm?abstract_id=2830291.

Krasner, Stephen D. 1978. *Defending the National Interest: Raw Materials Investments and US Foreign Policy*. Princeton, NJ: Princeton University Press.

Krieckhaus, J. 2006. "Democracy and economic growth: How regional context influences regime effects." *British Journal of Political Science* 36 (2): 317–40. doi: 10.1017/S0007123406000172.

Krueger, Anne O. 1979. *The Developmental Role of the Foreign Sector and Aid*. Cambridge, MA: Harvard University Press.

Krueger, Anne O. 1990. "Government Failures in Development." *Journal of Economic Perspectives* 4 (3): 9–23.

Krueger, Anne O. 1997. "Free Trade Agreements versus Customs Unions." *Journal of Development Economics* 54 (1): 169–87.

Krugman, P. 1998. "What's New about the New Economic Geography?" *Oxford Review of Economic Policy* 14 (2): 7–17. doi: 10.1093/oxrep/14.2.7.

Krugman, Paul R. 1993. "Regionalism versus Multilateralism: Analytical Notes." In *New Dimensions in Regional Integration*, edited by Jaime De Melo and Arvind Panagariya, 58–79. New York: Cambridge University Press.

Kwon, Chung S., and Tai S. Shin. 1999. "Cointegration and Causality between Macroeconomic Variables and Stock Market Returns." *Global Finance Journal* 10 (1): 71–81.

Kwon, Hyeok Yong. 2010. "Economic Perceptions and Electoral Choice in South Korea: The Case of the 2007 Presidential Election." *Pacific Review* 23 (2): 183–201.

Kwon, O. Yul. 2010. "Impacts of the Korean Political System on Its Economic Development: With a Focus on the Lee Myung-bak Government." *Korea Observer* 41 (2): 189–220.

Kyung-Sup, Chang. 2007. "The End of Developmental Citizenship? Restructuring and Social Displacement in Post-Crisis South Korea." *Economic and Political Weekly* 42 (50): 67–72.

Lee, Chang Kil, and David Strang. 2006. "The International Diffusion of Public-Sector Downsizing: Network Emulation and Theory-Driven Learning." *International Organization* 60 (4): 883–909.

Lee, Chung H. 1994. "Korea's Direct Foreign Investment in Southeast Asia." *ASEAN Economic Bulletin* 10 (03): 80–96.

Lee, Chung H., and Keun Lee. 1992. "Sustaining Economic Development in South Korea: Lessons from Japan." *Pacific Review* 5 (1): 13–24.

Lee, Hong-Bae, and Satoru Okuda. 2004. "Possibility of Realizing a Japan-Korea FTA." *Journal of East Asian Affairs* 131–56.

Lee, Hongshik, and Backhoon Song. 2008. "Quantitative Estimates of the Economic Impacts of a Korea–United States Free Trade Agreement." *Asian Economic Papers* 7 (2): 52–73.

Lee, Hyun-Chool. 2010. "Ratification of a Free Trade Agreement: The Korean Legislature's Response to Globalisation." *Journal of Contemporary Asia* 40 (2): 291–308.

Lee, Jaymin. 2011. "The Performance of Industrial Policy: Evidence from Korea." *International Economic Journal* 25 (1): 1–27.

Lee, Jeong Yeon. 2007. "Foreign Portfolio Investors and Financial Sector Stability in Asia." *Asian Survey* 47 (6): 850–71.

Lee, Jongseok, Iain Clacher, and Kevin Keasey. 2012. "Industrial Policy as an Engine of Economic Growth: A Framework of Analysis and Evidence from South Korea (1960–96)." *Business History* 54 (5): 713–40.

Lee, Jong-Wha. 2008. How to Design, Negotiate, and Implement a Free Trade Agreement in Asia: Office of Regional Economic Integration. Asian Development Bank. https://www.adb.org/sites/default/files/publication/27974/fta.pdf

Lee, Jong-Wha, and Innwon Park. 2005. "Free Trade Areas in East Asia: Discriminatory or Non-discriminatory?" *World Economy* 28 (1): 21–48.

Lee, Junkyu, and Hongshik Lee. 2005. *Feasibility and Economic Effects of a Korea-U.S. FTA. NRCS Joint Research Series on FTA Issues, 05–05–02.* Seoul: Korea Institute for International Economic Policy.

Lee, Seung-Myung. 2008. "Effects of the Korea-US Free Trade Agreement on the Korean Financial Market and the Financial Hub Initiative." *Journal of East Asian Affairs* 22 (1): 57–77.

Lee, Seyoung, and Hyun Soon Park. 2013. "Effects of Message Framing and Anchoring on Reaching Public Consensus on the Korea-U.S. FTA Issue." *Communication Research* 40 (2): 176–92.

Lee, Sook-Jong, and Taejoon Han. 2006. "The Demise of 'Korea, Inc.': Paradigm Shift in Korea's Developmental State." *Journal of Contemporary Asia* 36 (3): 305–24.

Lee, Yeon-ho. 2000. "The Failure of the Weak State in Economic Liberalization: Liberalization, Democratization and the Financial Crisis in South Korea." *Pacific Review* 13 (1): 115–31.

Lee, Yong-Shik. 2016. "The Long and Winding Road–Path Towards Facilitation of Development in the WTO: Reflections on the Doha Round and Beyond." *Law and Development Review* 9 (2): 437–65.

Lee, You-il, and Wan-soon Kim. 2010. "South Korea's Meandering Path to Globalisation in the Late Twentieth Century." *Asian Studies Review* 34 (3): 309–27.

Levi, Margaret. 2002. "Modeling Complex Historical Processes with Analytic Narratives." In *Akteure, Mechanismen, Modelle. Zur Theoriefähigkeit makro-sozialer Analysen*, edited by Renate Mayntz, 108–27. New York: Campus.

Levi, Margaret. 2004. "An Analytic Narrative Approach to Puzzles and Problems." In *Problems and Methods in the Study of Politics*, edited by Ian Shapiro, Rogers M. Smith, and Tarek E. Masoud, 201–26. New York: Cambridge University Press.

Li, Linyue. 2012. "A Comparative Analysis of Korea's Free Trade Agreements by CGE Models: New Challenges under Globalization." Paper presented at the *AKES Conference on Korea and the World Economy, XI*, July 13–14, Seoul Women's University, Seoul, Korea.

Lieberman, Evan S. 2005. "Nested Analysis as a Mixed-Method Strategy for Comparative Research." *American Political Science Review* 99 (3): 435–52. doi: 10.1017/S0003055405051762.

Lim, Haeran. 1998. "Politics of Industrial Transformation in Korea: Coalition and Industrial Policy." *Pacific Focus* 13 (2): 41–60.

Lim, Haeran. 2010. "The Transformation of the Developmental State and Economic Reform in Korea." *Journal of Contemporary Asia* 40 (2): 188–210.

Lim, Hyun-Chin, and Jin-Ho Jang. 2006. "Neo-liberalism in Post-Crisis South Korea: Social Conditions and Outcomes." *Journal of Contemporary Asia* 36 (4): 442–63.

Lim, Wonhyuk. 2012. "Chaebol and Industrial Policy in Korea." *Asian Economic Policy Review* 7 (1): 69–86.

Lim, Wonhyuk, and Joon-Ho Hahm. 2006. "Turning Crisis into Opportunity: The Political Economy of Korea's Financial Sector Reform." In *From Crisis to Opportunity: Financial Globalization and East Asian Capitalism*, edited by Jongryn Mo and Daniel I. Okimoto, 85–121. Stanford: Shorenstein Asia-Pacific Research Center.

Lindblom, Charles E. 1977. *Politics and Markets: The World's Political-Economic Systems*. New York: Basic Books.

Liu, Ling-Fang. 2007. "An Empirical Study of the Presidential Elections Effect on Stock Market in Taiwan, South Korea, Singapore, Philippine, and Indonesia." PhD diss., University of Nottingham.

Liu, Xuepeng. 2008. "The Political Economy of Free Trade Agreements: An Empirical Investigation." *Journal of Economic Integration* 23 (2): 237–71.

Low, Linda. 2001. "The Singapore Developmental State in the New Economy and Polity." *Pacific Review* 14 (3): 411–41.

Lukauskas, Arvid, and Susan Minushkin. 2000. "Explaining Styles of Financial Market Opening in Chile, Mexico, South Korea, and Turkey." *International Studies Quarterly* 44 (4): 695–723.

Mackinder, Halford John. 1919. *Democratic Ideals and Reality: A Study in the Politics of Reconstruction*. Vol. 46399: London: Constable and Company.

Maddison, Angus, and Associates. 1992. *The Political Economy of Poverty, Equity, and Growth: Brazil and Mexico*. Oxford: Oxford University Press.

Mah, Jai S. 2007. "Industrial Policy and Economic Development: Korea's Experience." *Journal of Economic Issues* 41 (1): 77–92.

Mansfield, Edward D., and Helen V. Milner. 2015. "The Political Economy of Preferential Trade Agreements." In *Trade Cooperation: The Purpose, Design and Effects of Preferential Trade Agreements*, edited by Andreas Dür and Manfred Elsig, 56–81. Cambridge: Cambridge University Press.

Mansfield, E. D., and H. V. Milner. 2012. *Votes, Vetoes, and the Political Economy of International Trade Agreements, Votes, Vetoes, and the Political Economy of International Trade Agreements*. Princeton: Princeton University Press.

Mansfield, Edward D. 1993. "Effects of international politics on regionalism in international trade." In *Regional Integration and the Global Trading System*, edited by Kym Anderson and Richard Blackhurst, 199–217. New York: Harvester Wheatsheaf.

Mansfield, Edward D., Jon C. Pevehouse, and David H. Bearce. 1999. "Preferential Trading Arrangements and Military Disputes." *Security Studies* 9 (1–2): 92–118.

Mansfield, Edward D., and Eric Reinhardt. 2003. "Multilateral Determinants of Regionalism: The Effects of GATT/WTO on the Formation of Preferential Trading Arrangements." *International Organization* 57 (04): 829–62.

Mansfield, Edward D., Helen V. Milner, and B. Peter Rosendorff. 2002. "Why Democracies Cooperate More: Electoral Control and International Trade Agreements." *International Organization* 56 (3): 477–513.

Manyin, Mark E. 2004. "South Korea-U.S. Economic Relations: Cooperation,

Friction, and Future Prospects." *CRS Report.* Washington, DC: Congressional Research Service.

Mardon, Russell. 1990. "The State and the Effective Control of Foreign Capital: The Case of South Korea." *World Politics* 43 (1): 111–38.

Marsh, David, and J. C. Sharman. 2009. "Policy Diffusion and Policy Transfer." *Policy Studies* 30 (3): 269–88.

Marshall, Monty, and Keith Jaggers. 2001. Polity IV Project: Political Regime Characteristics and Transitions, 1800–1999. http://www.systemicpeace.org/polity/polity4x.htm

Martin, Antoine, Antoine Martin, Bryan Mercurio, and Bryan Mercurio. 2017. "Doha Dead and Buried in Nairobi: Lessons for the WTO." *Journal of International Trade Law and Policy* 16 (1): 49–66.

Masih, Rumi, Sanjay Peters, and Lurion De Mello. 2011. "Oil Price Volatility and Stock Price Fluctuations in an Emerging Market: Evidence from South Korea." *Energy Economics* 33 (5): 975–86.

McKibbin, Warwick J., Jong-Wha Lee, and Inkyo Cheong. 2004. "A Dynamic Analysis of the Korea-Japan Free Trade Area: Simulations with the G-Cubed Asia–Pacific Model." *International Economic Journal* 18 (1): 3–32.

Mead, Walter Russell. 2014. "The Return of Geopolitics: The Revenge of the Revisionist Powers." *Foreign Affairs* 93: 69–79.

Milner, Helen V., and Keiko Kubota. 2005. "Why the Move to Free Trade? Democracy and Trade Policy in the Developing Countries." *International Organization* 59 (1): 107–43.

Mo, Jongryn, and Chung-in Moon. 2003. "Business-Government Relations under Kim Dae-jung." In *Economic Crisis and Corporate Restructuring in Korea: Reforming the Chaebol,* edited by Stephan Haggard, Wonhyuk Lim, and Euysung Kim, 127–49. New York: Cambridge University Press.

Mölders, Florian. 2012. "On the Path to Trade Liberalization: Political Regimes in International Trade Negotiations." No. 1245. DIW Berlin, German Institute for Economic Research.

Mölders, Florian, and Ulrich Volz. 2011. "Trade Creation and the Status of FTAs: Empirical Evidence from East Asia." *Review of World Economics* 147 (3): 429–56.

Moon, Chung-In. 1999. "Political Economy of East Asian Development and Pacific Economic Cooperation." *Pacific Review* 12 (2): 199–224.

Moon, Chung-In, and Sang-Young Rhyu. 2010. "Rethinking Alliance and the Economy: American Hegemony, Path Dependence, and the South Korean Political Economy." *International Relations of the Asia-Pacific* 10 (3): 441–64.

Moon, Woo-Sik, and Young-Seop Rhee. 2003. "Foreign Exchange Market Liberalization Policies in Korea: Past Assessment and Future Options." In *Globalization and the Asia Pacific Economy,* edited by Kyung Tae Lee, 102–19. New York: Routledge.

Nakagawa, Junji, and Wei Liang. 2011. "A Comparison of the FTA Strategies of Japan and China and Their Implications for Multilateralism." *Working Paper* 11, Bloomington: Indiana University Research Center for Chinese Politics & Business.

Newmark, Adam J. 2002. "An Integrated Approach to Policy Transfer and Diffusion." *Review of Policy Research* 19 (2): 151–78.

Nicolas, Françoise. 2009. "Negotiating a Korea-EU Free Trade Agreement: Easier Said Than Done." *Asia Europe Journal* 7 (1): 23–42.

Noble, Gregory W., and John Ravenhill. 2000. "The Good, the Bad and the Ugly? Korea, Taiwan and the Asian Financial Crisis." In *The Asian Financial Crisis and the Architecture of Global Finance*, edited by Gregory W. Noble and John Ravenhill, 80–107. New York: Cambridge University Press.

Noland, Marcus. 2007. "South Korea's Experience with International Capital Fows." In *Capital Controls and Capital Flows in Emerging Economies: Policies, Practices and Consequences*, 481–528. Chicago: University of Chicago Press.

North, Douglass C. 1990a. *Institutions, Institutional Change and Economic Performance*. New York: Cambridge University Press.

North, Douglass C. 1990b. "A Transaction Cost Theory of Politics." *Journal of Theoretical Politics* 2 (4): 355–67.

Oberdorfer, Don, and Robert Carlin. 2014. *The Two Koreas : A Contemporary History*. New York: Basic Books.

OECD (Organization for Economic Cooperation and Development). 2012. *Industrial Policy and Territorial Development: Lessons from Korea*. Paris: OECD Publishing.

OECD (Organization for Economic Cooperation and Development). 2014. *Industry and Technology Policies in Korea*. Paris: OECD Publishing.

Okazaki, Tetsuji. 2012. "Comment on 'Chaebol and Industrial Policy in Korea.'" *Asian Economic Policy Review* 7 (1): 87–88.

Olson, Mancur. 1965. *Logic of Collective Action: Public Goods and the Theory of Groups* Harvard Economic Studies vol. 124. Cambridge: Harvard University Press.

Pack, Howard, and Kamal Saggi. 2006. *The Case for Industrial Policy: A Critical Survey.* World Bank Policy Research Working Paper 3839. Washington, D.C. :World Bank Publications.

Park, Beomseob. 2008. "Beyond Economic Gains: True Leverage of Inter-Regional Free Trade Agreements in East Asia." Department of Government, London School of Economics and Political Science.

Park, Donghyun, and Insoo Kang. 2000. "Foreign Direct Investment in Korea: Recent Developments and Prospects." *Asian Affairs: An American Review* 27 (1): 3–16.

Park, Jinsoo. 2015. "Korea's Linkage Strategy between FTA Hub Policy and Middle Power Leadership in Regional Economic Integration." *Asia Europe Journal* 13 (4): 379–94. doi: 10.1007/s10308–015–0412–3.

Park, Mi. 2009. "Framing Free Trade Agreements: The Politics of Nationalism in the Anti-Neoliberal Globalization Movement in South Korea." *Globalizations* 6 (4): 451–66.

Park, Sung-Hoon, and Min Gyo Koo. 2007. "Forming a Cross-Regional Partnership: The South Korea-Chile FTA and Its Implications." *Pacific Affairs* 80 (2): 259–78.

Park, Sung-Hoon, and Sung-Won Yoon. 2010. "EU Perceptions through the FTA Lens: Main Results of Interviews among the Korean 'Elites.'" *Asia Europe Journal* 8 (2): 177–91.

Petri, Peter A. 2013. "The New Landscape of Trade Policy and Korea's Choices." *Journal of East Asian Economic Integration* 17 (4): 333–59.

Pfaff, William. 2001. "The Question of Hegemony." *Foreign Affairs* 80 (1): 221–32.

Pirie, Iain. 2005. "Better by Design: Korea's Neoliberal Economy." *Pacific Review* 18 (3): 355–74.

Pirie, Iain. 2007. *The Korean Developmental State: From Dirigisme to Neo-liberalism.* New York: Routledge.

Pirie, Iain. 2012. "The New Korean Political Economy: Beyond the Models of Capitalism Debate." *Pacific Review* 25 (3): 365–86.

Pitschas, Christian. 2016. "Transatlantic Trade and Investment Partnership (TTIP): The Devil in Disguise or a Golden Opportunity to Build a Transatlantic Marketplace?" *British Journal of American Legal Studies* 5 (2): 315–40.

Plummer, Michael G., David Cheong, and Shintaro Hamanaka. 2011. *Methodology for Impact Assessment of Free Trade Agreements.* Asian Development Bank.

Polo, C., and R. Viejo. 2015. "On the Accuracy of Cge Forecasts in Expansion and Recession: Spain 1990–1997." *Economic Systems Research* 27 (4): 525–42. doi: 10.1080/09535314.2015.1102126.

Pomfret, Richard. 1988. *Unequal Trade: The Economics of Discriminatory International Trade Policies.* Oxford: Basil Blackwell.

Putnam, Robert D. 1988. "Diplomacy and Domestic Politics: The Logic of Two-Level Games." *International Organization* 42 (3): 427–60.

Pye, Lucian W. 1997. "Money Politics and Transitions to Democracy in East Asia." *Asian Survey* 37 (3): 213–28.

Randerson, Claire, and Christopher M. Dent. 1996. "Korean and Japanese Foreign Direct Investment in Europe: An Examination of Comparable and Contrasting Patterns." *Asian Studies Review* 20 (2): 45–69.

Reich, Simon. 2000. "Miraculous or Mired? Contrasting Japanese and American Perspectives on Japan's Economic Problems." *Pacific Review* 13 (1): 163–93.

Rhodes, Martin, and Richard Higgott. 2000. "Introduction: Asian Crises and the Myth of Capitalist 'Convergence.'" *Pacific Review* 13 (1): 1–19.

Ricardo, David. 1891. *The Principles of Political Economy and Taxation.* London: George Bell and Sons.

Robertson, Jeffrey. 2012. "South Korean FTA Negotiations: Patterns of Negotiation Outside a South Korean Cultural Context?" *Asian Survey* 52 (3): 465–83.

Robertson, Justin Lee. 2012. "New Capitalist Processes, Interdependence and the Asia-US Private Equity Relationship." *Pacific Review* 25 (5): 637–59.

Rodriguez, Francisco, and Dani Rodrik. 2001. "Trade Policy and Economic Growth: A Skeptic's Guide to the Cross-National Evidence." In *NBER Macroeconomics Annual 2000*, edited by Ben Bernanke and Kenneth Rogoff, 261–338. Cambridge and London: MIT Press.

Rodrik, Dani. 2004. "Industrial Policy for the Twenty-First Century." Cambridge: Harvard University.

Rosenbaum, Chika Yamamoto, and Jonathan Krieckhaus. 2016. "What Explains South Korean Interest in FTA Partners?" *Asian Survey* 56 (5): 982–1004.

Rosnick, David, and Dean Baker. 2016. "Trade and Jobs: Can We Trust the Models?" Washington DC: Center for Economic and Policy Research.

Ross, Robert S. 2006. "Balance of Power Politics and the Rise of China: Accommodation and Balancing in East Asia." *Security Studies* 15 (3): 355–95.

Rozman, Gilbert. 2007. "South Korea and Sino-Japanese Rivalry: A Middle Power's Options within the East Asian Core Triangle." *Pacific Review* 20 (2): 197–220.

Russett, Bruce. 1994. *Grasping the Democratic Peace: Principles for a Post-Cold War World*. Princeton: Princeton University Press.

Sachs, Jeffrey D. 2003. "Institutions Don't Rule: Direct Effects of Geography on Per Capita Income." Working Paper No. 9490. National Bureau of Economic Research. doi: 10.3386/w9490.

Sally, Razeen. 2011. "Chinese Trade Policy after (Almost) Ten Years in the WTO: A Post-Crisis Stocktake." *ECIPE Occasional Paper* 2. Brussels: European Centre for International Political Economy.

Sartori, Giovanni. 1970. "Concept Misformation in Comparative Politics." *American Political Science Review* 64 (4): 1033–53.

Schott, Jeffrey J. 2007. "The Korea-US Free Trade Agreement: A Summary Assessment." *PIIE Policy Brief 07-7*. Washington, DC: Peterson Institute for International Economics.

Schott, Jeffrey J. 2010a. "KORUS FTA 2.0: Assessing the Changes." *PIIE Policy Brief 10-23*. Washington, DC: Peterson Institute for International Economics.

Schott, Jeffrey J. 2010b. "Prospects for Implementing the Korea-US Free Trade Agreement." *PIIE Policy Brief*. Washington, DC: Peterson Institute for International Economics.

Schott, Jeffrey, Scott Bradford, and Thomas Moll. 2006. "Negotiating the Korea-United States Free Trade Agreement." *PIIE Policy Brief 06-4*. Washington, DC: Peterson Institute for International Economics.

Schott, Jeffrey J., Euijin Jung, and Cathleen Cimino-Isaacs. 2015. "An Assessment of the Korea-China Free Trade Agreement." *PIIE Policy Brief 15-24*. Washington, DC: Peterson Institute for International Economics.

Sen, Rahul, and Sadhana Srivastava. 2009. "ASEAN's Bilateral Preferential Trade and Economic Cooperation Agreements: Implications for Asian Economic Integration." *ASEAN Economic Bulletin* 26 (2): 194–214.

Seo, J. 2015. "Security Ties or Electoral Connections? The US congress and the Korea-US Free Trade Agreement, 2007-2011." *International Relations of the Asia-Pacific* 15 (2):217-243. doi: 10.1093/irap/lcu024.

Sharman, Jason Campbell. 2012. "Chinese Capital Flows and Offshore Financial Centers." *Pacific Review* 25 (3): 317–37.

Shin, Gi-Wook. 2010. "Historical Disputes and Reconciliation in Northeast Asia: The US Role." *Pacific Affairs* 83 (4): 663–73.

Shipan, Charles R., and Craig Volden. 2012. "Policy Diffusion: Seven Lessons for Scholars and Practitioners." *Public Administration Review* 72 (6): 788–96.

Simmons, Beth A., and Zachary Elkins. 2004. "The Globalization of Liberalization: Policy Diffusion in the International Political Economy." *American Political Science Review* 98 (1): 171–89.

Simmons, Beth A., Frank Dobbin, and Geoffrey Garrett. 2006. "Introduction: The International Diffusion of Liberalism." *International Organization* 60 (4): 781–810.

Skocpol, Theda. 1979. *States and Social Revolutions: A Comparative Analysis of France, Russia and China*. New York: Cambridge University Press.

Smith, Adam. 1937 [1776]. *The Wealth of Nations*. New York: Random House.

Sohn, Chan-Hyun. 2001. "Korea's FTA Developments: Experiences and Perspectives with Chile, Japan, and the U.S." Regional Trading Arrangements: Stocktake and Next Steps, Trade Policy Forum, Bangkok. Bangkok, June 12–13, 2001. https://www.pecc.org/resources/trade-and-investment-1/21-koreas-fta-developments-experiences-and-perspectives-with-chile-japan-and-the-us/file.

Sohn, Chan-Hyun, and Hongshik Lee. 2010. "Trade Structure, FTAs, and Economic Growth." *Review of Development Economics* 14 (3): 683–98.

Sohn, Yul. 2014. "The Role of South Korea in the Making of a Regional Trade Architecture: Convening, Bridging, and Designing FTA Networks." *EAI Middle Power Diplomacy Initiative Working Paper 8*. Seoul: East Asia Institute.

Sohn, Yul, and Min Gyo Koo. 2011. "Securitizing Trade: The Case of the Korea-US Free Trade Agreement." *International Relations of the Asia-Pacific* 11 (3): 433–60.

Solís, Mireya. 2013a. "Business Advocacy in Asian PTAs: A Model of Selective Corporate Lobbying with Evidence from Japan." *Business and Politics* 15 (1): 87–116. doi: 10.1515/bap-2012–0045.

Solís, Mireya. 2013b. "South Korea's Fateful Decision on the Trans-Pacific Partnership." *Foreign Policy at Brookings* 31: 1–21.

Solís, Mireya, and Saori N. Katada. 2007. "Introduction: Understanding East Asian Cross-Regionalism: An Analytical Framework." *Pacific Affairs* 80 (2): 229–57.

Solís, Mireya, and Saori N Katada. 2015. "Unlikely Pivotal States in Competitive Free Trade Agreement Diffusion: The Effect of Japan's Trans-Pacific Partnership Participation on Asia-Pacific Regional Integration." *New Political Economy* 20 (2): 155–77.

Song, Byung Kwon. 2009. "Does the President's Popularity Matter in Korea's Local Elections?" *Pacific Affairs* 82 (2): 189–209.

Song, Yeongkwan. 2011. "KORUS FTA vs. Korea-EU FTA: Why the Differences?" *KEI Academic Paper Series* 6 (5): 1–15.

Souva, Mark, Dale L. Smith, and Shawn Rowan. 2008. "Promoting Trade: The Importance of Market Protecting Institutions." *Journal of Politics* 70 (2): 383–92.

Stoever, William A. 2005. "Restructuring FDI Policy in Emerging Economies: The Republic of Korea Case." *Thunderbird International Business Review* 47 (5): 555–74.

Stubbs, Richard. 2009. "What Ever Happened to the East Asian Developmental State? The Unfolding Debate." *Pacific Review* 22 (1): 1–22.

Sup, Shim Ui. 2004. "Thinking about Korea-Mongolia Free Trade Agreement." *Mongolian Journal of International Affairs* 11: 75–88.

Swank, Duane. 2006. "Tax Policy in an Era of Internationalization: Explaining the Spread of Neoliberalism." *International Organization* 60 (4): 847–82.

Taylor, Ian. 2006. "China's Oil Diplomacy in Africa." *International Affairs* 82 (5): 937–59.

Thurbon, Elizabeth. 2001. "Two Paths to Financial Liberalization: South Korea and Taiwan." *Pacific Review* 14 (2): 241–67.

Thurbon, Elizabeth, and Linda Weiss. 2006. "Investing in Openness: The Evolution of FDI Strategy in South Korea and Taiwan." *New Political Economy* 11 (1): 1–22.

Tsebelis, George. 2002. *Veto Players: How Political Institutions Work*. Princeton: Princeton University Press.

Ursacki, Terry, and Ilan Vertinsky. 1994. "Long-Term Changes in Korea's International Trade and Investment." *Pacific Affairs* 67 (3): 385–409.

U.S. International Trade Commission. 2001. *U.S.-Korea FTA: The Economic Impact of*

Establishing a Free Trade Agreement (FTA) between the United States and the Republic of Korea: Investigation. Washington, DC: U.S. International Trade Commission.

USTR. 2008. 2008 Trade Policy Agenda and 2007 Annual Report. USTR.

Vaughn, Bruce. 2011. "Australia: Background and U.S. Relations." In *Australia: Economic, Political and Social Issues,* edited by Lachlan J. Williams and Ethan N. Lee, 167–85. New York: Nova Science.

Wad, Peter. 2001. "The Political Business of Development in South Korea." In *Political Business in East Asia,* edited by Edmund Terence Gomez, 181–215. London: Routledge.

Wade, Robert. 1990. *Governing the Market: Economic Theory and the Role of Government in East Asian Industrialization.* Princeton: Princeton University Press.

Wade, Robert. 1993. "Managing Trade: Taiwan and South Korea as Challenges to Economics and Political Science." *Comparative Politics* 25 (2):147–67.

Warwick, Ken. 2013. *Beyond Industrial Policy: Emerging Issues and New Trends.* OECD Science, Technology and Industry Policy Papers, No. 2. Paris: OECD Publishing. http://dx.doi.org/10.1787/5k4869clw0xp-en

Watanabe, Matsuo. 2004. "Issues in Regional Integration of East Asia: Conflicting Priorities and Perceptions." *Asia-Pacific Review* 11 (2): 1–17. doi: 10.1080/1343900042000292515.

Waterbury, John. 1992. "The Heart of the Matter? Public Enterprise and the Adjustment Process." In *The Politics of Economic Adjustment,* edited by Stephan Haggard and Robert Kaufman, 182–217. Princeton: Princeton University Press.

Weiss, Linda. 1995. "Governed Interdependence: Rethinking the Government-Business Relationship in East Asia." *Pacific Review* 8 (4): 589–616.

Weiss, Linda, and Elizabeth Thurbon. 2006. "'Where There's a Will There's a Way': Governing the Market in Times of Uncertainty." *Issues and Studies* 40 (1): 61–72.

White, G. W. 2005. "Free Trade as a Strategic Instrument in the War on Terror?: The 2004 US-Moroccan Free Trade Agreement." *Middle East Journal* 59 (4): 597–616.

Williams, Brock R., Mark E. Manyin, Remy Jurenas, and Michaela D. Platzer. 2014. "The U.S.-South Korea Free Trade Agreement (KORUS FTA): Provisions and Implementation." *Congressional Research Service: Report*: 1.

Williamson, John. 1994. *The Political Economy of Policy Reform*: Washington, DC : Institute for International Economics.

Wilson, Jeffrey D. 2012. "Resource Security: A New Motivation for Free Trade Agreements in the Asia-Pacific Region." *Pacific Review* 25 (4): 429–53.

Wonnacott, Ronald J. 1996. "Trade and Investment in a Hub-and-Spoke System versus a Free Trade Area." *World Economy* 19 (3): 237–52.

Woo-Cumings, Meredith. 1991. *Race to the Swift: State and Finance in Korea.* New York: Columbia University Press.

Woo-Cummings, Meredith, ed. 1999. *The Developmental State.* Ithaca, NY: Cornell University Press.

World Bank. 1993. *The East Asian Miracle: Economic Growth and Public Policy.* New York: Oxford University Press.

World Bank. World Development Indicators. http://data.worldbank.org

Wren, Colin. 2001. "The Industrial Policy of Competitiveness: A Review of Recent Developments in the UK." *Regional Studies* 35 (9): 847–60.

Xiaotong, Zhang. 2015. "China's Views of the TPP: Take It or Leave It, That Is the Question." *International Spectator* 50 (1): 111–16. doi: 10.1080/03932729.2014.944384.

Xiaotong, Zhang, Zhang Ping, and Yang Xiaoyan. 2014. "The EU'S New FTA Adventures and Their Implications for China." *Journal of World Trade* 48 (3): 525–51.

Yamamoto, Chika. 2016. "Free Trade Agreements in Japan and East Asian Regionalism: Sino-Japanese Rivalry and Beyond." PhD diss., University of Missouri.

Yang, Jonghoe, and Hyun-Chin Lim. 2007. "Asian Values in Capitalist Development Revisited." In *East Meets West: Civilizational Encounters and the Spirit of Capitalism in East Asia*, edited by Kyong-Dong Kim and Hyun-Chin Lim, 121–36. Leiden, Netherlands: Brill. doi: 10.1163/ej.9789004160217.i-220.54.

Yaylaci, O., and S. Shikher. 2013. "What Would KORUS FTA Bring?" *International Economic Journal 28 (1): 161–82.* doi: 10.1080/10168737.2013.787108.

Yeung, Henry Wai-chung. 2000. "State Intervention and Neoliberalism in the Globalizing World Economy: Lessons from Singapore's Regionalization Programme." *Pacific Review* 13 (1): 133–62.

Yoon, Yeo Joon. 2015. "Evaluation of the Korea-Chile FTA and Its Implications." *KIEP Opinions* 55. Sejong: Korea Institute for International Economic Policy.

Yoshimatsu, Hidetaka. 2012. "Political Leaders' Preferences and Trade Policy: Comparing FTA Politics in Japan and South Korea." *Asian Politics and Policy* 4 (2): 193–212.

Yu, Hyun Seok. 2011. "The Korea-Australia Free Trade Agreement and Its Security Implications." *Korea Observer* 42 (1): 47–67.

Yub, LEE Kyu, LEE Joun Won, and CHUNG MinChirl. 2017. "Korea-China FTA in Its First Year and Effectuation." *World Economy Brief* 7 (4).

Zhang, Bo, Na Wei, and Lan Wei. 2010. 2010 2nd IEEE International Conference on Information Management and Engineering. Chengdu, China, 16-18 April 2010. INSPEC Accession Number: 11361237. doi: 10.1109/ICIME.2010.5477987.

Zhang, Xiaoke. 2002. "Domestic Institutions, Liberalization Patterns, and Uneven Crises in Korea and Taiwan." *Pacific Review* 15 (3): 409–42.

Zhao, Jun, and Timothy Webster. 2011. "Taking Stock: China's First Decade of Free Trade." *University of Pennsylvania International Journal of Law* 33: 65.

Zhao, Quansheng. 2014. "US-China Relations and a New Dual Leadership Structure in the Asia-Pacific." In *China's Rise and Regional Integration in East Asia: Hegemony or Community?*, edited by Yong Wook Lee and Key-young Son, 17–39. New York: Routledge.

Zhuang, Rui, Junjie Hong, and Guangyu Bai. 2014. "Sino-Korea Free Trade Agreement and Asia-Pacific Economic Integration: The China Perspective." *China Economic Journal* 7 (2): 237–50. doi: 10.1080/17538963.2014.928973.

Index

Note: Page numbers in italics refer to the illustrations and tables.

absolute advantage, 17
active hedging, 36, 121–23
activist states: developmental states as, 18, 62; ISI and EOI countries, 61; South Korea, 81
adjacent units, 9
Africa: geopolitical distance to U.S., 34, 35; import-substituting industrialization strategy, 60; as part of the World Island, 33; South Korean economic development vs., 49, *50*
Aggarwal, Vinod K., 104, 105, 107, 132–33
Agnew, John, 30–31, 33
agricultural sector: opposition to KORUS FTA, 115, 147ch7n1; role as veto player, 12, 25, 110, 115; role in lack of U.S.-Japan FTA, 110; South Korea-Chile FTA role, 78–79; South Korean state autonomy from, 63, 64
Airbus, 18
Alba, Joseph, 98
alliance hypothesis, 29
alliances: active hedging and, 36, 121–23; case study approach, 8–9; connection to geopolitical struggles, 11; counterintuitive effects, 119, 122, 126–27; influence on FTAs, 3, 5, 26, 28–30, 36–37; in statistical model, 41, 44, 45. *See also specific countries*

Amsden, Alice H., 53, 62
analytic narrative, use of, 9–10
anti-Americanism (South Korea), 115, 117
anti-neoliberal globalization movement (ANGM), 117
Armitage, Richard L., 110
ASEAN. *See* Association of Southeast Asian Nations (ASEAN)
Asia: future trade negotiations, 132–33; geopolitical security concerns in U.S. FTA policy, 109–12; as part of the World Island, 33; rise of China and, 35–36; role in Cold War containment policy, 34, 35. *See also* East Asia; *specific countries*
Asian Annual Forum (2004), 109
Asian financial crisis (1997), 54–55, 56, 64
Association of Southeast Asian Nations (ASEAN): China FTA, 72, 120–21; effect on international trade, 90; South Korea FTA, 72, 74, 78, 81, 85, 90
Atlantic region, future trade negotiations, 133–34
attractive forces: in comparative political economy, 27; in gravity model, 19–20
Australia: rise of China and, 35; U.S. FTA, *106*, 107, 112
autonomy. *See* state autonomy

Bae, Chankwon, 92
Bahrain-U.S. FTA, *106*, 107, 108
Bai, Guangyu, 132
Baldwin, Richard, 11, 22, 23, 91, 130
basic vs. full gravity models, 21. *See also* gravity model
Bates, Robert, 9–10
Baucus, Max, 109–10
Beck, Nathaniel, 144ch3n1
Belgium, as FTA-intensive country, *69*, 70, 145n6
bilateral trade agreements: defined, 140; proposed, 80, *80*; shift from multilateral agreements, 29, 30; South Korea trading partners, 74
binary time-series cross-sectional (BTSCS) models: data set and variables for, 136–140, 144ch3n2; method, 38–39; mis-prediction of South Korea-Japan FTA, 124; NAFTA application, 42–43; results, 39–42, *40*; South Korea application, 43–45, *43*
Black, Jeremy M., 7, 32, 33–34
Boeing, 18
Bolivia, as FTA-intensive country, *69*, 70, 71, 145n7
Brazil: as BRIC nation, 6; import-substituting industrialization, 18
Brezezinksi, Zbigniew, 13
BRIC nations (Brazil, Russia, India, and China): as emerging economies, 6; South Korea vs., 50. *See also specific countries*
Britain. *See* United Kingdom (UK)
BTSCS. *See* binary time-series cross-sectional (BTSCS) models
Bush, George H. W., 113
Bush, George W.: securitization of U.S. FTA policy, 3, 8, 107, 109; signing of U.S. FTAs, 104, 107, 109, 112, 113
business services, 95. *See also* service sector
Buthe, T., 11

Cambodia: rise of China and, 35; South Korea FTA, 78, 82

Canada: Mexico FTA, 43; U.S. FTAs, 42–43. *See also* North American Free Trade Agreement (NAFTA)
capital intensive factor endowments, 20
Carter, Ashton, 133
Carter, David B., 39
Carter, Jimmy, 34
case studies: adjacent units to, 9; analytic narrative approach, 10; covariational evidence for, 8–9; defined, 8. *See also* South Korea *entries*
central planning, as development strategy, 61
CGE. *See* computable general equilibrium (CGE) models
chaebol (South Korean industrial conglomerates), 25, 55, 114–15
Chang, Ha-Joon, 12
Cheong, Inkyo, 87, 99, 146n5
Chile: FTA strategy, 70, 78; U.S. FTA, 107. *See also* South Korea-Chile free trade agreement
China: ASEAN FTA, 72; as BRIC nation, 6; FDI to and from South Korea, 92–94; geopolitical security concerns in FTA policy, 109–10, 111, 120–21, *121*; good neighbor policy, 120–21; growing domestic market in, 94; Pacific region role, 132; relative share of global trade, 6; rise of, as geopolitical phenomenon, 7, 8, 35–36; sanctions against South Korea for THAAD, 122–23; service sector market, 131; as top ten exporting country, 50, *51*; top twenty trading partners, *73*. *See also* South Korea-China free trade agreement
Cho, Hyekyung, 50
Choi, Bo-Young, 94
Choi, Byung-il, 64, 65
Choi, Won-Mog, 67, 96
Chung, Jae Ho, 35–36, 123
Cimino-Isaacs, Cathleen, 94
The Clash of Civilizations (Huntington), 34
classic case for free trade, 16–17

clustering of production, 22

coalitions, 61

Cold War containment: effects on rim countries, 7, 143n5; as geopolitical phenomenon, 7, 34–35; international relations influenced by, 129; long telegraph, 47; pivot of history concept, 33; South Korean economic development and, 7, 34, 35, 46–49

Cole, David Chamberlin, 47

communism containment. *See* Cold War containment

comparative advantage: distributional consequences caveat, 18–19; dynamic trade theory caveat, 18; in explanation of South Korea-Chile FTA, 78; justification for free trade, 67; modeling of, 77, 145n10; principles of, 16–17; shift from two-country to three-country models, 131

comparative political economy: principles of, 24–28; in typology of geopolitical economy, *15*

comparative politics, unit of analysis, 28

comparative statics, as term, 85

computable general equilibrium (CGE) models: consequences of South Korean FTAs, 85–90, *86–89*, 146nn5, 6; hub effects, 99; Japan-South Korea trade, 125; service sector analysis, 96

Congressional Research Service, 108

constituencies, role in FTA passage, 114

consumption, unbundling from production, 22

containment, Cold War. *See* Cold War containment

Cooper, William, 105–6

coordination costs, 23

Correlates of War (COW) dataset, 39

covariational evidence, 8–9

Cox proportional hazards models: FTA proposals, 80, *80*, 146n12; overview, 39

cross-national statistical models, 25–26, 60

cross-sectional logistic analysis of South Korean signed FTAs: data set and variables for, 140–41; explanation of choice of partners, 76–77, *76*; misprediction of South Korea-Japan FTA, 78, 79, 82, 124

cubic polynomials, 39, 144ch3n1

Czech Republic, as FTA-intensive country, *69*, 70, 145n6

Deardorff, Alan V., 143ch2n2

Deltas, George, 98

democracy: in comparative political economy, 26–28; in cross-sectional logistic analysis, 76–77, *76*; influence on FTAs, 5, 11–12; in South Korea, 54–56, 64; in statistical model, 41

Democratic party (U.S.), 113–14

demonstrations against KORUS FTA, 115

Desmet, Klaus, 98

developmental states: development strategies, 61, 62; East Asia, 12, 18; South Korea, 52–54, 61; as term, 12

development strategy, FTA strategy as, 59–62, 70–71, *71*. *See also* South Korean free trade agreements, as developmental strategy

Deyo, Frederick, 53

disclosure of free trade agreements, 117

distance: in cross-sectional logistic analysis, 76–77, *76*; in gravity model, 4, 20; in statistical model, 41

distributional implications of free trade, 18–19

Doha Development Round, 4, 131

domestic political factors: China FTA policy, 120; FTA policy, 5, 11–12; South Korean FTA policy, 114–17; two-level games, 118; U.S. FTA policy, 113–14, 133, 134

dyad-years, as unit of analysis, 38

dynamic trade theory, 18

East Asia: developmental state approach to growth, 12, 18; export-orientated industrialization strategy, 60–61; privileged global position of, 7

Eastern Europe, as pivot of history, 32, 33

econometric models. *See* binary time-series cross-sectional (BTSCS) models

economic crises: Asian financial crisis, 54–55, 56, 64; effects on autonomy, 55–56

economic development. *See* development strategy, FTA strategy as; South Korean free trade agreements, as developmental strategy

economic geography, 11, 21

economic growth: South Korea FTA effects on, 84–90, *84, 86, 89*; worldwide twenty-first century rates, 83

economic miracle (South Korea), 49–52, *50, 51, 52*

economic rationality of FTAs as development strategy, 81–82, 116

economics: role in geopolitical economy, 14, *15*; unit of analysis, 28

The Economist (journal), 131

EFTA (European Free Trade Association), 74, 90

Egypt, U.S. foreign aid, 34

Eisenhower, Dwight D., 34

embeddedness, 65

emerging economies, 6

emerging geopolitical economy, 130–32

EOI. *See* export-orientated industrialization (EOI)

Eom, Jun Hyun, 95

EU. *See* European Union (EU)

Europe: future trade negotiations, 133–34; as part of the World Island, 33

European Free Trade Association (EFTA), 74, 90

European Union (EU): FTA-intensiveness for member countries, 70; geopolitical security concerns in FTA policy, 126; service sector, 134; shift from global multilateralism to regionalism, 29; statistical model application, 43, 45; support for Airbus, 18; top twenty trading partners, *73*; U.S. FTA proposal, 134

European Union-South Korea free trade agreement. *See* South Korea-EU free trade agreement

Evans, Peter, 12, 53, 62, 65

executive branch: division with legislative branch, 12; in South Korea, 64–65, 114, 116–17

export-orientated industrialization (EOI): in East Asia, 60–61; exports as percentage of GDP, 68, *69*; FTA strategy as variant of, 59; South Korea as subset of, 71–72

exports: as percentage of GDP, 68, *69*; in statistical model, 41; top ten exporting countries, 50–51, *51*

exports, role in South Korean economic development: FTA coverage, 68, *69*, 84–85, *84*; location among top ten exporting countries, 50–51, *51*; percentage of GDP, 51–52, *52*; value of exports, 3, 143ch1n1

Facchini, Giovanni, 98

factor endowments, 20

false negative cases, *77, 78*

false positive cases, *77, 78*

fast track authority, 64, 116

foreign direct investment (FDI): FTA effects on, 11, 91–95, *92, 93*; link to trade and service sector liberalization, 11

France: relative share of global trade, 6; statistical model application, 43, 45; as top ten exporting country, 51, *51*

Frankel, Jeffrey A., 20, 21

free trade, political debate over, 16–19

free trade agreements (FTAs): in cross-sectional logistic analysis, 76–77, *76*; determinants of, 36, 44–45; as development strategy, 59–62; disclosure of, 117; domestic political factors in, 11–12; as economic policies, 60; facilitation of FDI, 11; geopolitics and, 7, 10–11, 128–29; hub effects, 97–99; importance of studying, 4–5; increase in, 4; location in trade agreement continuum, 143ch2n2; political factors, 5; proportion of trade subject to, 68–70, *69*; proposals, 80, *80*; as variant of export-orientated industrialization strategy, 59. *See also specific agreements; specific countries*

FTA-intensive countries, 69, *69*

FTAs. *See* free trade agreements (FTAs)

Fukuyama, Francis, 34

full vs. basic gravity models, 21. *See also* gravity model

future trade negotiations, 132–34

GATT. *See* General Agreement on Tariffs and Trade (GATT)

GDP (gross domestic product): in cross-sectional logistic analysis, 76–77, *76*; isolating FTA effects on, 88–90, *89*; as proxy for size of market, 20; role in predicting FTAs, 79; service sector share, 131

GDP per capita: in BTSCS models, 39, *40*; in cross-sectional logistic analysis, 76–77, *76, 80*; differences in, 20–21; in South Korea, *50*

General Agreement on Tariffs and Trade (GATT): rounds of multilateral agreements, 4, 16; shift to semi-multilateral and bilateral agreements, 29; Uruguay Round, 30

geographic clustering of production, 22

geographic distance, in gravity model. *See* distance, in gravity model

geography, role in geopolitical economy, 14, *15*

geopolitical economy, 14–57; comparative political economy and, 24–28; emerging, 130–32; as extension of IPE perspective, 6–8; geographic specificity of security threats, 5; geopolitics and, 30–36, 37; gravity model, 4, 19–21; international political economy and, 28–30, 37; overview, 6–8; political debate over free trade, 16–19; second unbundling, 11, 21–24; typology of, 14–15, *15*

geopolitics: as belief system, 33; defined, 7, 32; development of field, 31–32; pivot of history concept, 32–33, 34; role in geopolitical economy, *15*, 30–36

Germany: pivot of history concept, 33; relative share of global trade, 6; statistical model application, 43, 45; as top ten exporting country, 51, *51*

Gerring, John, 8–9

Gilpin, Robert, 130

Global Europe initiative (2006), 126

globalization: opposition to, 16, 117; securitization of U.S. FTA policy and, 106–7. *See also* second unbundling

global supply chains: China involvement, 93; role in emerging geopolitical economy, 130–31; South Korea involvement, 91–92, 93

Going for Growth (OECD), 96

Gökmen, Semra Ranâ, 31–32

Gowa, Joanne, 7, 28, 29, 37

Grambsch and Terneau nonproportionality test., 146n12

The Grand Chessboard: American Primacy and Its Geostrategic Imperatives (Brezezinksi), 13

gravity model: in Chinese FTAs, 120; hypotheses from, 20, 144ch2n3; low prediction of South Korea-U.S. FTA, 46–47; principles of, 19–21, 143ch2n2; role in South Korea-Chile FTA, 79; as standard explanation for FTAs, 4, 82, 117–18; in statistical model, 39, 40; in typology of geopolitical economy, *15*

gross domestic product. *See* GDP (gross domestic product)

growth. *See* economic growth

Haggard, Stephan, 49, 54, 55

heartland thesis, 33

hedging, 35, 112. *See also* active hedging

hegemonic stability theory, 29–30

Henisz index, 27

Higgott, Richard, 106

Hirschman, Albert, 28, 37, 60, 122

Hong, Junjie, 132

Hong Kong, lack of South Korea FTA, 85
Horng, Der-Chin, 126
hub effects, 97–99
Huntington, Samuel P., 34
Hur, Jung, 98

Im, Tobin, 65
import-substituting industrialization (ISI), 18, 60, 61
increasing returns, 22
India: as BRIC nation, 6; South Korea FTA, 74, 81, 90
Indonesia: hedging by, 112; Singapore geopolitical concerns, 111
informal comparisons, usefulness of, 9
information and communications technology (ICT), 23
international political economy (IPE): competition for power, 5; extension to geopolitical economy perspective, 6–7, 28–30, 37; in typology of geopolitical economy, *15*
international relations (IR): Cold War containment policy influence on, 129; as field of study, 31–32; political realism tradition, 28, 31
international trade: FTA effects on, 90–91; future trade negotiations, 132–34; political nature of, 128. *See also* comparative advantage; gravity model
ISI (import-substituting industrialization), 18, 60, 61
island states, levels of trade, 144ch5n3, 145n8
Israel: FTA discussion with South Korea, 145n11; geopolitical security concerns in U.S. FTA policy, 104–6; hub effects, 98; U.S. foreign aid, 34, 48
Italy: statistical model application, 43, 45; as top ten exporting country, 51, *51*
iterative approach to research, 10

Jang, Yong Joon, 92
Japan: agricultural sector, 64; ASEAN FTA, 72; colonial history in South

Korea, 125; computable general equilibrium studies, 87–88; developmental state in, 62; FDI to and from South Korea, 92; geopolitical security concerns in U.S. FTA policy, 110; lack of South Korea FTA, 78, 79, 82, 85, 124–25; relative share of global trade, 6; Singapore FTA, 111; South Korea-China FTA influence on, 132; South Korean trade deficit, 125; static effects, 86
JETRO database, 139
Johnson, Chalmers, 6, 62, 66
Jones, Leroy P., 53
Jordan-U.S. free trade agreement, 106, 107
Jung, Euijin, 94

Kalinowski, Thomas, 50
Katz, Jonathan N., 144ch3n1
Katzman, Kenneth, 108–9
Kennan, George, 34, 47
Kennedy, John F., 34
Keohane, Robert, 144ch3n2
Kim, Chi-Wook, 114, 115
Kim, Do Hee, 95
Kim, Hyuk-Hwang, 95
Kim, Jong Duk, 92
Kim, Min-Hyung, 123
Kim, Young Gui, 88, 90, 95
Kim Dae-Jung: Asian financial crisis effects, 55, 64; commitment to FTA strategy, 62–63; liberal reforms, 55–56, 63, 64
Kim Hyun-chong, 66
Kim Young-Sam, 55
King, Gary, 144ch3n2
Kohli, Atul, 53
Koo, Min Gyo: industrial policy and FTAs, 67; South Korea-Chile FTA, 78, 79; South Korean FTA policy, 62, 145n11; South Korea-U.S. FTA, 36; U.S. security interest in Japan, 110
Korea Herald (newspaper), 115
Korean People's Republic (KPR), 47. *See also* South Korea

Korean War (1950–1953), 47

Korea-U.S. free trade agreement. *See* South Korea-U.S. free trade agreement (KORUS FTA)

KORUS FTA. *See* South Korea-U.S. free trade agreement (KORUS FTA)

KORUS FTA Industry Alliance, 115

Kotbee, Shin, 94

KPR (Korean People's Republic), 47. *See also* South Korea

Krugman, Paul: geography of trade theory, 130; new economic geography, 21–22; support for dynamic trade, 18

Kyung-Sup, Chang, 64

labor intensive factor endowments, 20

Laos: rise of China and, 35; South Korea FTA, 78, 82

Latin America: geopolitical distance to U.S., 34, 35; import-substituting industrialization, 18, 60; liberalism attempt, 61. *See also specific countries*

Lee, Hongshik, 96

Lee, Hyun-Chool, 64, 116, 117

Lee, Junkyu, 96

Lee Myung-bak, 63, 116

legislatures: division with executive branch, 12; role in KORUS FTA passage, 113–14, 116–17; as veto player, 64–65, 116

Levi, Margaret, 9

liberalization of trade: as development strategy, 61; difficulty of, 16; FTA strategy as shift toward, 59; Kim Dae-Jung policies, 55, 56; link to FDI and service sector liberalization, 11

logit analysis. *See* cross-sectional logistic analysis of South Korean signed FTAs

long telegraph (February 22, 1946), 47

Lyman, Princeton N., 47

Mackinder, Harold, 32–33, 34

Malaysia: free trade agreements, 5, 82; as FTA-intensive country, *69*, 71–72, *71*; Singapore geopolitical concerns, 111

Mansfield, Edward D.: datasets, 41; domestic political factors, 11, 12; hegemonic stability theory, 30; Henisz index, 27; importance of free trade agreements, 4; location of FTAs in trade agreement continuum, 143ch2n2; median voters, 26; political dimension of FTAs, 67; security-alliance politics role in FTAs, 28; security alliances, 29

manufacturing sector: limitations on extent of liberalization, 147ch9n1; South Korea, 25, 114–15; U.S., 25

Marxism, 24–25

Mattis, Jim, 128

median voters, 11, 26–27

Meeting on External Economic Affairs (2001), 65–66

Mercosur, 145n7

Mexico: free trade agreements, 5, 72–73, 82; as FTA-intensive country, *69*, *70*, *71*, 145n5; hub effects, 98; import-substituting industrialization, 18; proportion of trade subject to FTAs, 68–69, *69*; U.S. FTAs, 42–43. *See also* North American Free Trade Agreement (NAFTA)

Middle East: number of U.S. FTAs in, 103, 104, *105*, *106*; as part of the World Island, 33, 104; privileged global position of, 7; role in Cold War containment policy, 34, 35. *See also specific countries*

military alliances. *See* alliances

Milner, Helen V.: datasets, 41; domestic political factors, 11, 12; foreign direct investment, 11; hegemonic stability theory, 30; Henisz index, 27; importance of free trade agreements, 4; location of FTAs in trade agreement continuum, 143ch2n2; median voters, 26; political dimension of FTAs, 67; security-alliance politics role in FTAs, 28; security alliances, 29

ministerial meetings, 65–66

Ministry of Foreign Affairs and Trade (MOFAT) (South Korea): capacity of, 66; consultation with business over FTA policy, 65; creation of, 63; power of, 65; support for KORUS FTA, 115
MITI and the Japanese Miracle (Johnson), 6, 62
Mo, Jongryn, 54
models. *See* binary time-series cross-sectional (BTSCS) models; computable general equilibrium (CGE) models; cross-sectional logistic analysis of South Korean signed FTAs; gravity model
MOFAT. *See* Ministry of Foreign Affairs and Trade (MOFAT) (South Korea)
Mölders, Florian, 139, 145n4
Moon, Chung-In, 47
Morocco-U.S. free trade agreement, *106*, 107, 108
multilateral trade agreements: shift to semi-multilateral and bilateral agreements, 29, 30; uncertainty of, 129. *See also specific agreements*
Muscarà, Luca, 30–31, 33

NAFTA. *See* North American Free Trade Agreement (NAFTA)
National Power and the Structure of Foreign Trade (Hirschman), 28
neoliberalism: developmental state perspective vs., 53–54; role of development strategies, 61; views of FTAs, 67
nested-inference research design, 9
Netherlands: as FTA-intensive country, *69*, 70, 145n6; membership in top ten exporting countries, 51, *51*
new economic geography, 21–22
New Zealand: FTA discussion with South Korea, 145n11; lack of U.S. FTA, 112
Nixon, Richard, 34
North American Free Trade Agreement (NAFTA): comparative advantage explanation, 103; gravity model explanation, 117–18; hub effects, 98; impor-

tance to Mexico, 72–73; KORUS FTA similarities, 113; shift from global multilateralism to regionalism, 29; statistical model application, 42–43, 45; Trump, Donald criticism of, 129
North Korea, threat from, 122, 123, 128
Nye, Joseph S., 110

Obama, Barack, 128
OECD (Organisation for Economic Co-operation and Development): productivity recommendations, 96, 97; recent economic growth rates, 83; South Korea membership, 49, *50*
Office of the Minister for Trade (OMT) (South Korea), 65
Oh, Jennifer Sejin, 64, 65
Oman-U.S. free trade agreement, *106*, 107, 108–9
OMT. *See* Office of the Minister for Trade (OMT) (South Korea)

Pacific region, future trade negotiations, 132–33. *See also* Asia
Park, Donghyun, 98
Park, Jinsoo, 98
Park, Mi, 117
Park, Sung-Hoon, 78, 79, 145n11
Peru: South Korea FTA, 90; U.S. FTA, 104
Pinkston, Daniel, 55
pivot of history concept, 32–33, 34
political geography, 30–32
political realism tradition: anarchy of the international system, 28; influence on Cold War containment policy, 34; IPE reliance on, 31–32
political science, role in geopolitical economy, 14, *15*
Portugal, absolute vs. comparative advantage example, 17, 18–19
production, unbundling from consumption, 22
productivity benefits of free trade, 67
Putin, Vladimir, 133–34
Putnam, Robert D., 113, 118, 134

rationality of FTAs as development strategy, 81–82, 116

RCEP (Regional Comprehensive Economic Partnership), 133, 147ch9n2

Reagan, Ronald, 34, 105–6

realism tradition. *See* political realism tradition

redistribution, role in comparative advantage theory, 19

Regional Comprehensive Economic Partnership (RCEP), 133, 147ch9n2

regionalism, shift to, 29–30

Republican party (U.S.), 113–14

Republic of Korea. *See* South Korea

residual analysis of South Korean signed FTAs, 77–79, *77*

resistant forces: in comparative political economy, 27–28; in gravity model, 19–20

Rhyu, Sang-Young, 47

Ricardo, David: comparative advantage theory, 16–17, 18, 19, 67; first unbundling, 22–23

Roh Moo-hyun: commitment to FTA strategy, 36, 63, 66; public relations campaign for KORUS FTA, 110

Rosenbaum, Chika (formerly Yamamoto), 29, 135

Rueschemeyer, Dietrich, 12

Russia: as BRIC nation, 6; future trade negotiations, 133–34; as top ten exporting country, 50, *51*. *See also* Soviet Union

Sakong, Il, 53

Samsung, 91, 95

Sanders, Bernie, 26, 134

Schott, Jeffrey, 94, 96–97, 131

second unbundling: growth in, 91; overview, 11; principles of, 21–24; role in emerging geopolitical economy, 130–31; in typology of geopolitical economy, *15*

security alliances. *See* alliances

semi-bilateral trade agreements, defined, 140

semi-multilateral trade agreements: shift from multilateral agreements, 29, 30; South Korea trading partners, 74; uncertainty of, 129

Seo, Jungkun, 55, 113–14

service sector: effects of South Korean FTAs on, 96–97; FDI in South Korea, 94, 95; liberalization of, 11; role in emerging geopolitical economy, 130, 131–32; South Korea-EU FTA effects on, 119, 126, 127, 147ch8n3; TTIP importance, 134

Signorino, Curtis S., 39

Singapore: free trade agreements with major world economies, 5, 72, 73, 82; geopolitical security concerns in FTA policy, 111–12; service sector market, 132; South Korea FTA, 63, 66, 74, 81, 90

size of market, in gravity model, 20

Skocpol, Theda, 12

Smith, Adam, 17

societies vs. states, 24–25

Sohn, Chan-Hyun, 36

Sohn, Yul, 110

Solís, Mireya, 66

South Korea: active hedging, 36, 121–23; colonial history with Japan, 125; developmental state period, 52–54, 61; difficult geopolitical position of, 35, 46; early democracy period, 54–56; economic miracle, 49–52, *50, 51, 52*; economic sectors and political interests, 25; financial crisis, 54–55; FTA effects on economic growth, 84–90, *84, 86, 89*; move from authoritarianism to democracy, 26, 54; proportion of trade subject to FTAs, 68, *69*; recent economic growth rates, 83; relative share of global trade, 5–6; role in Cold War containment policy, 7, 34, 35, 46–49; service sector market, 131; THAAD-related sanctions by China, 122–23; trade deficit with Japan, 125; U.S. foreign aid, 48–49; U.S. occupation, 7, 47, 48; value of exports, 3, 143ch1n1

South Korea-ASEAN free trade agreement, 86, *89*, 90

South Korea-Chile free trade agreement: bilateral nature of, 74; effect on international trade, 90; learning experience from, 63, 66, 81, 82, 145n11; legislative controversy over, 65; mis-prediction of, in model, 78–79

South Korea-China free trade agreement: dynamic effects, 87, 146nn5, 6; economic rationality of, 81; importance of, 5, 13, 74, 122–23; KORUS FTA influence on, 119, 122, 123, 127; limitations on extent of liberalization, 147ch9n1; negotiations for, 63; percentage of Korean exports, 85; pressure on Japan from, 132; signing of, 36; South Korean reluctance for, 121; static effects, 86; statistical model prediction of, 44, 45; unsurprising nature of, 21

South Korea-EU free trade agreement: economic rationality of, 81; effect on international trade, 90, 91; EU motivation for, 126; gravity model explanation for, 21; importance of, 5, 13; percentage of Korean exports, 85; semi-multilateral nature of, 74; service sector effects, 119, 126, 127, 147ch8n3; static effects, 86

South Korean free trade agreements: case study approach to, 8–9, 10; data set of trading partners, 73–75, *74, 75*; domestic political factors, 12; dominance of Korean trading system, 84–85, *84*; geopolitical security concerns, 7, 110–11; importance of studying, 5–6; lack of FTA with Japan, 78, 79, 82, 85, 124–25; recency of, 29; response to global events, 12; statistical model application, 43–45, *43*

South Korean free trade agreements, as developmental strategy, 59–82; concept of developmental strategy, 59–62, 70–71, *71*; data set of partners, 73–75, *74, 75*; economic rationality of, 81–82,

116; explanation of choice of partners, 75–80, *75, 76, 77, 80*, 145n11; export-orientated industrialization, 71–72; FTA coverage, 68–70, *69*; industrial policy role, 62, 66–68; state autonomy role, 62, 64–65; state capacity role, 62, 65–66; as state-led project, 62–63, 129–130; uniqueness of FTAs with three world economy leaders, 5, 72–73, 82

South Korean free trade agreements, consequences of, 83–99; economic growth effects, 84–90, *84, 86, 89*; FDI effects, 91–95, *92, 93*; hub effects, 97–99; international trade effects, 90–91; overview, 83; service sector effects, 96–97

South Korea-Singapore FTA: bilateral nature of, 74; effect on international trade, 90; learning experience from, 63, 66, 81

South Korea-U.S. free trade agreement (KORUS FTA): dynamic effects, 87; economic rationality of, 81, 116; effect on international trade, 90–91, 132; far-reaching provisions of, 112–13; geopolitical security concerns, 8, 11, 110–11; gravity model explanation for, 21; importance of, 5, 13, 74; influence on South Korea-China FTA, 119, 122, 123, 127; MOFAT role, 66, 115; percentage of Korean exports, 85; productivity motivation for, 67; service sector effects, 96, 126; signing of, 63; simultaneous goals of, 103; South Korean political perspective, 114–17, 132; static effects, 86, 87; statistical model prediction of, 44, 45; U.S. political perspective, 113–14, 132; war on terror role, 35

Soviet Union: U.S. containment policy, 7, 33, 34–35, 46–49; U.S. geopolitical response to, 7. *See also* Russia

Standard Chartered Report (2005), 91

state autonomy: democratization effect on, 54; economic crisis effects on, 55–

56; role in development strategies, 62, 63–65; in South Korea, 63–65

state capacity: role in development strategies, 62, 65–66; in South Korea, 65–66

states: economic development and, 12; FTA strategy as statist project, 129, 130; motivation to intervene in domestic economies, 130; societies vs., 24–25; as unit of analysis in international relations, 28; veto players within, 12

static effects: discuss ion, 86; dynamic effects vs., 85–86

statistical models. *See* binary time-series cross-sectional (BTSCS) models; cross-sectional logistic analysis of South Korean signed FTAs

Stein, Ernesto, 20

Stolper-Samuelson theorem, 18–19, 25

The Strategy of Economic Development (Hirschman), 60

Taiwan: as activist state, 62; rise of China and, 35, 133; successful development of, 5, 17

tariffs: in continuum of trade agreements, 143ch1n2; Global Europe initiative goals, 126; KORUS FTA provisions, 112; NAFTA provisions, 98; role in import-substituting industrialization, 60; rounds of multilateral agreements, 4, 16; South Korea-China FTA provisions, 146n5; South Korean economic development and, 53

temporal comparisons, as covariational evidence, 9

Terminal High Altitude Area Defense (THAAD), 122–23

Thailand: as FTA-intensive country, *69*, 71–72, *71*; South Korea FTA negotiations, 145n11

three-party trade, shift from two-party trade, 11, 23

TPP. *See* Trans-Pacific Partnership (TPP)

trade deficits, 91, 125

trade-investment-services-IP nexus, 11

Transatlantic Trade and Investment Partnership (TTIP), 134

Trans-Pacific Partnership (TPP): geopolitical motivation for, 132–33; third-party trade effects, 147ch9n2; U.S. presidential campaign arguments, 26; U.S. withdrawal from, 129, 131, 132, 133

transportation costs, in gravity model, 4

Truman, Harry S., 34

Trump, Donald, 26, 128, 129, 133, 134

TTIP (Transatlantic Trade and Investment Partnership), 134

Tucker, Richard, 144ch3n1

Tunisia, as FTA-intensive country, *69*, 70, 71, 145n7

two-level games: KORUS FTA, 113, 118; South Korea-China FTA, 120; U.S.-EU FTA proposal, 134

two-party trade, shift to three-party trade, 11, 23

typology of geopolitical economy, 14–15, *15*

United Kingdom (UK): absolute vs. comparative advantage examples, 17, 18–19; relative share of global trade, 6; as top ten exporting country, 51, *51*

United States (U.S.): absolute advantage example, 17; decision to pursue preferential trade agreements, 30; economic sectors and political interests, 25; EU FTA proposal, 134; FDI to and from South Korea, 92, 95; geopolitical security concerns in FTA policy, 7–8, 34–35, 103–9, *105*, *106*; legislative restraint on FTA policy, 64; Pacific region role, 132–33; pivot of history concept, 33; post-WWII liberal multilateral trading leadership, 7; relative share of global trade, 6; service sector, 95, 134; summary of FTAs, 104, *105*, *106*; THAAD proposal, 122; as top ten exporting country, 50, *51*; top twenty trading partners, *73*; war on

terror, 7–8, 35, 103, 106–9, 112. *See also* Cold War containment; *specific trade agreements*
United States-Bahrain free trade agreement, 108
United States-Canada free trade agreements, 42–43. *See also* North American Free Trade Agreement (NAFTA)
United States Congress, 113–14, 115, 116
United States-Israel free trade agreement, 104–6
United States-Jordan free trade agreement, 107
United States-Mexico free trade agreements, 43. *See also* North American Free Trade Agreement (NAFTA)
United States-Morocco free trade agreement, 108
United States-Oman free trade agreement, 108–9
United States-Singapore free trade agreement, 111–12
United States-South Korea tree trade agreement. *See* South Korea-U.S. free trade agreement (KORUS FTA)
Uruguay Round (GATT), 30
U.S.. *See* United States (U.S.)
USSR (Union of Soviet Socialist Republics). *See* Soviet Union

Verba, Sidney, 144ch3n2
veto players: agricultural sector power, 12, 25, 110, 115; anti-Americanism as, 115, 117; Asian financial crisis effects on, 64; influence on FTAs, 5, 11–12; legislatures as, 64–65, 116; as resistant forces, 27–28; in statistical model, 41
Vietnam: as FTA-intensive country, *69,* 71–72, *71;* South Korean FDI in, 92, 94–95; U.S. foreign aid, 48

Wade, Robert, 53, 62, 67
Wang, Yunjong, 87
war on terror: as geopolitical phenomenon, 7–8, 35; securitization of U.S. FTA policy and, 103, 106–9, 112
Washington Declaration (1994), 107
Wei, Shang-Jin, 20
Western Europe: privileged global position of, 7; role in Cold War containment policy, 34, 35. *See also specific countries*
White, G. W., 108
Williams, Brock R., 132
Williamson, John, 49
Wonnacott, Ronald J., 98
Woo-Cumings, Meredith, 53
World Bank, 67, 68
World Island: defined, 33; U.S. FTAs, 104, *106. See also specific countries*
World Trade Organization (WTO): Doha Development Round, 4, 131; rounds of multilateral agreements, 4; shift to semi-multilateral and bilateral agreements, 29
World War II (1939–1945): economic and political environment prior to, 28; growth of political realism tradition after, 31
WTO. *See* World Trade Organization (WTO)

Yamamoto, Chika (now Rosenbaum), 29, 135
Yoon, Yeo Joon, 90
Yoshimatsu, Hidetaka, 110

Zhuang, Rui, 132
Zoellick, Robert, 3, 107, 147ch7n1